Radical *Brown*

SERIES | RACE AND EDUCATION

Series edited by H. Richard Milner IV

Radical *Brown*

Keeping the Promise to America's Children

MARGARET BEALE SPENCER
NANCY E. DOWD

Harvard Education Press
Cambridge, Massachusetts

Paperback ISBN 9781682538715

Library of Congress Cataloging-in-Publication Data
Names: Spencer, Margaret Beale, author. | Dowd, Nancy E., 1949– author.
Title: Radical Brown : keeping the promise to America's children / Margaret Beale Spencer, Nancy E. Dowd.
Other titles: Race and education series.
Description: Cambridge, Massachusetts : Harvard Education Press, [2024] | Series: [Race and education] | Includes bibliographical references and index.
Identifiers: LCCN 2023053525 | ISBN 9781682538715 (paperback)
Subjects: LCSH: Brown, Oliver, 1918–1961–Trials, litigation, etc. | Topeka (Kan.). Board of Education–Trials, litigation, etc. | Educational equalization–United States. | Racism in education–United States. | Educational change–United States.
Classification: LCC LC213.2 .S667 2024 | DDC 370.890973–dc23/eng/20231227
LC record available at https://lccn.loc.gov/2023053525

Published by Harvard Education Press,
an imprint of the Harvard Education Publishing Group

Harvard Education Press
8 Story Street
Cambridge, MA 02138

Cover Design: Endpaper Studio
Cover Image: FG Trade/E+ via Getty Images

The typefaces in this book are Legacy Serif ITC and Futura

To those who have fought for justice on whose shoulders
we stand; and to all children, who deserve
the reality of full humanity

Contents

Foreword

The US Supreme Court decision in *Brown v. Topeka Board of Education* shook the very foundations of America's racial order. Whereas the Court's 1896 *Plessy v. Ferguson* decision declared that "Blacks have no rights Whites are bound to respect," *Brown* struck down the "separate but equal" doctrine flowing from this ruling. On its face, *Brown* restored the full citizenship rights originally granted to former slaves by the Thirteenth, Fourteenth, and Fifteenth Amendments to the Constitution and the 1866 Civil Rights Act. Following Reconstruction, southern Whites employed concerted legal and extra-legal methods to systematically erode and reverse Black citizenship and human rights. *Plessy* was the final nail in the coffin, signaling the North's full capitulation and the total return of Blacks into the clutches of former slave owners. Although Blacks played outsized roles in the North's victory over the South, White interests converged after the Civil War to present a united front in opposition to Black Civil and Human Rights. The old wine of "chattel slavery" was poured into the "new bottles" of a rigid racial caste system.

Radical Brown sees the seventieth anniversary of *Brown v. Topeka Board of Education* as a time to reflect on contradictions between soaring ideals of racial equality and the stubborn reality of persistent racial inequality. Why are Black communities and Black people in America still "separate and unequal" compared to Whites on every important indicator of social justice, well-being, and quality of life, education and achievement, income and wealth, morbidity and mortality, arrest and incarceration, environmental cleanliness and safety, child development and family stability, unemployment and underemployment? Over the years, careers and fortunes have been built on the social research and social policy *industry* that claims to be dedicated to the eradication of racial inequality in America. Yet the status quo persists.

After studying eighty years of records from US Congressional annual debates about the "slavery question," the eminent historian John Hope Franklin concluded that the true purpose of the exercise was merely to prolong debate, thus forestalling any real progress toward ending slavery.

Radical Brown argues for an expansive reading and implementation of the *Brown* decision, which moves beyond limited, conservative reading and implementation. The authors believe *Brown* was "a mandate for comprehensive equality grounded in *shared, common, equal humanity.*" The authors suggest that *Brown* demands recognition and implementation of "*a vision of common humanity.*" It was not sufficiently transformative to simply declare as unconstitutional "systems, structures and culture grounded in inhumanity and hierarchy centered on the assumed inferiority of Blacks and the supremacy of Whites. This radical declaration needed to be followed by similarly radical, full-scale change to implement a system of equality." Ironically, Reconstruction represented stumbling national progress toward Black equality. Former slaves and free negroes made tremendous advances in political, economic, legal, and social rights. Blacks were even elected to some of the highest offices in the land. However, the specter of Black equality enraged and frightened Southern Whites, who resolved to turn back the clock. They found sympathy among many Northern Whites, also conflicted by—if not outright hostile to—this notion. The emerging identity of American "exceptionalism," read "Whiteness," could not and would not accommodate visions of Black equality *and* humanity.

This volume powerfully asserts that the US Supreme Court decision in *Brown v. Topeka Board of Education* has lost its way. "*Brown* as an icon has been drained of its meaning. Trotted out as an example of powerful constitutional change, its historic meaning has devolved into a cramped, minimized view of equality that has become a rationalization for inequality. Understanding *Brown* as mandating anything less than profound and necessarily radical comprehensive change ironically reduces its meaning to an apology for sustaining inequality dressed up as equality, reifying a false narrative of racial progress and shared humanity" (chapter 1). The authors reach this conclusion after rereading *Brown* to excavate and expose its true radical meaning.

Rereading is a process lawyers commonly use to explore, dissect, and examine constitutional cases, to understand meaning in the context when decided, as well as contemporary applications. This volume pays careful attention to the social science supporting the *Brown* decision, as well as post-*Brown* developmental science. In the fullest sense, rereading requires a focus on the legal, philosophical, psychological, physical/structural, and cultural contexts impacting the meaning of equality advanced in *Brown*. The authors' radical rereading and reassessment of the *Brown* decision identifies key unfinished, unrealized aspects of *Brown*. They attribute these failures to *both* conservative application of the legal doctrine and uncritical acceptance of supporting social science data/interpretations.

Spencer's phenomenological variant of ecological systems theory (PVEST) situates development in relation to identity, context, and history. Emphasis is placed on comprehensive, inclusive conceptualization of the development process. This perspective recognizes the humanity of all children, framed by the unfolding life course and developmental tasks to be mastered at each stage of life. PVEST provides essential scaffolding for rereading *Brown* to recognize Black children's shared humanity. The Court's "uncritical adoption of a deficit perspective converting children of color into 'problems' shifted the focus from structural and cultural racism to blaming the victims. It also ignored the harms of segregation to all children" (chapter 1). As a result, "*Brown*'s efficacy has been woefully inadequate both for the victims of the system as well as those privileged by it."

Radical Brown persuasively argues the necessity to go beyond radical change in education to encompass comprehensive, radical change across society. Fully supporting children's foundational, developmental needs is only possible after centuries-old systems of structural, cultural, and psychological racism are torn down. The full scope of centuries-long anti-Black racism embedded in this society's DNA must be acknowledged and "rooted out." Equality for all children requires first protecting each child's humanity and healthy development. Successful life-long personal growth and development, physical and psychological health, and full societal and civic participation rest on successful completion of early developmental tasks. Systemic racial inequality blocks essential interconnected, developmental "life steps" that are foundational for positive life course competence, healthy identity formation, and motivation.

The vision emanating from *Radical* Brown identifies and reframes the past, present, and future of US racial inequality. The Court's fundamental definition of inequality in *Brown* was based on unexamined assumptions about humanity, for example, Whose humanity matters? Whose humanity is recognized? Historically, slavery, Jim Crow segregation, mass incarceration, and destructive child development contexts/outcomes have normalized Black denigration and subjugation—while denying Black humanity. By contrast, the construction of White humanity has been grounded on unchallenged assumptions of racial supremacy, privilege, and "divine destiny." This volume recognizes how problems with the reasoning underlying the *Brown* decision, and implications for remedy, have been hidden, narrowed, marginalized, and ignored. Such faulty reasoning and missteps are at the very core of contemporary inequality.

The law can be a blunt instrument for social change. This from a nonlawyer sociologist with four decades' experience testifying as an expert witness in higher education cases before the courts. From my uninformed vantage point, interpretation and application of legal findings or rulings are influenced—within limits of course—by personal factors. I am on firmer ground making such assertions regarding social science research and policy. The adage "data speak for themselves" is a misnomer. Interpretation and application of social science research findings, even from the most rigorously executed study, often reflect the slanted worldviews of particular "spirit mediums" who presume to objectively channel—or summarize—"what this all means." *Radical* Brown links racist attitudes to the "go slow," "two steps forward, one step back," approach characteristic of the ambivalent history of efforts to tear down US *apartheid*. The "with all deliberate speed" caveat in

Brown II is a perfect example; this "get out of jail free card" effectively neutralized enforcement of the Court's courageous, unanimous decision to outlaw racial segregation.

Radical Brown attributes America's largely uninterrupted, pervasive, and persistent, racial inequality to refusal to recognize the humanity of Black people. While not without difficulty, it is possible to legislate "behaviors"; racist actions can be controlled and sanctioned. On the other hand, it is impossible to legislate "hearts" and "minds." Racist attitudes, values, and emotions are internal states difficult to ascertain and attribute. You cannot—and should not—police individual thoughts and worldviews. However, people must be held accountable when racist beliefs lead to racist behaviors toward others. Similarly, societies must be held accountable for "racist scripts" that justify racist policies, practices, and outcomes. This book articulates how and why a system, which for centuries refused to see Black children as humans, does such violence to their self-image, health, and well-being. Laws are an essential, but not sufficient, corrective for systemic racial inequalities in actions, policies, practices, and outcomes. What then is the solution?

The most radical "takeaway" from *Radical* Brown is the challenge for fundamental changes in how Americans feel and think about *race*. To achieve this shift would be truly profound and radical. It would create a "beloved community," a community where all are cared for, where poverty, hunger, and hatred are eliminated. It would also be a community without racism, where Black children are precious and thrive. It is often assumed that beloved communities, characterized by *agape*, or selfless love, can only be found in Reverend Dr. Martin Luther King's theology or in Toni Morrison's novels—not in the *real world*. This volume boldly challenges us to imagine, and work towards creating, a society where children are not penalized from cradle to crypt by race, zip code, or language. The authors propose an important step toward this goal, the reinterpretation and expansion of mandates from *Brown v. Topeka*. America, the richest and most powerful nation on earth, has the means to make the dream of Black Equality a reality. The challenges are daunting, but not insurmountable. What has been lacking is the will.

James Baldwin reminds us, *"Not everything that is faced can be changed; but nothing can be changed until it is faced."* As eyes turn toward the future, hope for real, sustained change in America's racial order springs eternal. At the heart of the Black ethos, central to our survival, is the belief, *"Troubles don't last always."*

Walter Allen

Introduction

$B_{ROWN\ V.\ BOARD\ OF\ EDUCATION}$ famously stands for the principle of the equality of all. Yet as we near the seventieth anniversary of *Brown*, we are far from equality. This contradiction between the embrace of equality and the reality of inequality rests upon a limited, conservative reading and implementation of *Brown*. Radical *Brown* argues that *Brown* instead stands for a mandate for comprehensive equality grounded in *shared, common, equal humanity*. We aim in this volume to expose and elaborate on this rereading of *Brown*.

Most fundamentally, we argue *Brown* commands that we recognize and implement *a vision of common humanity*. Four hundred years of systems, structures, and culture grounded in inhumanity and hierarchy centered on the assumed inferiority of Blacks and the supremacy of Whites were declared unconstitutional in *Brown* as violative of equality. This radical declaration required an equally radical full-scale replacement, a system of equality. For each child, it means the full support of foundational developmental needs. Those needs are interconnected with the accomplishment of developmental tasks essential to successful life course competence, healthy identity formation, and motivation. Linked successes include lifelong personal growth and development, physical and psychological health, and full societal and civic participation.

Support of every child's humanity and development requires dismantling embedded structural and cultural racism to build a system of equality for all children. *Brown* commands not only radical change in education, but comprehensive radical change. The full scope of four hundred years of embedded inequality had to be addressed.

We begin in chapter 1 with our rereading of *Brown*'s mandate. We provide essential scaffolding for *Brown*'s radical imperative of common humanity. This requires attentiveness to the complex layers of ecology that impact individual development that require sophisticated, deep change to achieve equality for all. This means dismantling and reconfiguring structures, systems, and cultures for both Whites and Blacks (and all people of color) with policies and practices organized and infused with the belief in, and dedication to, common humanity. Critical to Radical *Brown*, as this scaffolding establishes, is attention to our context and history, as well as a focus on how to implement common humanity on an individual level through the fully supported development of every child.

After articulating this scaffolding in chapter 1, we elaborate on its critical components and implementation in parts I and II. In part I (chapters 2–4), we focus on context and history, detailing the linked systems of slavery and segregation, the stated embrace of a comprehensive humanity-based definition of equality in the Thirteenth, Fourteenth, and Fifteenth Amendments, and the glimpse of radical change during Radical Reconstruction. This leaves no doubt of the validity of our rereading of *Brown*. At the same time, we expose the utter failure to achieve equality by the reassertion of slavery in all but name under Jim Crow. Segregation, a system of racial regression named "Redemption" by its supporters, is what *Brown* utterly rejected. *Appreciating the comprehensiveness of this system of racial hierarchy is essential to understanding the meaning and scope of the radical mandate of* Brown. The consequences of centuries of failed equality at the moment *Brown* was decided deeply affected Blacks *and* Whites—dramatically differently by race as to who gained and who lost, but a harm to all. But inequality did not end there. Despite affirmation of the radical meaning of *Brown*, comprehensive equality was resisted, denied, and undermined. The denial of *Brown*'s radical mandate continues to this day. This profound contradiction generates nothing short of developmental chaos at the individual level. This deep chronosystem defines the scope of what Radical *Brown*

requires as well as exposing the challenge for every person in a continuing racialized system of hierarchy based in inhumanity.

In part II (chapters 5–8), we elaborate on the scope of the change
needed to implement the mandate of common humanity. We add to the
common humanity scaffolding of chapter 1 core developmental tasks
that define self, community, and ultimately, our country. We explore the
developmental science, foundational to *Brown*, essential to a robust,
comprehensive system of support for every child's full humanity. Our
analysis centers the failure to fully embrace Blacks' humanity in the
wake of *Brown* and what the full recognition of Blacks' humanity means
for successful practice and policy. The troubled and established practice of making Whites' lives and meaning-making the "standard of
humanity" remains pervasive. When life course processes for people of
color are ignored as well as the enveloping role of history in their lives,
inequality sustains itself.[1] There continues to be a virtual absence of
Black child human status. To the contrary, more frequently maintained
have been assumptions of Black psychopathology, as well as ignorance
of historical conditions fomenting coping processes and identity at the
individual and collective levels of the socially constructed hierarchy of
race.[2] The long-standing concept of Blacks' inhumanity has contributed to perspectives about Black life as well as to the perpetuation of
Whiteness as the presumed standard of humanity.[3] Our rereading of
Brown takes as foundational, operational, and substantive an acknowledged shared humanity across groups and the implications of a failure
to do so, including "inequality presence denial."[4]

After our robust exploration of Radical *Brown* in parts I and II, in
part III (chapters 9 and 10), we suggest policies and strategies that
embody Radical *Brown*. We provide not a comprehensive plan but, rather,
exemplars of how Radical *Brown* might be applied in a complex, sophisticated, and sustained process of change to achieve the radical goal of
common humanity. At a policy level, we suggest a framework for legislation and voluntary implementation even in the absence of legislation.
Our focus is guided by the vision of a system that equally supports and
values the common humanity of all children, acknowledges the deep-
seeded and comprehensive character of dehumanizing traditions, and

recognizes that goal cannot be color-blind but must be color conscious of the differential construction of Black and White identity. The focus must remain on this core underlying requirement of equality. We suggest that educational policies and systems are linked to other systems. While we focus on education, education is tied to other critical systems that have long foundered in inequality and, thus, have untoward implications for domains of human functioning for Blacks and Whites. At a practice level, we highlight ideas that in whole or part are examples of implementation of Radical *Brown* that might be adopted bottom up, community by community, without waiting for political actors to engage to achieve Radical *Brown*.

Brown v. Board of Education: The Facts and the Decision

We reread *Brown* to expose its radical meaning. "Rereading" is a process common to lawyers by which constitutional cases are explored, dissected, and examined to understand their meaning in the context in which they were decided, as well as their contemporary application. Rereading is also critical to focusing social science research and strategies for remediation—particularly considered from a context-sensitive and human development perspective—based upon the realities of current conditions and a reframed goal of comprehensive change. Our rereading includes legal, philosophical, psychological, physical/structural, and cultural contexts that impact the meaning of equality that *Brown* represents. We reread with particular and careful attention to the social science so critical to the decision in *Brown*, as well as post-*Brown* developmental science.

As prelude to our analysis, it is good to remember that *Brown* was not simply one case but a collection of four state cases, commonly referred to as the Segregation Cases. Coming from Kansas, South Carolina, Delaware, and Virginia, the cases represented a cross-section of the nation, challenging the segregation required by law from kindergarten to high school. A fifth case, from the District of Columbia, *Bolling v. Sharpe*, challenged segregated high schools in the nation's capital. The Segregation Cases most directly questioned the practical *application* of the constitutional doctrine of "separate but equal." Segregation in practice had meant only separation and never equality. The Segregation Cases also challenged the underlying *doctrine* of separate but equal: the notion that equality as a principle is not violated by the involuntary separation of individuals and groups solely on the basis of race as long as all are treated equally, that racial separation has no negative meaning, no social or cultural message of privilege, subordination, or hierarchy solely for the benefit of Whites. In *Brown*, however, the plaintiffs argued that separate but equal violates the very meaning of equality in our Constitution.

The Supreme Court unanimously agreed: "We conclude that in the field of public education the doctrine of 'separate but equal' has no place. Separate educational facilities are inherently unequal."[5] The Court based its decision most squarely on the evidence that segregation communicates inequality and inferiority to Black children, grounding its conclusion on social science evidence. "Our decision . . . cannot turn on merely a comparison of . . . tangible factors. . . . We must look instead to the effect of segregation itself on public education."[6] Separation imposed harm and stigma: "To separate them [Black children] from others [White children] of similar age and qualifications solely because of their race generates a feeling of inferiority as to their status in the community that may affect their hearts and minds in a way unlikely ever to be undone."[7] The meaning and impact of segregation was particularly egregious given the importance of education to children and their development. "In these days, it is doubtful that any child may reasonably be expected to succeed in life if he is denied the opportunity of an education. Such an opportunity, where the state has undertaken to provide it, is a right which must be made available to all on equal terms."[8] Overturning the principle of "separate but equal," the Court found the true meaning of equality embodied in its earliest decisions interpreting the scope and meaning of the Equal Protection Clause of the Fourteenth Amendment shortly after the amendment's passage: a comprehensive, robust, all-embracing concept of equality. In the companion case of *Bolling v. Sharpe*[9] the Court linked this broad concept of equality to liberty: "Liberty under law extends to the full range of conduct which the individual is free to pursue, and it cannot be restricted except for a proper governmental objective. Segregation in public education is not reasonably related to any proper governmental objective."[10]

Brown was a monumental decision considering the comprehensive practice of segregation North, South, East, and West in *every* aspect of life. The overturning of "separate but equal" in education triggered the immediate dismantling of segregation in other areas. In education, however, the Court signaled that the remedy would not be immediate, by setting for argument the issue of implementation of its decision. A year later in *Brown II*, the Court affirmed the courts' broad equity powers to enforce comprehensive remedies but opened the door to delay and limitation by finding that the remedy could be implemented "with all deliberate speed" and that localized conditions prevented setting a single set of remedial guideposts.[11] *Brown* provoked widespread, long-term resistance that morphed from violent defiance and constitutional crisis to persistent racially coded policies and neutral policies with disproportionate racial impact.

Our Current Context

Inequality persists due to the failure to implement the radical, comprehensive remedy mandated by *Brown*. Our current context is one of deep, persistent inequality on the basis of race compounded and interlaced with inequality on the basis of poverty. Inequality is linked to the limited vision of the scope of *Brown* and the meaning of equality as applied to education. It is also linked to inequalities, subordination, and systemic racial hierarchy in other systems that similarly failed to implement comprehensive radical change to remedy segregation, especially in housing, employment, health, wealth, and income.

Focusing just on schools, inequality continues measured by *tangible* factors, while *intangible* factors at the core of *Brown*'s radical mandate have never been addressed. The failure to address the intangible, the common humanity core of *Brown*, may be what infects and sustains tangible inequality measures. Children of color are less likely to receive a high-quality education that supports their full developmental potential compared to White children, irrespective of the wealth of the school district where they attend school. Both children of color and White children are likely to be unequally developmentally supported to a full, robust expression of their developmental capacity, because children of color are treated as less human and White children are imbued with crippling lessons of inhumane racial supremacy.

Inequality starts long before kids begin public school, as evidenced by school readiness data. Children are not equally situated as they begin school,[12] and that is related to uneven availability and differential quality of preschool education as well the impact of income characteristics on families and neighborhoods.[13] Schools not ready to serve all children do not close gaps but instead perpetuate or exacerbate them. A Casey Foundation report labels preschool racial inequities "a national crisis."[14]

The racial demographics of the school population are changing toward a more racially diverse population of students.[15] This means a multiracial, not biracial, configuration of students. Particularly in the South and West, Latinx students are the fastest growing student group, and in the West sometimes the largest proportion of students.[16] No matter the configuration, White students attend school with more Whites than is their representation in the student population. "Segregation, modified" is the dominant pattern in terms of who is attending school with whom, as a result of de facto policies and practices and the intersection and mutual reinforcement of education and housing patterns. Thus, even under the limited interpretation of *Brown* post-1954, focused on bodies and racial mixing, implementation has been a near total failure other than sustaining White segregation.

As resegregation and intense segregation have increased, so too has the "achievement gap."[17] College readiness levels vary dramatically by race and poverty.[18] These differences should not be viewed as "achievement gaps," as one study points out, but as a "receivement gap," the predictable results of structural inequities and differential support of students by race and poverty.[19] Differences in resources, teachers, and classroom size, less challenging courses and curricula, and fewer advanced classes all contribute to this gap. Funding for schools is highly unequal: "the wealthiest 10% of school districts . . . spend nearly 10 times more than the poorest 10%, and spending ratios of 3 to 1 are common within states."[20] Teacher effectiveness is also highly unequal. "By every measure of qualifications, unqualified and underprepared teachers continue to be found disproportionately in schools serving greater numbers of low-income or minority students."[21] Inexperienced and not as highly credentialed teachers are more common in schools with high concentrations of kids of color.[22] In addition, the most ironic impact of desegregation was to undermine Black teachers, principals, and other school personnel. Today, the teaching workforce is dominantly white and female.[23]

Black students also are more often and disproportionately disciplined, suspended, or expelled.[24] The disparities begin in preschool and are especially dramatic for Black boys.[25] Black students have a higher rate of the harshest discipline of suspension and expulsion and a dramatically higher rate of referral to law enforcement.[26]

There are social and school culture consequences to the pattern of resegregation. "Racial isolation . . . can also perpetuate stereotypes and deny students the opportunity to learn different viewpoints and perspectives. Segregation undermines the important idea of a shared future and a joint society . . . and the perpetuation of stereotypes, fears, and ignorance."[27] Integration, on the other hand, "promotes cross racial understanding, breaks down stereotypes, eliminating bias and prejudice."[28] Inattention to attitudes, culture, bias, and stereotypes has thus far characterized the process of integration. Academic resources are not paired with support for common humanity in cultural and social environments.[29] Lower levels of self-esteem among Black students are characteristic when they attend majority white schools versus schools with a majority of students of color.[30] A recent compilation of research on racism in schools reinforces the dynamics and manifestations of what is called the "new racism" that has emerged post-*Brown*. The unequal educational culture reinforces racial hierarchy to the detriment of children of color and the reinforcement of White supremacy for White children.[31]

Overwhelmingly, what we know, what we have counted in comparing schools and comparing outcomes for students, has been about numbers. Research on school culture and climate is far outweighed by research that focuses on the tangible aspects of education. There is limited research about attitudes, stereotypes, bias, and how inhumanity is embedded in structural inequality. The evidence of inequality, in other words, goes far deeper than what we have presented here *because we have failed to ask whether real equality defined as common humanity exists.* Central to Radical *Brown* is whether and how schools can support the humanity of *every* child and assure *every* child's equal maximum development. Everything that has been measured demonstrates inequalities that intersect, proliferate, and ignore the mandate of Radical *Brown*. Yet the focus has been on bodies and numbers, not on outcomes of equality and the valuing of every child's humanity. We have perpetuated educational inequality, with a segregated system that identifies White with success and the perpetuation of White supremacy, and identifies children of color with failure, lesser education, less developmental potential, and a bottom line of inadequate and under-acknowledged developmental support mired in assumptions of inhumanity.

Radical *Brown*

The change that is necessary to confront and address blatant inequality is the reframing of our vision emanating from *Brown*. It is Radical *Brown* that we find and expose in detail in the following chapters: *radical in its identification of the problem and the scope of the mandate to achieve equality.* Fundamentally, the definition of inequality in *Brown* was undergirded by particular assumptions about humanity. Inequality is grounded in unacknowledged philosophical assumptions about whose humanity matters—whose humanity is recognized. Irrespective of conscious or unconscious awareness, Blacks are viewed as not human; that is the core assumption of slavery and Jim Crow. This assumption remains unchallenged and unresolved today. Its corollary is the construction of White identity grounded upon the assumption of racial supremacy and privilege, similarly unchallenged and unresolved. This is the foundational issue to be addressed in this volume. The recognition of this problem in *Brown*, and its implications for remedy, has been hidden, narrowed, marginalized, and ignored. Nonetheless, it is at the core of contemporary inequality.

Unearthing this radical understanding suggests that embedded in the *Brown* decision is a transformative understanding of the developmental make-up and capacities of children. Although framed as exclusively a concern about the negative impact of segregation on Black children, inherently, this principle of the *unfair and unconstitutional impact of structural inequality encompasses the impact on all children; it acknowledges, as well, the diverse representations and sources of human vulnerability.* This includes the construction of privilege—and costs of privilege—for White children, as well as the resistance to subordination of Black children. Recognition of developmental implications as the radical message of *Brown* mandates a *close, critical, and differentiated understanding of the human developmental process itself; it interrogates how that knowledge must be used to radically change education to equitably support the humanity of all children.* We unearth and articulate this radical understanding of *Brown.*

The developmental argument is grounded in the full analysis of the work of Dr. Kenneth P. Clark, as well as the developmental science research since *Brown* that underscores the key insight of the decision that the *intangibles* of inequality matter most. Dr. Clark's full report submitted to the Supreme Court suggested actions relevant to the impact of segregation *on both Black and White children.* Recognition of Black humanity is incomplete without confronting and dismantling White supremacy at the core of White identity.

The legal argument that builds upon this developmental insight is the recognition that freedom and equality must be defined in relation to slavery and segregation. In addition, the Supreme Court's support for developmental science in a range of recent decisions provides support for the assertion that our contemporary understanding of *Brown* not only should recognize this historical broad definition of equality but should be grounded in our understanding of the needs of children informed by both developmental science and what we know of our contemporary context of inequalities.

Brown as implemented, undeniably was a significant, monumental step forward. We can acknowledge this affirmative contribution, but it is essential that we confront and interrogate its failure. To do so undergirds our primary point: *Brown* must be radically reread to achieve meaningful equality, or it becomes yet another tool to rebuild and maintain systems of *in*equality. A first step of the process is an acknowledgement of the inhumanity status historically and contemporarily associated with Black bodies.

Independent of life course stage considered, the existence and viewpoint of *Black inhumanity beliefs* and the consequences of *"inequality presence denial"* continue unacknowledged, unabated, and uninterrogated irrespective of their functional ever-presence. Functioning as if invisible, this accepted social obliviousness reinforces racial hierarchy and destructiveness for all citizens.

As observed from the school room (re: troubling school traditions and achievement differences) to the board room (i.e., hiring traditions and salary discrepancies), and as practiced in daily navigated life spaces (e.g., walking, driving, or shopping while Black), resistance to individual and collective coping and competence efforts are obstructed or demonized. Meeting developmental tasks and thriving goals—given the contextually operationalized inhumanity status beliefs of Blacks and other minorities—collectively, represents nothing less than intergenerational trauma and misuse of tax dollars. Representing both tangibles and intangibles, it takes a toll and matters.

Brown's failure is not due to the decision, but rather to how *Brown* has been read and used. It has been frozen in time and meaning, instead of being understood in the chronology and evolving shape of racism and White supremacy. There were multiple sources of harm from segregation: individual, familial, proximal, and distal damaging ecologies of development and macro-level enduring belief systems. They were the result not only of the failure of equal protection but also of active strategies to do harm. Harm was coupled with benefits to Whites and the construction of structures and systems that embedded racial hierarchies and beliefs to support racial inequalities as justified. The full scope of this harm has been ignored. It is not because the evidence was not there but rather—given the absence of a human development lens—how it was described, in a way that encouraged misapprehension of the harm and therefore defined equality in limited and ultimately unequal ways. Yet the harm and the equitable remedies necessary to address the injuries and achieve equal protection of the law with respect to education are nevertheless present in the case. *Brown* challenged segregation as a principle and as a holistic system. Indeed, cases that followed *Brown* systematically dismantled other manifestations of Jim Crow. The scope of the case, then, comprehensively includes all the harms of segregation; the meaning of the case extends to the full scope of the harm.

Because the harm identified in *Brown* is the impact of segregation on identity, the decision requires us to understand not only the legal mechanisms of segregation, but also its philosophical assumptions and justifications. That leads to justifications for slavery that are fundamentally grounded on the inhumanity of Blacks, and the corollary assumption of White supremacy. The harm of segregation can only be resolved by addressing the intangible impact of this philosophical assumption on all children, White and Black, creating race privilege for Whites and justification for race subordination for Blacks. Equality requires challenging this philosophical assumption and its structural and cultural manifestations in the life course of children. Because of the developmental impact of this refusal to recognize and value the humanity of Black children, and confront the inhumanity central to White identity, genuinely equitable solutions must be grounded in close examination of the developmental realities of identity and concurrent functioning in the world to determine whether equality has been achieved.

The philosophical meaning and developmental consequences of slavery and segregation sustained over centuries are the heart of the opinion. The intangible was the focus of *Brown*. Educational achievement, as *Brown* recognized, is linked to support for identity, to each child's humanity. Yet that is what has been missed in the implementation of *Brown*. Identity thus is inextricably linked, then and now, to the scope of the remedies required by *Brown*.

Although *Brown* is focused on intangible factors, tangible factors are not irrelevant but simply are insufficient. Tangible factors reveal wildly unequal schools within districts, between districts, and between states. Moreover, if the concept of equality also means equity, then tangible factors must be responsive to the needs of children rather than imagine the equivalence or sufficiency of universal supports.

The developmental message of *Brown* is linked to a broad reading of the meaning of equality in the Fourteenth Amendment. Equality was both prohibitory and affirmative. Rights of equality were intended to prevent racial inequality or subordination but also imposed a duty to achieve racial equality. The positive rights protected by the Fourteenth Amendment are critical to the affirmative steps needed to accomplish Radical *Brown*.

As *Brown* says, we cannot look at equality in terms of when the Fourteenth Amendment was passed, but rather must assess our context now. Added to that imperative is the seventy years since *Brown*, three more generations of inattentiveness to our common humanity. The context now is more highly segregated schools. "Neutral" policies are responsible for this, as well as the limited focus of "integration" on numbers, not on developmental goals. Teachers represent a proximal level of the context. The context contributes to unequal opportunity and unequal achievement, linked to tangible and intangible factors. The tangible must be addressed by an unpacking of the philosophical underpinnings supporting teacher trainings and school financing efforts with the goal of providing equitable supports.

Inequalities are rife, and the hard conversations about the deeply entrenched teachings of racism remind us that those lessons often are grounded in the multiple levels of the social ecology of American life. The seamless embeddedness of the messages includes what public education *has taught every child who comes through its doors during the formation of identity*. The school-based process is variously linked with socialization experiences in the home and community. Students' unavoidable meanings made of their experience make the critically important identity process a complex task.

The acceptance of the vision of Radical *Brown* and its implementation undoubtedly will generate resistance. Together with resistance, however, there is broad support for living our principles of equality and justice, not only with respect to education but in the other interconnected systems that have sustained racial hierarchy for far too long. The very breadth of the current movement for change also supports the view that this is precisely the time for a different vision and concrete means to achieve that vision. The proposals we present are examples, not a comprehensive plan; comprehensive change requires the engagement of multiple constituencies, stakeholders, and disciplines committed to a common vision.

This is *"Radical* Brown": a mandate grounded in a developmental understanding of identity and the humanity of all children that represents the broad meaning of equality inherent in the Fourteenth Amendment. Inequalities in education are rampant not because of *Brown* but in spite of *Brown*: patterned inequities are a misreading of the scope of *Brown* when decided, as well as its meaning today.

Radical Brown *is premised on the core assumption of Black people as fully human and, thus, equal. It assumes that White identity can be recast as fully human, and therefore Whites also can be equal.* The dismantling of inequality, and the importance of the core assumption of common humanity, has never been more important than at the present. We see as fundamental the reorientation of the meaning of equality in education. *Brown v. Board of Education* requires the implementation of equality that ensures the perception *by* every child, and the perception *of* every child, *that their humanity is equally valued and supported.* The acceptance and implementation of that vision and belief in common humanity require radical change in policy and practices, top down and bottom up.

CHAPTER 1

A Scaffolded Rereading
of *Brown*

We come then to the question presented: Does segregation of children in public schools solely on the basis of race, even though the physical facilities and other "tangible" factors may be equal, deprive the children of the minority group of equal educational opportunities? We believe that it does. (*Brown*, 493)

To separate them from others of similar age and qualifications solely because of their race generates a feeling of inferiority as to their status in the community that may affect their hearts and minds in a way unlikely ever to be undone. (*Brown*, 494)

We conclude that in the field of public education the doctrine of "separate but equal" has no place. Separate educational facilities are inherently unequal. (*Brown*, 495)

Brown AS AN ICON has been drained of its meaning. Trotted out as an example of powerful constitutional change, its historic meaning has devolved into a cramped, minimized view of equality that has become a rationalization for *in*equality. Understanding *Brown* as mandating anything less than profound and necessarily radical comprehensive change ironically reduces its meaning to an apology for sustaining inequality dressed up as equality, reifying a false narrative of racial progress and shared humanity.

The need to recognize the radical meaning of *Brown* has never been more consequential. We face constant reminders of our failure to implement *Brown*'s comprehensive command to achieve equality, as well as an unparalleled reemergence and visibility of a White supremacy movement reminiscent of the post–Civil War era.

Exposing the radical meaning of *Brown* then is essential. *Brown* commands equality. Achieving equality in our current context is inextricably linked to four centuries of relentless inhumanity. We have not achieved equality because we have not sought it, have not worked for it, have not confronted what is essential to achieve it. Our rereading of *Brown* exposes the comprehensive scope of equality mandated by *Brown* centered unequivocally on common humanity.

Brown v. Board of Education's declaration of the unconstitutionality of segregation rests on the meaning and impact of segregation, particularly the impact on intangible developmental factors. This conclusion was validated with the authority of developmental science. This core reasoning is the essence of our re-reading of *Brown*'s meaning: the constitutional harm is the failure to recognize the humanity of Black children as integral to the equal and common humanity of all children, and the developmental harm of this inequality to Black and White children. The remedy required is its opposite: recognition of shared humanity and its implementation in public education.

Brown's use of social science and reliance on what the opinion called "psychological knowledge" as justification for the Court's judgment opened the door to developmental research as the mechanism for understanding the nature and impact of the harm and constructing the remedy. Nevertheless, the particular language and characterization of the developmental research and its meanings, and the Court's singling out only of harm to Black children, (1) invigorated misunderstanding of the human development findings, (2) inappropriately interpreted, conceptualized, and framed descriptions of the harm of slavery and segregation, and (3) severely compromised and affected the character of the remedy and its enactment.

Implementation ignored, misinterpreted, and limited the core meaning of shared humanity, generating profound failure. This was a failure of all essential actors: politicians at all levels of government, school boards, school administrators, teachers, parents, and students.

Violent resistance gave way to segregation by design using zoning, attendance rules, and other facially neutral tools. Biases and attitudes fostering discrimination and racial hierarchy remained rarely if ever addressed.

Historical context was denied, multiple levels of the ecology of human development were overlooked, and the impact of the nature of Blacks' enslavement and subsequent long-term treatment as chattel was profoundly ignored. The result guaranteed the persistent color-bias-based subordinate-superior American social dichotomy. Rather than critical incorporation of developmental research, further elaborated over time, the courts embraced uncritically the social science research in *Brown* without the benefit of data conceptually linked to developmental science insights: perspectives which assume shared humanity irrespective of social status. Heavily stereotypic analytic shortcomings severely hampered the design and implementation of the remedy.

Uncritical use of social science treated its application as a scientific tool as "objective." Assumptions and perspectives of research design went unchallenged. Much social science incorporates a deficit perspective about children of color and rarely examines White children's challenges, coping processes, and character of racial identities. The failure to be self-reflective or consider potential unconscious bias of (predominantly White) researchers profoundly impacts research. This does not render social science valueless but does require that it be used critically.

There are both unfinished and unrealized aspects of *Brown* due to both conservative usages of the opinion and the limited critical lens used for interpreting the social science data presented. For example, conservative usage of *Brown* began with the Court's delay in ordering remedies, followed by its failure to set implementation guidelines. The view that oversight must end supported minimal change. The uncritical adoption of a deficit perspective converting children of color into "problems" shifted the focus from structural and cultural racism to blaming the victims. It also ignored the harms of segregation to all children. *Brown*'s efficacy has been woefully inadequate both for the victims of the system as well as those privileged by it.

We provide this missing analysis in this framing chapter. We begin by identifying ecological insights and human development theorizing concerning the power of context and human "meaning making" processes. *Brown*'s efficacy (or its absence for the children of those considered human chattel) is interrogated both for appreciating the myriad expressions and processes of human vulnerability and the requirements for successful resiliency promotion. In subsequent chapters we expand upon this foundational scaffolding by delving further into colorism, identity, and intersectionality.

The PVEST Frame for Scaffolding Radical *Brown*

Our rereading of *Brown* is framed by the perspective that humanity and vulnerability are inextricably linked: vulnerability is a globally shared and an unavoidably present human status irrespective of resource level. Humanity membership and linked vulnerability align with challenges associated with navigating diverse environments in order to thrive. Thriving refers to those efforts intended to meet and address everyday needs as one engages in the fulfillment of life-course-specific developmental tasks. Navigating the life course and responding to necessary developmental tasks is not free of potholes; difficulties and myriad challenges are rampant. The process represents humanity in its unapologetic messiness.[1] Individual and collective efforts to thrive reflect different levels of vulnerability, defined as the balance or imbalance between risks and protective factors.

Our conceptual orientation of the development process is captured by the use of inclusive human development theorizing, Spencer's phenomenological variant of ecological systems theory (PVEST; pronounced P-VEST) (figure 1.1).[2]

Rather than presuming a model of child development centered around a "neutral" child, unraced and ungendered, PVEST situates development in the realities of identities, context, and history. This infuses the unfolding life course pattern and the addressing of developmental tasks to be mastered with a humanity frame that incorporates and recognizes the humanity of all children. PVEST provides

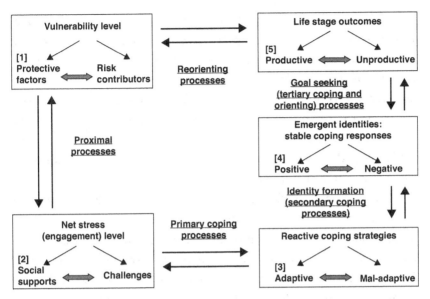

Figure 1.1 Processes emphasizing: phenomenological variant of ecological systems theory (PVEST). *Sources*: Margaret B. Spencer and Vinay Harpalani, "Nature, Nurture, and the Question of "How?": A Phenomenological Variant of Ecological Systems Theory," in *Nature and Nurture: The Complex Interplay of Genetic and Environmental Influences on Human Behavior and Development*, ed. Cynthia Garcia Coll, Elaine L. Bearer, and Richard M. Lerner (Mahwah, NJ: Lawrence Erlbaum Associates, Inc., 2004), 53–77; Margaret B. Spencer, "Phenomenology and Ecological Systems Theory: Development of Diverse Groups," in *Handbook of Child Psychology*, vol. 1: *Theoretical Models of Human Development*, 6th ed., ed. Richard M. Lerner and William Damon (New York: Wiley Publishers, 2006), 829–93.

essential scaffolding to implement our rereading of *Brown* to require the recognition of shared humanity.

PVEST's phenomenological focus emphasizes the development of human consciousness and awareness.[3] As progressively more complex sense-making of the world, development occurs through the interaction of identity, context, and experience.[4] As early socio-emotional processes, critical identity factors affect individual perceptions of self and opportunities, imposed expectations or stereotypes, and normal maturational processes. As an identity-focused cultural ecological perspective,

Spencer's PVEST emphasizes that—understood as a bidirectional process—identity can both impact risk and be impacted by risk level: "risk is best viewed as an *exacerbation of normative challenges and competencies due to larger sociopolitical processes and/or lack of resources* and resilience as successful coping with these exacerbated challenges."[5] This is critical: the normative developmental process can be exacerbated, even disrupted, by identity linked to systemic inequality manifested through differentiated (or even absent) supports for individuals and communities based on racial hierarchy.[6]

Spencer identifies five interdependent identity-linked component processes or influences: vulnerability character, stress, coping, identity, and life (stage-specific) outcomes. Critical to acknowledge is that vulnerability represents the balance or imbalance between risk and protective factors or assets and not singularly risks; particularly for Blacks, the strengths of families and individuals are real but are habitually ignored.[7] The interaction of these components translates into net vulnerability, net stress management, reactive coping mechanisms, emergent identities, and adverse or productive life-stage-specific coping products.[8] In the process of creating one's identity, these components are supported or reinforced, or not. "Identity lays the foundation for future perception, self-appraisal, and behavior, yielding adverse or productive life-stage-specific coping outcomes."[9]

Within the PVEST framework, both vulnerability level and stress are influenced by systemic and institutional factors, and systemic factors also come into play with respect to coping mechanisms. If systems (such as school or police authorities) view a coping mechanism as maladaptive, this can have serious consequences. What is considered maladaptive can vary by identity: while all children develop in the context of culture, not all do so in the same way or in the same relation to culture: "Some children develop in a cultural context in which their culture, race or ethnicity are considered privileged over other cultural and racial groups. This privilege is, unfortunately, neither recognized as such nor acknowledged as a significant life-course asset."[10] Although there are a few recent exceptions, this means that the cultural socialization of Black and minority children frequently is ignored or not adequately represented in developmental science. At the same time, the socialization of racial hierarchy continues to be overlooked. Specifically, neither privilege nor subordination has been explored in most mainstream developmental scholarship.[11] The dominant questions have been geared to "what" or outcomes due to subordination status given human tasks confronted in developmental processes, but not the "how" of the outcome.[12]

The problem of internalized hierarchical beliefs means that vulnerability is too frequently viewed as synonymous with risks and associated narrowly with minority status. However, net vulnerability status applies to all humans. At present, the state is responsive only to certain groups of "We the People," reinforcing hierarchy and inhumanity. Vulnerability level (high or low) represents factors that depend on the individual's interaction with society,[13] such as their response to stereotypes and biases linked to factors including race as well as privilege.[14] This is also associated with stress factors from neighborhood dangers, social supports (or their absence), and daily hassles; in other words, underacknowledged are challenges and support level differences.[15] Identity— particularly racial-hierarchy-linked awareness—triggers or increases risk; context-associated structural factors trigger stress. The level of vulnerability (specifically degree of risk versus protective factor accessibility) and stress identified in PVEST comes from the state. This includes systems created by the state, as well as responsive cultural traditions generated by state policies, actions, and inactions. PVEST connects state action (and inaction) to individual, granular consequences that multiply and aggregate into community and broader patterns.[16]

As a function of vulnerability level, navigating risks and stress given inequities in contexts of inequality can be daunting but can also be cause for developing resilience (i.e., given the accessing of protective factors and supports, the production of good outcomes in the face of significant risk and challenge). As Spencer has observed:

Structural racism in American society stems from systematic, institutionalized practices resulting in the subordination and devaluation of minority groups and the setting up of life course barriers for all of its members' life course experiences. The consequences of structural racism for minority youth are twofold. First, minority youth in America often live and mature in high-risk environments characterized by systemic, structural barriers to individual success [thus, resulting in "thin" effective protective factors and accessible asset presence]. Second, instances of resilience . . . often go unrecognized, thus, denying individuals a sense of success and accomplishment.[17]

The PVEST framework exposes structural and cultural factors that must be addressed to implement Radical *Brown*'s core meaning of the support of the common humanity of all children. Dislodging the embedded inhumanity norm attached to Blackness that perpetuates racial hierarchy is mandated by the state's role in creating and sustaining hierarchy and the constitutional mandate to correct this foundational and persistent inequality.

Risks, Supports, and the Recursive Process

Specific aspects of PVEST are critical to Radical *Brown*. First, in navigating stage-specific normative and unique developmental tasks and confronting challenges, assets and opportunities contribute to a manageable process, make probable the possibility of resiliency (i.e., good outcomes albeit difficulties), and result in varied levels of success. If assets and opportunity are not present, they contribute to patterned failures. Outcomes include demonstrations of everyday thriving as intermediate processes including reactive coping and ego identifications, which are associated with developmental-stage-specific outcomes that may be productive and demonstrate resilience. Again, the alternative and untoward consequences appear as unproductive and challenging outcomes.[18] Critical to acknowledge is that context, cultural traditions, and "human sense-making" contribute to responsiveness and flexibility. Bidirectional changes as opportunity and/or trauma contribute mutability. A positive aspect of the "disorderliness or messiness" in the pursuit of developmental tasks is that unexpected experiences require coping and become linked with an individual's motivational process given varied developmental tasks to be mastered as life course experiences unfold.[19]

There is always a "back and forth" or a *recursive process* between efforts and outcomes. This recursive process interacts with the multiple linked and overlapping aspects of our human functioning (cognitive, bio-neuro-physical, and psycho-social/affective domains). Ultimately, there is something to be said about successful efforts and positive outcomes (or not) achieved. Effective effort relates to having a sense of positive impact by expended efforts. Affective effort refers to the emotional/affective results emanating from the process of trying to make a difference and to impact outcomes. Another framing of the process is one of personal causation suggesting the benefits from having an impact or making a difference (i.e., as personal causation).[20] In addition to the contributions of human cognition and affective attributes, the process has biological sequalae as well (i.e., biological basis for attempts to "make a difference" or to "impact the environment"). Thus—as a recursive system—the undergirding motivational dynamic has *humanity-relevant implications*. All three domains of human development show linked, simultaneous effect, so individuals are engaged in particular activities as culturally relevant and context-aligned processes.

There is another aspect of the recursive process which acknowledges the contributions of human motivation as a source of energy, as individuals engage varying environments in the pursuit of satisfying culturally defined and developmentally linked life course human developmental tasks. Unevenness or dissonance in the experience of achieving outcomes may occur and are important. Critical is an awareness of the "goodness of fit or non-fit" between the goals of the individual (or collective) and the supports (or not) provided by the context.[21] Lack of "fit" usually causes tension and stress and may complicate the pursuit of human development tasks. Complications evoke individual as well as collective responses as reactive coping activities. Life's "messiness" creates redundancies, which precipitate stable responses characterized as identifications. Ultimately, human development-stage-specific patterned identifications function as stable identities as our lives continue to unfold.[22]

Context Matters: The Chronosystem

A second critical component of the developmental framework is context and the chronosystem. The various domains of our humanity are conjoined, unfold in multiple contexts, and are activated as meaning-making efforts associated with our cognitive, psycho-social, and bio-neuro-physical domains. The processes are necessarily aligned with the nature of the context including the psycho-historical moment.[23]

Bronfenbrenner's ecological insights make clear that history—providing the chronosystem to ecological systems theory—is a core aspect of our environment that matters at every level of the ecology. The chronosystem represents a major part of the human experience.[24] Bronfenbrenner identified multiple interacting ecological levels: the micro- (individual, first-hand experiences), meso- (stable links among micro-system-level connections), exo- (policy/decision-making level), and macro-level (amorphous and encompassing beliefs, attitudes, and assumptions about others disseminated through levels of connectedness, encompassing and impacting what happens at the other three levels). The chronosystem level penetrates across all four levels, contributing from an individual's or the collective's perspective "all-encompassing history" from the micro- outward to the macro-level. Parallel with the all-inclusive role of the macro-system level of the ecology, the chronosystem's "historical footprints" envelop all others and profoundly impact the context and character of life course learning, as well as development— and stage—specific outcomes. Without question, both individual and collective memories represent and reflect the chronosystem and the ecology.

Within an ecology of a particular era, including its threats and opportunities, the degree of "fit" or "non-fit" of individuals and communities always matters for survival and development. The process of meeting everyday tasks includes the requirement to cope with both planned and unexpected challenges given accessible or limited supports. The upside of the disorderly human process is that it allows for the honing of positive and productive coping skills and hones their internalization as stable responsive identities over time. The character of context-individual linked interactions (as productive interactions or not) as well as the candid interrogation of conflicts matters; the character of resolution provides core contributions to human vulnerability. Thriving efforts—given stress encounters and endemic coping strategies accessed, pivoted to, and engineered to address challenges—may be assessed as "successful and positive" and suggest resiliency (i.e., good outcomes in a context of high risk).[25] At the same time, others may be characterized as "adverse" and unproductive. As our PVEST framework underscores, context and the chronosystem differentiate risks, supports, and outcomes by race individually and collectively.[26] A foundational point, serving to scaffold our perspective on *Brown* and its radical rereading is specific: *it matters deeply to consider everyone's humanity given coping needs linked with the character of ecologies relevant to healthy processes and supportive policies.* The failure to do so reincorporates the impact of inhumanity and inequality.

Overlooking the fact of shared humanity introduces long-term individual and collective conditions of social fragility. Myrdal's characterization of the nation's systemic racism as an American dilemma represents the character of this social fragility.[27] Foundational to Radical *Brown*, the recognition of a shared humanity status matters—as especially relevant and foundational to diverse communities of unequal power statuses. It is particularly salient when a socially constructed racial classification system is created and operationalized for the sole purpose of securing economic assets and its harsh character and control defended by narrowly defining humanity along color lines. An essential shared humanity and vulnerability perspective, which includes the nation's color-based definition of humanity, requires acknowledging and explaining past harms for Blacks *and* Whites. This is foundational and necessary scaffolding to our radical rereading.

The chronosystem as a source of environmental risk (i.e., as well as unrealized opportunity for decreased vulnerability for Blacks *and* Whites*, albeit for different reasons) frames the stable sources of antagonism and inequality. This was in place when *Brown* was decided, characterized by both trauma producing and assistance providing everyday practices conferring collective White privilege *and* individual-level ego fragility.

One missed opportunity of *Brown* so far includes underemphasizing the role of history as a long-term influencer of all aspects of life in America for everyone.[28] This includes, for Whites, the downside of structured inequality traditions on the group's human vulnerability level, which is critical to acknowledge for joint and collective thriving and resilient outcomes. The definition of vulnerability and its conceptual framing acknowledge the importance of a balance between protective factors and supports versus exposures to risks and challenges. The level as a balance or its absence has implications for coping needs, thriving processes, and patterned outcomes fostering resiliency.[29] Historical contributions and their implications for human vulnerability as protective factors and supports reveal that concepts of Whiteness habitually scaffold Whites' ego-identity-enhancement opportunities as linked with inequality. Risk factors linked with Whiteness, although generally ignored, include ego-identity processes supported by beliefs of superiority, moral fortitude concerns (i.e., given the lack of blame, shame, pain, and guilt), empathy implications significant for the nation's social fabric, and potentially underhoned productive coping strategies in response to normative and atypical life course challenges.[30] The risks experienced as life course challenges for Whites—in the conduct of meeting developmental tasks—serve to further exacerbate and institutionalize conditions of inequality given the habit of "inequality presence denial" as a White coping tradition. It is no wonder that being called "racist" continues as a significant slur to White identity.[31]

A full seventy years following *Brown,* concerns about integration continue, including fears about "brown bodies" as well as "displacement fears" given population estimates of minority and nonminority Whites by the middle of the twenty-first century. The coping mechanisms of Whites blame Blacks and cast aspersions and mistrust of the government. Thus, the January 6 Capitol rioters' chants that "you will not displace us" may represent both a fear of population shifts and, as well, uncomfortableness with expectations linked with the fragility of an internalized belief of White superiority and, thus, the displacement of the multisourced identity-relevant uncomfortableness onto others.

Empathy and Whiteness

A final critical insight from the PVEST framework is the developmental importance of social cognition and empathy and the particular developmental evolution of Whiteness as a racial identity. Ignoring the chronosystem and the impact of historical practices feeds a tradition to overlook prior events that favor those having power and to discount its process of attainment and maintenance. A humanity orientation, on the other hand, fosters empathy and caring as well as accurate historical knowledge. Attentiveness to empathy and how it is acquired is revealing.[32] At the start of life, the emergent process of developing empathy occurs in social contexts and practices with "similar and dissimilar" others and helps to frame life course ego processes.[33] The interpersonal experiences and skills implicit in interactions and mutual practices represent both developmental linked achievements and evolving socialization-based experiences within families and communities. Empathy develops as the capacity to see another's point of view. This is a normative growth process from ego-centered thought processes to those encompassing "independent others."[34]

Interesting and illustrative of the importance of empathy, the observations and analyses of the nation's forty-fifth president demonstrate the significance of an absence of empathy or selected unawareness of "the other" outside of opportunities narrowly serving the self.[35] The end of the nation's second decade of the twenty-first century was, as well, a period preoccupied with suggestions of narcissism in elected leadership. From the outside, it communicated fears of peril both for a nation threatened by the global pandemic COVID19 as well as national security concerns during a period of transition of presidential power unlike anything previously observed in the nation's modern era.[36]

An absence of empathy, caring, and concerned treatment—in fact, a reluctance to bestow compassionate status particularly to "unlike others"—functions as a refusal to acknowledge their status of basic humanity. In our rereading of *Brown* grounded in context, we take into consideration that American slavery was more brutal than other national models and represented a collective identity tied to significant economic and global benefits from agricultural products, as well as individuals' inferred beliefs in an assumed superiority. The assumed superiority of Whites and inferiority of slaves and the defined superiority status of Whites based upon skin color difference was, additionally, associated with an inferred standardized human status. Most significantly, the linkage of the institution of slavery, labor needs, and control concerns regarding Black bodies created socially constructed racial hierarchies and colorism beliefs that remain powerful. The failure to incorporate and implement the necessary humanity-recognition at the core of *Brown* has meant that *Brown* has functioned primarily at a level of aspiration. The actual operationalization of inferior beliefs concerning Blacks and assumptions of superiority of Whiteness precipitate sources of significant stress for both Whites and Blacks albeit for different reasons. Problematic is the uninterrogated bonus of "wages of Whiteness" for Whites as well as the history of Black inhumane treatment, without consequences, that reinforces perceptions of uneven power and everyday violence for Blacks.[37]

Irrespective of race, for both groups, effective reactive coping is required. Specific protective factors enjoyed by Whites—and set into motion by enduring traditions supportive of particular reactive coping strategies—continue. Reducing African slaves from a human status to de jure and de facto chattel slavery status endures as linked with social traditions of work opportunities, educational access, family formation, health supports, and economic traditions. Historical memory lapses provide "cover" from addressing criminal justice traditions and disproportionate incarceration rates and unequal economic traditions that continue to satisfy cheap labor needs. All create sources of stress and reactive coping needs given developmental tasks to be met, which are associated with education, housing, and employment inequality traditions. Given social cognition processes and the ability to infer potential threats of economic loss, and linked ego needs given under-interrogated beliefs of superiority, the situation precipitates and secures structured inequality. It is an extraordinary individual and collective reactive coping response and linked set of practices more associated with expectations for "beasts of labor" versus human beings having basic humanity needs.

The strategy of linking white skin color with life course human status has been and continues to be an effective strategy for the continuation of racist traditions. More specifically and totally ignored post-*Brown*, continuing to treat non-White positionality as a "beast of labor" status produced an identity for Whites—albeit as a fragile ego status—as one of assumed superiority. The color-based characterization generates determinative policies and de jure and de facto inequality-supportive practices. Guaranteed have been persistent inhumane practices and inauthentic (White) identifications scaffolding unacceptable traditions.

From a theoretical perspective that recognizes the role of stress for reactive coping processes, stripping individuals from a human status based solely on the construction of status defined by skin color differences institutionalized the identification of "Whiteness" as a powerful source of a "fragile ego identity." It communicates both superiority for self and a vehicle for minimizing cognitive dissonance potentially generated by the mistreatment of Blacks. There is minimal dissonance about those for whom humanity remains unrecognized. Individuals cannot easily feel guilty about someone who is not considered human. Accordingly, lacking discernible identification with "the other," there is no reason for empathy, caring, or any human consideration.[38]

The attendant and evolved four-hundred-year-old uninterrogated collective White identity remains intact. Missed are opportunities for dissection and analysis. Recursively linked reactive coping virtually guarantees institutional instability, the honing of a problematic and fragile ego identity for Whites, and collectively, a lack of success in recognizing and practicing traditions of shared humanity. Legitimizing the use of a particular reactive coping strategy and continuing the extraordinary control of context that disproportionately denies access to supports and protective factors reinforces the norm of inequality. Its consistency benefits individual and collective identity processes (internalized beliefs of White superiority) for the maintenance of uneven power statuses between Whites and Blacks. Infrequently addressed as well are successful strategies in White families and communities dissuading beliefs of Black inhumanity. Rarely if ever explored are the supports for White resiliency traditions that result in beliefs of shared humanity status irrespective of race and skin color.

America's brand of slavery was powerful and sustaining of a fragile ego status.[39] It served to scaffold identifications of superiority and the presumed standard for humanity. Constructed race-associated practices intended to deny the essence of the humanity of unlike others is pregnant with meaning for White identity and those possessing Brown and Black bodies.

The "fragility of self" and collective "fragile group identity" processes imply the extreme situation of denying the humanity of others for the purpose of sustaining beliefs of White human superiority and, thus, "to claim or own as exclusive," the standard as the representative of humanity. The psychological reactive coping vehicle scaffolding the ego processes communicates a normalized mindset suggesting "self" as the successful standard against which all others are compared. Reactive coping strategies may be honed, broadened, and protected by uninterrogated beliefs of White superiority. Assisted by socially constructed systems reinforcing conditions of structured inequities, social-psychological systems abetting learning, including school curricula content and family socialization, serve to increase and sustain viewpoints and values. In a character flawed-like manner, the process works brilliantly.[40]

Conclusion

The lack of an appreciation of Black children's humanity and the failure to confront White children's socialization in a White superiority-identified manner led to the misuse and misreading of *Brown*. Its true radical meaning was at best merely aspirational versus a blueprint for change that acknowledges the significant impact of ecological considerations and the role of history. Colorism and an imposed inhumanity status imposed upon Blacks and superiority status afforded Whites allows everyday de jure and de facto traditions to endure. The lived and under-interrogated beliefs aid a particular identity process, comfortable mindset and uncritical thriving conditions for Whites. At the same time, for Blacks, practices suggesting their inhumanity continue unaddressed, and conditions of chattel slavery persist given the many examples of structured inequalities. Most certainly, the questions posed by social science assist the system. Questions about how slavery imbued superior identity processes for Whites are ignored, and the strategies of the social sciences persist that demonstrate the greater human vulnerability of Blacks with explanation of outcome differences fueling beliefs of inferiority.

Radical *Brown* mandates the unrealized radical reconstruction of comprehensive equality. It is constructed on the scaffold of the PVEST frame of what is needed for developmental equality based on common humanity. As we have established, risks and supports operating in a recursive process require ongoing focus and change. The variable experience of our current context must attend to achieving common humanity for both Blacks and Whites, both oppressed but highly differentiated by the inhumanity of the persistence of beliefs integral to slavery and segregation. The theoretical scaffolding provided exposes the ecological levels essential to establish common humanity as complex and interconnected. One of the aspects that pervades all levels is the impact of history, the chronosystem, which creates the footings for our contemporary context. The past continues to govern our present because we have not destroyed our foundational belief in the inhumanity of Blacks, nor have we embraced the common, equal humanity of all. We establish the links between past and present, as well as the reminder that the vision of common humanity, the clear intention to adopt a radical reorienting to a new, inclusive "We the People," has been articulated for over two hundred years yet has been persistently subverted. We identify the individual, human, developmental consequences of sustained beliefs concerning inferiority and sustained conditions of privilege for the task of constructing common humanity. These complex consequences cannot be ignored lest we repeat the process of reconstructing inequality.

PART I

Context

CHAPTER 2

Slavery, Emancipation, and Reconstruction

THREE AND A HALF CENTURIES of slavery and segregation embed racial hierarchy in a deep chronosystem that underlies the developmental challenge to achieve individual and collective shared humanity that is *Brown's* command. History also defines the scope of what *Brown* declared unconstitutional. History infuses the legal scope of *Brown*, the takedown of a comprehensive system which the law had been instrumental in constructing and defending. Jim Crow reflected a continuation and deepening of the rationale and practice of slavery. The history of slavery and segregation together dictate the content of equality and freedom, infusing the scope of the constitutional mandate as well as the ecology of harm in need of comprehensive reconstruction. *The scope of the harm defines the scope and depth of the remedy.*

We must know our past because it governs our present. Only by identifying the linked systems of slavery and segregation, and their underlying foundational beliefs of presumed Black inhumanity and White supremacy, can *Brown* be understood as standing for its opposite: systemic comprehensive equality grounded in *common humanity.* Radical *Brown's* affirmation of common humanity requires a completed comprehensive Reconstruction to end the subordination of Blacks and the false elevation of Whites. Reconstruction can only occur by grasping the developmental impact of sustained inhumanity, in order to understand the task before us.

Slavery

Slavery is not a distant historical footnote to contemporary racial inequality; to the contrary, it is foundational to the contemporary structure of beliefs of racial inferiority, inhumanity, and hierarchy. While slavery was not unique to the United States, the uniqueness of American slavery was its racialization. The mark of slavery was Blackness, justified by beliefs of Black racial inferiority that rationalized racial oppression. All who were not Black were constituted over time out of multiethnic origins into becoming "White." Whiteness was defined at its core as racial superiority. The power of this underlying racial foundation permitted the White revolutionary patriots and the drafters of the Constitution simultaneously to proclaim the equality of all while practicing racial slavery as well as racial hierarchy. Emancipation ended slavery but left the system of racial hierarchy grounded in racial inferiority and inhumanity intact, as well as the core definition of Whiteness as racial supremacy. The Reconstruction Amendments were intended to complete the step from unequal emancipation to equal humanity. By definition, in order to displace racial hierarchy, they were intended to radically shift personhood for Whites as well as for Blacks. This step is yet incomplete. Radical *Brown* mandates that move to completion.

We can only know what equality/freedom means by reference to inequality/slavery. Understanding slavery, defining it, knowing how it operated, and comprehending its impact on African Americans and on Whites, is critical. Key aspects of slavery included the following:

1. Slavery was diffuse, uneven, and differentiated depending on the specific colony and region of the country, in terms of its extent, legal framework, and everyday manifestation. It was comprehensive, a national system—the US was a slave republic or state, because in every state the core feature of the distinctive US system, that slavery was racially defined and all African Americans were presumed slaves, was foundational.
2. Slavery was intimately intertwined with economic growth and capitalism. It was integral to the ability to expand and change the

economy with the assurance of cheap labor and absolute control over labor.[1]

3. There was no colony or territory where Blacks were free and equal. It was not possible to escape slavery by becoming a freeman. A freeman (or free man) meant not being subject to slavery but, nevertheless, subject to the assumption that one was a slave. Even if known to be free, one was not an equal to Whites, one was not fully free. While not all Whites enjoyed the same level of freedom, the potential to transcend one's status was theoretically possible. For a Black person, it was not. The Fugitive Slave Acts were emblematic of this mark of status: they enforced the slave system nationally; no Black person was safe under these statutes. The infamous *Dred Scott* decision[2] similarly expressed the assumed inhumanity, inferiority, and therefore justified exclusion of all Black people from "We the People," and the corresponding racial superiority of Whites. Many abolitionists as well could not imagine comprehensive equality. Coexisting with fervent opposition to slavery was the idea that a reconstructed system of inequality would mirror the treatment of freemen. Black inferiority and White supremacy would continue.

4. Slavery was total, reinforced socially as well as legally. It evolved over a period of several centuries and was deeply embedded in institutions, practices, social norms, and cultural beliefs. Extra-legal control was as important, even more important, than legal control. Legal control meant courts supported slavery (civilly, by the use of contract and property law; criminally, by walling off criminal law or applying it differentially, including the inability of slaves to testify or to bring claims for maltreatment or death). Law also enacted specific slave codes to supplement existing laws. Insulating slaveholders from legal consequences and allowing custom and social norms to control slaves was another way the law reinforced the broad and corrosive total system.

5. Slavery constructed racial identity as critical and highly differentiated. For Whites, identity was grounded in White supremacy. Whiteness evolved over time as a racial identity but always was marked, during slavery and post-slavery, by the core belief and

expression of superiority and hierarchy. Racial solidarity enabled class control by conferring racial privilege that operated to prevent class solidarity between former slaves and indigent Whites. Embracing equality would require relinquishing or destroying racial privilege and a fundamental redefinition of Whiteness. It also would require Whites to confront their own dehumanization and self-value tied to a false sense of worth. The acceptance of slavery and its racial privilege was dehumanizing to Whites. For Blacks racial identity meant social death, physical and psychological harm, and degradation. As Orlando Patterson explains:

> The social death of slavery was a prolonged assault on every . . . elementary human needs. Social death did not destroy them . . . rather, it hung like the sword of Damocles over the head of every slave who ever lived. . . . All ties were precarious . . . experienced as an ever-present sense of impending doom that shadowed everything, every thought, every moment of her existence. This is the essence of natal alienation, which, in addition to its crushing psychological impact for every individual slave, also entailed their inability as a group to "freely integrate the experience of their ancestors into their lives.[3]

> Slavery was grounded in a presumed lack of humanity. And yet there was resistance to subordination, the creation of racial identity, human-ness and sense of self in spite of White subordination, the creation of Black culture out of multiple African cultures and languages, and a lived reality not controlled by Whites, differentially developed regionally. It also meant that there was a clear Black concept of freedom and equality that was grounded in essential humanity.[4]

6. This totalistic system was replicated, rather than eliminated and replaced, after Emancipation and the failure to sustain Radical Reconstruction. Segregation represented a morphing, reconstituted system of slavery. The two are inextricably intertwined.

Slavery emerged in a context of "unfreedom," where law defined multiple statuses of limited freedom, including apprenticeship and indenture. Slavery was a relationship of domination but also of parasitism, where slaveholders had to construct stereotypes designed to ignore or render invisible the domination at the heart of the relationship.[5] As Judge Leon Higginbotham Jr. underscores, inferiority was the foundation of all else.[6]

Intersecting imperfectly with economic and class lines, slavery hardened over time along race lines. Slavery and race merged.[7] Slave law, then, created a racialized status that was the opposite of freedom: "white liberty and black slavery [became] ... reciprocals."[8] Freedom became twisted into the notion that republican liberty *required enslavement*. The ultimate justification for slavery was its morality, reinforced by religion. It was a "just" system essential to the creation of "republican equality," meaning the equality of all Whites.[9] It was claimed to be essential to Whites who believed they were racially superior, and thus inferior Blacks required, and were benefitted by, White masters.[10]

Moreover, Whites deemed slavery essential to prevent crime, by assuming and associating criminality on the basis of race.[11] All Blacks were presumed to be slaves; this racial mark made certain behavior presumptively criminal and imposed "a presumption of guilt based on race."[12] This assumption applied to free Blacks as well. This meant the judicial system for Blacks did not operate fairly or neutrally but, instead, assumed guilt and punished more onerously by race.

Yet these justifications pale beside the economic dynamic: slavery was economically essential.[13] Edward Baptist demonstrates the crucial intersection between slavery and capitalism; slavery was intertwined with economic expansion and development, a more efficient, less costly system than indenture.[14] Baptist calls this "the half that has never been told":

The massive and cruel engineering required to rip a million people from their homes, brutally drive them to new, disease-ridden places, and make them live in terror and hunger as they continually built and rebuilt a commodity-generating empire—this vanished in the story of a slavery that was supposedly focused primarily not on producing profit but on maintaining its status as a quasi-feudal elite, or producing modern ideas about race in order to maintain white unity and elite power.[15]

The harm of slavery is then not only denial of rights, Baptist argues, but also its function economically and structurally.

[The practices of white enslavers for picking cotton] rapidly transformed the southern states into the dominant force in the global cotton market, and cotton was the world's most widely traded commodity at the time, as it was the key raw material during the first century of the industrial revolution. The returns from cotton monopoly powered the modernization of the rest of the American economy . . . *In fact, slavery's expansion shaped every crucial aspect of the economy and politics of the new nation.*[16]

This is the story of how "commodification and suffering and forced labor of African Americans is what made the United States powerful and rich."[17] This is a radically different version of American history: "Enslaved African Americans built the modern United States, and indeed the entire modern world, in ways both obvious and hidden."[18]

Irrespective of slave-holding patterns and the presence or absence of significant slave populations, slavery and racial hierarchy were national in scope and integral to territorial expansion. Colonial slave law had three core characteristics:

First, law had to create a new form of property that recognized the ownership of human beings. Next, the men who made law imposed a regime of race control, deliberately suppressing the human spirit's impulse to freedom, dignity, and autonomy by whatever violence was necessary. Finally, to make its control of the subordinate race effective, the dominant race had to impose extensive restrictions on its own liberty in order to deny liberty to others.[19]

Although in some instances a separate body of law, such as the Virginia slave codes, governed slavery, the law of slavery primarily constituted the application of existing legal categories to enable private control, especially through the law of property and contract,[20] what one

scholar calls "the banality of evil."[21] Slave owners were given broad dis-
cretion in the treatment of slaves, because they were simply property
with which the owner could do as he wished.[22]

The very law used to oppress was sometimes used as a tool of
resistance. Adrienne Davis has identified estate cases where formerly
enslaved women and their children successfully sued for their rights to
wealth and property.[23] The notorious 1850 Fugitive Slave Law was successfully used to establish the status of free Blacks: four of every ten persons prosecuted under the Act ended up declared free.[24] Freedom suits
under state law were a means to use the law to shift from slave to free
Black status and to articulate the concept of freedom.[25]

Law also validated social practice and custom. "Statutes were not
necessarily the only or the most dynamic vehicle of change, and they
contained only a fraction of the "law." Custom was a coequal form
of law-making through the period of slavery."[26] Examples of custom
include "almost any activity or aspect of slave life," such as food rations,
the amount of work time and free time, and the operation of public
markets by slaves.[27] The lived reality of slavery thus was far more comprehensive than the legal recognition of slavery and legal support of slavery. The mark of race justified exploitation, violence, family division, and
the denial of social and cultural freedom. The disregard of family was
particularly cruel and egregious. As Peggy Cooper Davis notes:

> The moral voice of the slave was therefore silenced in two ways, First,
> parents were prohibited from teaching freely chosen values to their
> children. Second, slave children were denied both the moral and
> social heritage of their families and the freedom to develop values
> in the more flexible and intimate environment of family.[28]

The imposition of such harm also generated consciousness, including
fostering autonomous values and family values.[29] "For children, civil
freedom brings nothing less than the right to grow to moral autonomy, because the child-citizen, like the child-slave, flowers to moral
independence only under authority that is flexible in ways that slaves
and masters cannot manage, and temporary in ways that slaves and
masters cannot tolerate."[30] So if slavery assumes a lack of personhood

and humanity, freedom is a recognition of full capacity, choice, and morality.

Amidst this oppressive system was resistance and creation: "what enslaved people made together—new ties to each other, new ways of understanding their word—had the potential to help them survive in mind and body . . . But the road on which enslaved people were being driven was long. It led through the hell."[31] They created a collective body that continued to survive and demand more; they were political because "African Americans had a story that made them a people."[32] What was learned and created is linked to survival of slavery and segregation.[33]

Racial identity was critical in the construction of Whiteness and the scope of Blackness. This was foundational to slavery and has been sustained ever since. Because racial identity was constructed, it was determined in the nineteenth century by racial performance.[34] "Proving one's whiteness meant performing . . . While the essence of white identity might have been white 'blood,' because blood could not be transparently known, the evidence that mattered most was evidence about the way people acted out their true nature."[35]

The evolution of Whiteness occurred over the colonial period through the establishment of the republic and into the nineteenth century. It shifted from a notion of multiple White races with distinct "temperaments" to the concept of a single White race by the early twentieth century.[36] However defined, it was critical. The earliest American immigration statute, the Naturalization Act of 1790, authorized citizenship only for "free white persons."[37] Defining who was "White" by law was then a critical determination.[38] Whiteness was defined against Blackness or, alternatively, by racial superiority, two variations of a core racial theme. At best it evolved into a sense of a lack of racial identity, erasing recognition of racial privilege so that self-value was "objective," neutral, and real. At worst, it was the justification of inhuman practices by slave owners and their successors in the Klan, as well as White supremacists of our day.[39] So a critical part of White identity, born in slavery and its beliefs about Blackness, is the belief in racial superiority.[40] There is no content in Whiteness that is egalitarian; superiority is always present. While who is White has been constructed, fluid, and evolutionary, the meaning of White has remained inextricably linked to *in*equality.

Robin Lenhardt identifies the principal source of racial injury as racial stigma.[41] The consequence of stigma is *social dehumanization*: "a racially stigmatized person becomes socially spoiled, dishonored, and 'reduced in our minds from a whole and usual person to a tainted, discounted one.'"[42] The nature of the harm imposed is both individual and group harm, including a deprivation of full personhood and citizenship.

Amidst the oppressiveness of slavery, history is rife with "battles for freedom, equality and inclusion [as well as ideals of] self-determination, self-governance, and self-defense."[43] One of the most widespread patterns of resistance was rebellion during the Civil War, which dramatically shifted the outcome of the war as well as the necessity and scope of emancipation.[44] The agency of slaves during the war suggests distinctive and sophisticated political agency and the importance of defining freedom and equality from the perspective of Black people.

Throughout the period of American slavery, while all Blacks were presumed to be slaves, not all Blacks were slaves. In the first census, in 1790, there were nearly 60,000 free Blacks in the US. By 1810, the number was 186,000.[45] More lived in the South than in the North.[46] The status of free Blacks starkly illustrates the racial hierarchy created by slavery that transcended slavery, because not only were free Blacks subject to the challenge that they were slaves, but also they were legally, as well as socially, not treated as equals. The framework of the treatment of freemen was the precursor to what the post-slavery world became.[47] Limitations were not uniform but, rather, were more restrictive generally in the Lower South than in the Upper South or the North.[48] The other alternative was to encourage colonization; seeing the coexistence and equal personhood of Blacks and Whites as unimaginable.[49]

Ibram Kendi views American history as characterized by two historical forces, racial progress and the progression of racism, embodying antiracist equality and racist inequality.[50] According to Kendi, racial discrimination generates racist ideas, which generate ignorance and hate. Acts precede the articulation of ideas; the powerful direct those without power.[51] Isabel Wilkerson names the issue in different terms, as caste, but like Kendi, she underscores the depth of the belief system and its structural manifestations, grounded in slavery as the origin story recast over time.[52] The construction of caste is traced to White supremacy and the reassertion of slavery's caste system through segregation to the present. Caste operates as unseen but central, baked in, like the core structure of a house, a structure of hierarchy.[53]

Slavery is foundational; it reappears transformed but undefeated. It morphs, what Elise Boddie calls "adaptive discrimination," a constant that persists, resists, and fights equality.[54] This is critical to defining the scope of *Brown*: the condemnation of segregation reaches backward to segregation's goal to replicate slavery. Rather than separating slavery from the meaning of *Brown*, it is integral to its meaning. *Brown* was critical for recognizing that after slavery there was not progression but regression as segregation reinscribed and deepened the inequality of slavery.[55]

Slavery reaches into the present, due to the unresolved and incomplete transformation to comprehensive equality. Achieving Radical *Brown* requires achieving the unrealized promise of comprehensive, systematic equality, consistent with the vision but unattained goal of Reconstruction. Achieving *common* humanity requires addressing the interlocking threads of inhumanity present in the construction of Black and White identities.

Reconstruction

Two competing trends emerge after the Civil War, converging in *Brown*. The dominant trend was the reassertion of slavery in all but name, through the infamous Black Codes after the assassination of Lincoln, followed by Jim Crow after Reconstruction ended. Subordination was accomplished by disfranchisement, violence, and the hardening of customary and legal rules of separation, all in the service of sustaining White supremacy. The competing trend was Emancipation and Reconstruction, understood as substantive, affirmative, and grounded in equality and freedom. This included restructuring the Constitution by enacting the Thirteenth, Fourteenth, and Fifteenth Amendments and the extraordinary effort to reconstruct the Union as a multiracial democracy during the brief period of Radical Reconstruction.

Both of these trends are critical to Radical *Brown*. The persistence of inequality, its morphing into segregation and the deepening of beliefs and practices of White supremacy, is a reminder that the comprehensive system of racial inequality during slavery continued and evolved under segregation, and defines the scope of the harm *Brown* was to correct. At the same time, the scope and understanding of Radical Reconstruction underscore the broad vision of systemic equality embodied in the Reconstruction Amendments. Even if imperfect in execution, Radical Reconstruction remains as an embodiment of comprehensive equality. We identify here the links between Reconstruction and Radical *Brown*.

The Reconstruction Amendments (the Thirteenth, Fourteenth, and Fifteenth Amendments) fundamentally rewrote the Constitution, aiming to reconstitute American society and culture to embrace racial equality. This was transformative constitutionalism. Eric Foner, the preeminent historian of Reconstruction, argues that the Reconstruction Amendments amounted to a "second founding," because of the effort to create an equal society as well as the expansion of federal power.[56] The Emancipation Proclamation, issued January 1, 1863, only applied to states in rebellion, not nationally. More than two years later, after the end of the Civil War, national emancipation was achieved with the ratification of the Thirteenth Amendment. The Fourteenth Amendment, guaranteeing substantive rights of equal protection, due process, birthright citizenship, and the privileges and immunities of citizenship, was ratified three years later, along with the final Reconstruction Amendment, the Fifteenth Amendment, guaranteeing the right to vote to Black men.

If the goal of the Reconstruction Amendments is understood as giving newly freed men Constitutional support to be treated fully not only as "citizens" of the United States, but also as whole persons or human beings, and ensuring that such treatment would be manifest in the real world, then it embodies a radical rather than limited understanding of emancipation and of the society that would follow.[57] Social reform would encompass substantive conditions necessary to human dignity.[58] That would require common humanity, triggering not only a reconceptualization of Blackness but also a redefinition of Whiteness in egalitarian terms.

The Reconstruction Amendments established the principle of racial equality, fundamentally and radically reforming the racial foundation of our country. The attempt to implement this radical constitutional vision of comprehensive equality, removing Blackness as stigma and presumed inferiority, dismantling White supremacy, and embracing equal humanity, was short-lived in the brief, imperfect effort at Radical Reconstruction. Not only was Reconstruction limited to the South, but it failed to include essential tools for equality. Nevertheless, it stands as a remarkable effort dedicated to systemic equality.

W. E. B. Du Bois characterized Reconstruction as an "idealistic effort to construct a democratic, interracial political order . . . as well as a phase in a prolonged struggle between capital and labor for control of the South's economic resources."[59] It was a period of movement, flow, and complexity, a window on both a radical understanding of freedom and equality and the challenges of the embedded racism of slavery. Economic shortcomings were critical: the lack of a strong economic component to Reconstruction significantly undermined its efficacy.[60]

Freedom and equality were defined by former slaves and free Blacks as inclusion: "Freedom meant inclusion rather than separation. Recognition of their equal rights as citizens quickly emerged as the animating impulse of Reconstruction black politics . . . demanding civil equality and the suffrage as indispensable corollaries of emancipation."[61] Particularly strong was a desire for autonomy, individually and collectively, rooted in efforts to achieve economic independence.[62] Furthermore, there was a strong movement to achieve basic literacy as well as establish schools for children.[63] A robust set of self-generated goals regarding the meaning of freedom included freedom of physical movement, self-determination, recognition and respect for family, religious freedom, including the establishment of separate Black churches, literacy education for adults and schools for children, and full civil and political rights. This defining of freedom emerged prior to formal

Reconstruction of any kind. It is all the more remarkable because it emerged within "a wave of violence that raged almost unchecked in large parts of the postwar South."[64]

The economic consequences of freedom were especially contested. Freedmen and freedwomen advocated for land redistribution to ensure their independence, as well as defining free labor in terms of fair wages and freedom of contract and movement. Whites, on the other hand, resisted all aspects of economic freedom. One of the most flawed characteristics of Reconstruction was the lack of land redistribution, in conjunction with the implementation of labor practices that re-created conditions mimicking slavery, designed to perpetuate Black dependency and poverty.

Radical Reconstruction began only after enactment of the Reconstruction Act of 1867, establishing military districts and requiring states to take certain steps prior to rejoining the union, including writing new constitutions that guaranteed universal manhood suffrage and the right to education, and ratifying the Fourteenth Amendment, to ensure equality for freed persons equivalent to the rights of Whites. This was "a stunning and unprecedented experiment in interracial democracy."[65] Engagement was immediate and profound. Radical Reconstruction facilitated an incredible shift in political participation, and the goals of that participation were clear. "We claim exactly the same rights, privileges and immunities as are enjoyed by white men—we ask nothing more and will be content with nothing less. . . . The law no longer knows white nor black, but simply men, and consequently we are entitled to ride in public conveyances, hold office, sit on juries, and do everything else which we have in the past been prevented from doing solely on the ground of color."[66] Historian Eric Foner claims that the ultimate, utopian goal was color-blindness, meaning the end of racial hierarchy. While that vision was remarkably broad, there were conflicts between radicals and moderates about the speed and substance of change. So, for example, the right to education was included in the new Southern states' constitutions, but the question of whether education would be integrated or segregated was often sidestepped. The strongest, clearest, and most immediate demand was suffrage.

Steven Hahn underscores how Reconstruction is a window into the transformative actions of Black communities, their construction of what equality meant, how it was experienced, and how it was compromised and resisted.[67] Hahn argues that extraordinary Black political activity during Reconstruction is rooted in Black political activity during slavery, in the course of the Civil War, and immediately at war's end. "The black military role in support of the Union made possible a revolution in American civil and political society that was barely on the horizon of official imagination as late as the middle of 1864."[68] Emancipation as originally conceived did not translate into full humanity or citizenship; that definition emerged because of the role of Black soldiers: "A new relationship between their grassroots aspirations and a nation-state was being imagined. In the history of slavery and freedom in the Atlantic world, there never had been nor ever would be anything quite like it."[69]

The advent of universal male suffrage energized communities at all levels. Freedmen registered in high numbers, mostly as Republicans, helped to write new state constitutions that were dramatically egalitarian, and "began to build—with an assortment of tensions and conflicts—new political relations, institutions, and aspirations within their own communities."[70] The first Black US senator was seated in 1870; by this time there were Black officeholders at every level of government, a model of biracial political engagement. This was possible due to proportionate majority status or by collaboration with Whites. As Hahn argues, how former slaves accomplished these tasks remains one of the most remarkable, though still relatively unexplored, chapters in American history."[71] They also consolidated kinship ties, changed labor patterns, and collectively settled on available land, building kinship ties and associations and societies creating community organizations. Their vision of equality embraced community social welfare.[72]

What the Klan did in response was not new or unique but part of an ongoing pattern of terrorism: "Paramilitary organization had been fundamental to the social and political order of slavery; it remained fundamental to the social and political order of freedom."[73] When Radical

Reconstruction ended, what followed was horrific. The period from 1877–1901 was one of severe repression.

For the Black community, Reconstruction was a period of assertiveness and transformation, tempered with the recognition of limitations, contradictions, and failures. Black political activity was tied to family and community, work and religion, and land. Violence and paramilitary activity were deeply embedded in the White South. The collapse of Reconstruction and the fierceness of Redemption triggered patterns of separation and emigration, culminating in the Great Migration. The Great Migration fundamentally changed the configuration of the African American population: it became national, urban, and industrial, engaging in new political forms.[74] At the same time, there was evolving consciousness: "Relying on the relations and institutions that they had built and that enabled them over many decades to endure oppression and make themselves as a people, they challenged the nation—as their slave and freed forebears had done—to confront the meaning of its own democracy."[75]

Things had forever changed, and that change reached a high point during Reconstruction. The low point, and deepest failing of Reconstruction, was the lack of economic policies to ensure empowerment (in addition to racial violence). As Kathy Franke argues, freed people recognized that property rights were essential to their freedom.[76] So too, she argues, was repair for the harms of slavery: "The failure to provide any kind of meaningful reparation to formerly enslaved people in the 1860s has ongoing structural effects today . . . the original sin from which the evil of structural racism has grown is clear.[77]

This was justice never received and unfair advantage perpetuated. It was the difference between being a *free*man and a *freed*man: a freeman had civil and political rights; a freedman was not a slave but not a freeman.[78] "The badge of being freed has produced intergenerational forms of disadvantage for which reparation remains past due."[79] In addition to and intertwined with this economic failure was the failure to interrogate Whiteness, to separate White identity from White supremacy and White privilege. The deepening of White inhumanity toward

Blacks was the lack of reckoning with Whites' own sense of self. As W. E. B. Du Bois lamented, "Instead of standing as a great example of democracy and the possibility of human brotherhood America has taken her place as an awful example of its pitfalls and failures, so far as black and brown and yellow peoples are concerned."[80] Du Bois saw Reconstruction as the opposite of this failure, a period of enduring significance:

> The most magnificent drama in the last thousand years of human history is the transportation of ten million human beings out of the dark beauty of their mother continent into the new-found Eldorado of the West. They descended into Hell; and in the third century they arose from the dead, in the finest effort to achieve democracy for the working millions which this world had ever seen.[81]

Reconstruction was an enormous failure, and the consequences of that failure persist to this day. The harsh, enduring inequality and racial hierarchy that reasserted itself at Reconstruction's end is mirrored in resistance to the implementation of *Brown* and the evolution of a limited notion of the mandate of *Brown*. But Reconstruction also succeeded. Reconstruction remains relevant to the scope and meaning of equality. Reconstruction suggests what is possible while it exposes the unfinished scope of the project that defines Radical *Brown*.

The implications individually and intergenerationally of successive generations from 1619 to Emancipation are essential to our understanding of the contemporary context within which we function. If 20 to 30 years is the average period of a generation, the 250-year period from 1619 to Emancipation encompasses roughly eight to twelve generations. This deep intergenerational pattern challenges us to imagine family and community history magnified for generations and its consequences for culture, structures, and systems that frame the life course. This perspective only gets us to Emancipation—and the enormity of the failure to reverse and replace this monstrous context. This is the foundation on which we stand.

The consequences of slavery ground identity in hierarchy. This is sharply differentiated by race. Blackness is defined as marking inferiority and inhumanity, a status similar to but lower than, that of animals, rationalizing sexual, physical, and mental abuse. This generated resistance and resilience as well as survival. Whiteness is defined as humanity, and humanity is defined as exclusively White. Centuries of identity were grounded in racial superiority and hierarchy, with no value to White identity in and of itself without its core worth in relation to hierarchy. It is a pattern of unremitting centuries of self/identity tied to embracing one's own inhumanity justified by the constructed inhumanity of others. As our developmental scaffolding outlined in chapter 1 suggests, it is essential to think about the consequences of this chronosystem for individuals. How deeply ingrained is the racial code for us all?

With Emancipation, the intent was complete, total comprehensive equality that would erase nearly three centuries of embedded culture, psychology, law, inhumanity, and inequality. The contradiction of the Founding was to be resolved; the "People" were to be inclusive of all. Admittedly, gender equality was not part of this, but comprehensive racial equality was. Yet even the most rabid opponents of slavery found it difficult to embrace full equality; that paradox exemplifies the depth of the destructive rationalization of inhumanity defined by race. Nevertheless, the comprehensive, humanity-based definition of emancipation is exemplified by Radical Reconstruction. That definition of freedom reflected the perspective of the drafters of the Reconstruction Amendments and the interpretation of the Amendments by the Supreme Court close in time to their passage.

The inferiority/inhumanity system reasserted itself and intensified after Radical Reconstruction ended. Imagine the personal context and chronosystem of Emancipation, Radical Reconstruction, and then the flood of "Redemption" in the South, as well as regression in the North and reconstructed inequality in the West. Imagine the chaos, contradictions, confusion, possibilities, and denials; empowerment met with violence, the sense of dual consciousness, of dissonance. Most importantly,

CONTEXT

the reassertion of inhumanity/inferiority intensified. That was the intent of Jim Crow, manifested in both facially racial and facially neutral forms. What does that do to individual lives and meaning-making? For Blacks and Whites? What are the developmental consequences of this context? We turn to the context of segregation in Chapter 3 to consider the impact of adding to this foundational inequality and inhumanity one hundred years of segregation before we arrive at *Brown*.

CHAPTER 3

Segregation

JIM CROW IS THE OPPOSITE OF EQUALITY, an anti-equality system. Its comprehensive inequality speaks to the power of Radical Reconstruction and the virulent backlash against it. Segregation as a new comprehensive system of subordination rebuilt racial hierarchy on slavery's foundation, in many respects creating an even harsher system. This comprehensive system negatively defines the scope of what *Brown* mandates.

Jim Crow conventionally defines the practice of legal segregation. It includes de jure, facially racial segregation (school segregation mandated by statute or constitution), as well as de facto or facially neutral laws with intended racially segregated effects (voting regulations) and the biased administration of laws (policing). Legal rules are only the half of it, however; custom or social practice (often supported by law) also was critical.

Segregation was comprehensive and national. While regionally differentiated, segregation was not exclusively Southern. It began in the North, with the unequal treatment of free Blacks prior to the Revolution, rationalized by differentiating the humanity and citizenship of free Black persons compared to Whites. Northern statutes prohibited segregation and discrimination, so segregation was law*less*, but in practice, segregation and discrimination were practiced without fear of legal consequence. Social conduct in defiance of antidiscrimination law was commonplace. In addition, facially neutral laws were used to ensure separation and hierarchy.

In the South the implementation and administration of facially neutral laws characterized the first phase of segregation immediately after Reconstruction ended. Disenfranchisement, disproportionate use of criminal laws and punishments, and severe racial violence epitomized this period. Segregation evolved into a formalized, facially discriminatory statutory system after 1890 and flourished in the early 1900s. The last Jim Crow statute was enacted in the 1950s.

In the creation of segregation, the US Supreme Court was not merely complicit, but was instrumental, with its decision in *Plessy v Ferguson*[1] and other cases upholding the constitutionality of segregation as a form of equality (!), just as the Court had been instrumental in upholding slavery in *Dred Scott*. Jim Crow reflects the exacerbation, intensification, and worsening of subordination, hierarchy, and racial violence after Reconstruction as part of "Redemption." Redemption was an effort to reassert, solidify, and intensify the racial bargain of the Founding, and to deny Radical Reconstruction's vision of comprehensive racial equality.

Northern Origins

C. Vann Woodward opens his classic study, *The Strange Career of Jim Crow*,[2] with this definition of segregation:

> "Segregation"... means physical distance, not social distance—physical separation of people for reasons of race.... The concept of segregation in connection with race is not an absolute—though it approached that extreme during a period of nearly a half century of American history.[3]

As Gunnar Myrdal observed, segregation was a White problem, not isolated, but integral to White American society.[4] It was an expression and defense of Whiteness as White supremacy.

After Reconstruction ended, southern Whites made it clear that there was to be no equality in any aspect of life; suffrage, in particular, was to be withdrawn.[5] Segregation laws were extremely rigid: "racial ostracism... extended to virtually all forms of public transportation, to sports and recreations, to hospitals, orphanages, prisons, and

asylums, and ultimately to funeral homes, morgues, and cemeteries. . . .
The new Southern system was regarded as the 'final settlement,' the
'return to sanity,' the 'permanent system.'"[6]

This imposed systemic hierarchy had originated in the North.[7] It
developed there and then moved South. "The Northern Negro was made
painfully and constantly aware that he lived in a society dedicated to
the doctrine of white supremacy and Negro inferiority . . . One of these
ways was segregation, and with the backing of legal and extra-legal
codes; the system permeated all aspects of Negro life in the free states
by 1860."[8] This included being

> systematically separated from Whites. They were either excluded
> from railway cars, omnibuses, stagecoaches, and steamboats or
> assigned to special "Jim Crow" sections; they sat, when permitted,
> in secluded and remote corners of theatres and lecture halls; they
> could not enter most hotels, restaurants, and resorts, except as ser-
> vants; they prayed in "Negro pews" in the white churches, and if par-
> taking of sacrament of the Lord's supper, they waited until the
> whites had been served and bread and wine. Moreover, they were
> often educated in segregated schools, punished in segregated pris-
> ons, nursed in segregated hospitals, and buried in segregated
> cemeteries.[9]

Segregation was coextensive with abolitionist sentiments; one did
not necessarily lead to the elimination of the other.[10] The end of slavery
in the North left segregation and racial hierarchy firmly in place.
Resistance to equality coexisted with abolition, especially with respect
to schools.[11] As Purnell and Theoharis explain:

> Northerners wove Jim Crow racism into the fabric of their social,
> political, and economic life in ways that shaped the history of the
> region, and the entire nation. Jim Crow, outside of the South, coex-
> isted, even thrived, alongside efforts to reform its worst manifesta-
> tions in social and political life. This characteristic distinguished
> it from its southern version. . . . In the North, black people could get
> as "uppity" as they want . . . so long as they did not try to get too

close to whites, as their neighbors, sexual partners, classmates, or
union brothers. . . . Jim Crow, whether in the North or in the South,
demanded that black people remain in their "place."[12]

In addition to statutes and customary practices, Northern segregation fostered social distinctions with derogatory names.

> The word "nigger" as a derogatory term for all black people first
> gained political, cultural, and social currency in the Jim Crow
> North, "precisely at the moment when gradual abolition and eman-
> cipation began to free people of color in the North." In the 1820s
> and '30s, white northerners used the word . . . to describe all black
> people "as backward and beyond redemption . . . incapable of achiev-
> ing real freedom and citizenship."[13]

Critically, distinctive to Northern segregation is its "color-blind" version
of Jim Crow.[14] This Northern model was *the* model of segregation before
Southern Jim Crow, and became the national model in the post-*Brown*
period.

Southern Jim Crow

It was more than a decade after Reconstruction ended before the first
facially racial Jim Crow laws appeared in the Southern states and more
than two decades before the older coastal Southern states adopted such
laws.[15] Initially, segregation was enforced by custom and the administration of "neutral" laws. Over time, things got worse—the "adoption
of extreme racism."[16]

One of the strongest early steps taken was disfranchisement, which
was virtually total, together with the toleration, and increase, of racial
violence. Facially racial laws were enacted in the 1890s and early 1900s
and accelerated in the 1920s. The scope of the laws was extensive and
comprehensive. "The movement had proceeded in mounting stages of
aggression, 'Its spirit is that of an all-absorbing autocracy of race, an
animus of aggrandizement which makes, in the imagination of the
white man, an absolute identification of the stronger race with the very
being of the state."[17]

Jim Crow requirements affected everyone:

The legislation of Jim Crow affected all classes and ages, and it tended to be thorough, far-reaching, even imaginative: from separate public school textbooks for black and white children and Jim Crow bibles on which to swear in a black witness in court to separate telephone booths, separate windows in the banks for black and white depositors, and Jim Crow elevators in office buildings, one for whites and one for blacks and freight. New Orleans went so far as to adopt an ordinance segregating black and white prostitutes. . . . Even as the laws decreed that African American babies would enter the world in separate facilities, so blacks would occupy separate places at the end of their lives.[18]

Separation was so powerful that during World War II, there were efforts to separate blood by race to prevent Black blood being given to White soldiers.[19]

Segregation included residential segregation, unequal education, a segregated military until 1945, massively unequal employment with Blacks relegated primarily to lower, menial jobs, and exclusion from the benefits of the New Deal and GI Bill. Federally, President Woodrow Wilson ordered the federal government to be segregated. The intensity of this inhumanity and its taken-for-granted expression by Whites is captured in the remark made just before the *Brown* decision by President Eisenhower to Chief Justice Warren: "[Segregationists] are not bad people. All they are concerned about is to see that their sweet little girls are not required to sit in school alongside some big, black bucks."[20]

Segregation was public; it was the active role of the state in both public and private life.[21] The proliferation of laws continued virtually until the year *Brown* was decided, continually additive and worsening.[22] The intensification of inhumanity came on top of centuries of inhumanity.

While the role of the state was critical, private social enforcement was equally powerful. The "etiquette of Jim Crow" required carefully observing the rules of racial interaction. Every Black child had to learn this etiquette to survive.[23] Etiquette had the purpose to ensure that Black people proffered obeisance to White people and thereby marked their relative inferiority . . . lapses in race etiquette resulted in many of the criminal assaults that beset Black American life: the so-called back talk or sassing that Whites were taught from earliest childhood not to tolerate from Blacks, the "crime" of Blacks getting above themselves whether with a too new or too fancy car or a suit of too fine a cut, or—deadliest of all for the transgressor—an inadvertent or casual or misplaced indication of a Black man's interest in a White female.[24]

This meant not sharing sidewalks, entering through back doors, limiting where one shopped, and denial of the courtesy of a name or title by using a first name or the generic "gal" or "boy." "The etiquette of Jim Crow maintained a cardinal rule: *Whites first*."[25] Race was pervasive in the organization of life, including the customs that Blacks and Whites did not shake hands, publicly interact, or walk together.[26] Even boarding the train had to be done carefully: as George Swanson Starling left Wildwood, Florida, in 1945 for the North, "A railing divided the stairs onto the train, one side of the railing for white passengers, the other for colored, so the soles of their shoes would not touch the same stair."[27] Black men removed their hats in public places, while White men did not do so even when in Black homes. Whites thought of segregation not as a throwback to slavery, but as modern, well-managed race relations.[28]

The constant specter of violence *against* Blacks ironically was tightly linked to the myth of violence and criminality *by* Blacks and the "condemnation of blackness." This powerful racist mythology morphed from unfounded belief to "scientific racism."[29] Fear for the safety of children was acute within the Black community in light of the pervasiveness of "racialized dangers." The dangers were brutal—two 14-year-old Black boys that a White motorist observed playing with a 13-year-old White girl were arrested for attempted rape. They were seized by a mob from jail and lynched, including cutting off their genitals and pulling skin from their bodies. This was in 1942, a decade before Emmett Till was murdered after a false accusation of whistling at a White woman in a store.[30] Violence was widespread, sexual and physical, triggered by slight infractions or outright lies. Lynching was commonplace, often public, a constant threat and a practice of torture and inhumanity treated as acceptable and justifiable by many Whites. White mob rule and rioting erupted frequently to destroy signs of Black empowerment, epitomized by the destructive 1921 Tulsa Massacre.

Survival and coping strategies were essential to African Americans, embedded in their culture.[31] These are collective memories that emphasize violence, discrimination, personal and property losses, and socioeconomic struggles. This is not to say that affirmative, distinctive culture was not a part of the community as well. Anders Walker emphasizes the value of separation, of affirmative community.[32] This generated a vision of equality but not of the necessity of integration if integration meant assimilation and sameness, given the negatives and bankruptcy of White culture.

One other distinctive aspect of Jim Crow was ensuring cheap labor and minimizing economic opportunity and self-sufficiency. A notorious part of economic subordination, interfacing with the discriminatory criminal justice system, was the convict leasing system. Douglas Blackmon's history of this system links it to the prison labor system that persists to this day.[33] Segregation dovetails with the rise of racial capitalism in the South. The convict leasing system was linked to disproportionate arrest and conviction for neutral criminal infractions.[34] Blackmon labels this the "Age of Neoslavery," lasting until shortly before *Brown*.[35] Although convict leasing practices ended with changes in industrial practices, contemporary prison labor practices challenge that conclusion.

National Patterns of Segregation

Segregation changed significantly as the result of Black migration north coupled with racialized New Deal policies, creating a new segregation structure in housing, employment, education, and law enforcement.[36] As resistance to de jure segregation emerged in the South, de facto segregation hardened in the North.[37] Although the North was framed as the Promised Land, an escape from Southern Jim Crow, "Black migrants found Pharaoh on both sides of the river."[38] Not better, just different; or in the words of Rosa Parks, who left Montgomery for Detroit, the "Northern promised land that wasn't."[39] So, for example, the membership of the Klan was larger in the North than in the South.[40] This northern pattern is critical to a comprehensive understanding of segregation just as slavery was a deeply embedded national system.[41]

Two critical studies that expose the role of federal and local housing policies sustaining segregation are Richard Rothstein's *The Color of Law*[42] and Jessica Trounstine's *Segregation by Design*.[43] Rothstein comprehensively explores de jure government policies creating and sustaining segregated housing.

> Until the last quarter of the twentieth century, racially explicit policies of federal, state, and local governments defined where whites and African Americans should live. Today's residential segregation in the North, South, Midwest and West is not the unintended consequence of individual choices . . . but of unhidden public policy that explicitly segregated every metropolitan area in the United States. . . . Segregation by intentional government action is not de facto. Rather it is what the courts call de jure: segregation by law and public policy.[44]

Trounstine adds complexity to this picture by exposing the local intersection of housing segregation and city services.

> The preferences of white property owners have been institutionalized through the vehicles of local land use policy, shaping residential geography for more than 100 years. . . . These institutions persist, narrowing options for some residents and creating and recreating inequality and polarization today.[45]

Segregation was not created by choice or economic inequality; rather, this was *"segregation by design."*[46] Place has a powerful influence on intergenerational inequality, correlating to income and wealth inequality, employment instability, political polarization, and the underfunding of public goods.[47]

One final part of this national pattern is its multiracial character. Every group deemed non-White was assigned a place in the Black/White binary of segregation. In the West and Southwest segregation was directed against Mexican Americans, Native Americans, and Asians. "The dispossession of Mexican and American Indian land and property rights was endemic of a widespread tendency of the American West's legal regime to racialize Mexican, Asian, and American Indians as "foreign" to all Anglo-Saxon, Protestant "American" values and beliefs."[48] Non-Whites were seen as "incompatible," foreign, often using language as markers for racialization.[49] This was in addition to the dispossession, subordination, and exclusion of Native Americans, who were rendered "different" and noncitizens until 1924, under a unique constitutional framework that subjected them to separation, annihilation, and forced assimilation of their children.

Similarly, Mexican-Americans were racialized and victimized, rendered "permanent outsiders."[50] Active white vigilantes claimed the West as "Whites only." Exacerbated by the Gold Rush, these actions by White settlers resulted in the active takeover of both Mexican and Native American lands and the exclusion of Chinese and Mexican miners. Oregon went so far as to establish itself as a White homeland with an exclusion law that remained in effect until 1926.[51]

Texas is a particularly horrific example of this pattern. Slavery was incorporated in the Texas constitution after the Texas revolution of 1835–36. Free Blacks were regulated by statute. After emancipation, racist patterns worsened with stringent forms of segregation.[52] In this Black/White binary, one form of resistance by Mexican-Americans was to legally identify as Caucasian.[53] Language subordination was integral to educational segregation.[54] "Segregation was practiced throughout the Southwest to isolate Mexican-American children and to retard their educational progress … to reproduce the caste society of the Southwest, with Anglos at the top and Mexican, Indians, and Blacks at the bottom."[55]

Monica Munoz Martinez's compelling history of the evolution of "Juan Crow" details both public and private violence, with special attention to the role of the mythologized Texas Rangers.[56] The Rangers were organized to protect White settlers and White supremacy; Mexicans and Native Americans were enemies. Violence occurred within the context of contested creation of the border, economic control, and the eventual US acquisition of half of Mexico's territory, transforming a multiracial geography into a territory of White supremacy.[57]

Asians were the target of segregation as well, in the south as well as in the West. Their strategy, like Mexican Americans, was to argue that they were White, a strategy that largely failed.[58] The Chinese were treated as utterly foreign and likely disloyal. Japanese migration in the late 1800s and early 1900s triggered hostility equal to that of the Chinese, leading to land laws intended to exclude them from property ownership and laying the groundwork for internment.

Segregation was a comprehensive, national system, reinforced at every level of government, a combination of law, policy, and custom. It was justified by the same belief system foundational to slavery. The many ways that this philosophical and social system of presumed inhumanity, inferiority, and hierarchy functioned included interlocking systems that sustained separation, racial isolation, and racial polarization.

Segregated Education

Segregated education, like segregation generally, originated in the North. The education of free Blacks was separated from that of Whites. Although the North enacted anti-segregation statutes, segregation persisted.[59] In the South, where public education was uncommon before the Civil War, a mixture of segregated and integrated schools after the war gave way to mandated segregation by statute or by state constitutional amendments enacted after Radical Reconstruction ended.

Segregated education was never equal. Inequality was reflected in buildings, books, the length of the school day, the number of months in the school year, the number of students per teacher, the education and experience of teachers, as well as the content and goals of education. The subjective factors—valuing each child, valuing development of capacity, supporting equal citizenship, valuing each child's community and language—were presumed unequal, reinforcing White supremacy and imposing racial harm. For Black children, self-sustenance, self-identity, and culture nevertheless were fostered in this separate environment. Most teachers in Black schools were Black, and they supported the children in their care and responsibility. In the intangibles, therefore, there is a record of the benefit of separation, a record of resistance, the resilience of Black education, and the valuing of Black children despite the intent to communicate that they were lesser than their White peers.

White insistence on segregated education ran deep. School was an arena where Whites and Blacks would have had interaction over significant periods of time. Schools were distinctive because they represented a possible melting pot, at a very significant phase in the life course. Education represented a unique danger, the danger of all children becoming equally competent, as well as the danger of social interaction that might disrupt the social hierarchy. White fears of physical danger to White girls and women based on racial stereotypes of Black men transferred to even very young Black boys, as reflected in the previously noted statement of President Eisenhower to Chief Justice Warren prior to the *Brown* decision.

The *purpose* of segregation represents the blatant, clear, powerful link to slavery: its purpose was to replace, restore, and "redeem" White supremacy and racial hierarchy. The purpose was dehumanization and psychological harm. The prohibition and criminalization of the education and literacy of Black people during slavery was replaced with meagre, inferior, and separate schools that resulted in high illiteracy, limited or no opportunity, and a clear communication of inferiority. Resistance and a countervailing positive culture of support for some Black children occurred in spite of, not because of, this deliberate systemic structure of inequality and developmental harm. Over time, systemic inequality strengthened, solidified, and rigidified. Segregated education became a critical component sustaining the comprehensive segregation system, intended to support White supremacy and Black subordination. The focus on subordinating Blacks ignored the impact on Whites, undermining White humanity. The radical mandate of *Brown* necessitated not just opening schoolhouse doors but changing systems, culture, and developmental outcomes comprehensively.

Linking Slavery and Segregated Education

In *Self Taught* Heather Williams exposes the patterns originating in slavery of Black community efforts to support the education of their children as well as the self-education of adults.[60] The education of slaves was criminally prohibited during slavery, calling for the punishment of anyone teaching a slave to read, write, or do math and punishment of slaves who acquired these skills. Statutes prohibiting the education of slaves were enacted as early as 1739. A South Carolina statute outlawed teaching literacy or employing a slave to write; it was amended in 1800 to also prohibit any meeting for "mental instruction" for slaves or free Blacks.[61] Prohibitions were not limited to the South, as evident by litigation against Prudence Crandall in Connecticut, who had admitted Black girls to her boarding school in 1833.[62] Nevertheless, some slaves became educated, including some educated at the behest of their masters. Literacy had practical consequences, as well as intellectual and spiritual meaning.[63]

During the Civil War, in areas of Union control or as a result of self-emancipation, many former slaves sought to become literate. In addition, Black soldiers pursued literacy in preparation for full citizenship. As they learned they taught others. The same pattern emerged after the Emancipation Proclamation, postwar, and during Reconstruction. Thus, Blacks played a leading role in the evolution of public education. The impetus came from freedpeople, triggering calls to northern missionaries to send teachers. Mostly White female missionaries came to the South to teach from 1862 to 1870.[64]

Freedpeople not only defined their freedom rights as including suffrage and jury service, but also identified a new right: the right to attend school.

Across the South, African Americans employed the literacy they possessed to argue for a meaningful freedom, and, realizing the limits of their self-taught literacy, they urged the federal government to acknowledge and protect their right to education. Simultaneously, they appealed to state governments to provide public schooling. The idea of a right to education was a radical one indeed. Most slave states . . . had also failed to confer on whites anything resembling a right to education.[65]

Freedpeople articulated a three-part concept of education: education for their children, literacy for adults, and preventing literacy requirements from disqualifying adults from participation in governance.[66] Defining characteristics of this push for education were self-help and self-determination. Freedpeople saw "freedom as meaning self-determination, not subordination to paternalism."[67]

Teaching was a political act. Black teachers were targeted by southern Whites because "they embodied change: their public presence proclaimed that African Americans were free."[68] Teaching was not limited to teachers: learning imposed responsibility, so as one learned, one was expected to become a teacher to another. In pursuit of literacy, many older students and even adults attended school.[69]

The Black community, despite their lack of resources, were instrumental in establishing schools.

Freedpeople's commitment to education took both white southerners and northerners by surprise, but it was particularly stunning to those from the South who thought they knew the black people who lived among them. . . . African Americans' insistence on establishing schools transformed education throughout the southern states.[70]

When taxes were imposed to establish schools, there was resistance largely based on race. "At its core, White opposition to Black education lay in much more than hostility toward taxation; it was born of jealously, fear, and insecurity in a radically shifting social order."[71] The very advancement, opportunity, and self-sufficiency sought by Blacks was feared by Whites.

If black children no longer recognized themselves as inferior, and were in fact surpassing white children in measurable ways, and if white children, through intermingling with black children, had begun to doubt their superiority, how long could white adults hope to hold on to power?[72]

Blacks understood that resistance to their education was designed to sustain racial hierarchy, to regulate Black behavior and restore pre-emancipation norms.[73] Underfunding was endemic before the end of Reconstruction. But things were to get much worse. While schools were not eliminated; vastly different funding, facilities, transportation, and support were the result of enactment of statutes requiring separation. Disenfranchisement also removed Black leadership from local education politics, resulting in further drops in funding, shorter school terms, and lower teacher salaries.

W. E. B. Du Bois's classic 1911 study of segregated schools found that most Black children did not attend school,[74] due to lack of facilities, poverty, or the fact that children could not be spared from contributing to family income. Teachers were poorly trained, and buildings were inadequate, with little funding or oversight. School terms ranged from three to six months, and the focus was on manual training. To the extent that there was any progress in public education in the South it was reserved for Whites. Black education was limited in many areas to the elementary level and was geared to acceptance of a subordinated "place" in society.[75]

The scope of education envisioned by the Black community, part of their larger vision of freedom, was obliterated in this harshly unequal system. Instead, as William Watkins emphasizes in his work on the White architects of Black education from 1865 to 1954, Black education was framed and justified to serve White interests.[76] It was crafted by Whites concerned with profit, economic gain, labor peace, and the acceptance of Blacks' "proper" place. Teaching reinforced "conformity, sobriety, piety, and the value of enterprise. . . . The curriculum was thus geared to social engineering . . . America's apartheid had to be made workable. It needed to appear natural and ordained."[77]

Northern School Segregation

In theory, segregated education was solely a Southern phenomenon. Segregation was prohibited by law in the North by statutes enacted during abolition. But the assignment of children by race in defiance of those statutes was common into the 1950s, a blatant contradiction between law and practice.[78] The abolition-era statutes prohibiting discrimination and segregation were upheld in numerous court decisions. But practice did not change. Segregation was sustained by a range of devices including residential segregation, separate classrooms, divided playgrounds, separate buildings, and school zone line-drawing. By *Brown*, there was little explicit, facially racial segregation based on statutory mandates, but facially neutral statutes and practices achieved the same result.[79]

Before the Civil War, Black children were excluded or separated from Northern schools. Segregation was famously judicially approved in the Boston school case, a challenge brought by free Blacks to the denial of access to schools.[80] The Massachusetts Supreme Court held that whether to integrate or segregate was a discretionary decision up to the local school committee and deemed racial segregation not a state constitutional violation. The Boston school case became a touchstone for other state court decisions, as well as a leading case cited by the US Supreme Court for the proposition that the segregation principle of "separate but equal" was constitutionally sound.[81] On the eve of the Civil War, just over one-third of free Black children attended school in the North, half the rate of White children.[82] After the war, Northern segregation continued, and worsened from 1890 to 1940, especially solidifying in response to the Great Migration.[83]

The Northern model of segregation was not simply different. Rather, the Northern model played a more destructive role: it became the national model.

> For much of the early twentieth century, . . . the myth of de facto segregation formed the heart of a broader narrative of regional exceptionalism—one that effectively defended racial segregation in the North and West by categorically differentiating it from the legal Jim Crow that reigned in the South.[84]

As with the overall comprehensive system of segregation, the North played a critical role by using "neutral" statutes and policies to accomplish comprehensive segregation in schools and other systems. This is the model that has persisted.[85] *"Colorblind" forms were used to sustain racial inequality as a long-term practice.*[86] The Northern model became the "cure" that perpetuated segregation post-*Brown.*[87]

The Value of Black Education

As noted earlier, part of the Black cultural tradition is the value of Black-identified schools and the affirmative value of Black children being educated together. What has been missing from understanding the command of *Brown* is the full support of the development and humanity of all children. This would imagine development as including affirmative racial identity and embracing racial equality, rather than the privilege/subordination inhumanity model that is the hallmark of educational inequality.

Lessons from Black education during segregation are instructive, particularly the pedagogical models of Black teachers under conditions hardly designed to support the well-being and development of Black children.[88] Fairclough describes Black teachers' role and practices amidst poor working conditions, shortcomings in training, and personal hardship. Vivian Gunn Morris and Curtis Morris identify four themes of excellence: outstanding teachers, the content of curriculum and extracurricular activities, strong parental support, and the school's role in community leadership.[89] Most important for students were caring and supportive teachers.[90]

Vanessa Siddle Walker similarly challenges the notion of the inferiority of Black schools during segregation.[91] Caring was a critical characteristic of Black teachers, along with high expectations connected to the goal of racial uplift.[92] "Black teachers promoted the acquisition of a form of capital that could not only be used in exchange for jobs, rights and social power but could also strengthen racial pride and mutual progress. Situated pedagogies refer to teachers 'creating responses and initiatives' in classrooms, schools and communities 'shaped by a particular history of oppression and privilege in the lives of their students.'"[93] Morris and Morris cite the parallels in a contemporary study of successful low-income predominantly Black elementary schools: those schools demonstrate some of the same characteristics of excellence as schools during the segregation era.[94]

Despite all odds, Black teachers played a key role and engaged in quiet resistance to Jim Crow. Upon desegregation, most either lost their jobs or were demoted, due to the inability of Whites to imagine Black teachers as qualified or able to teach Whites. Their leadership and methods were lost. Desegregation as implemented caused "social and emotional loss."[95] "Whites took the concept of integration and hijacked it. Furthermore, they dropped the educational components that Blacks had assumed would go hand in hand with integration."[96] Black inferiority persisted as a cultural norm, making Black teachers presumptively unqualified.[97] The loss of Black teachers post-*Brown* was never recovered; today's public education teachers are overwhelmingly White women.[98]

Segregated Education for Other Students of Color

Segregated education was used to subordinate all children of color. Other racial groups deemed non-White (Latinx, Asian Americans) or completely excluded (Native Americans) fit within segregated education as subordinated children. This varied regionally with the distribution of racial groups. In addition, language was used as a factor to justify segregation. The focus on the Black/White binary subordinated language and culture issues as justifications by Whites, and those issues remained subordinated and contribute to current inequalities. They must be taken into account in Radical *Brown* or we will be perpetuating that erasure.

Native Americans had a unique educational trajectory.[99] The focus of Native American policy was couched in racist justifications to "civilize" Native children.[100] Children were "rescued," taught to read, write, and speak English, to adopt individual rather than tribal identity, and to adopt Christianity.[101] Extinguishing Native languages was considered critical. Forced assimilation began at the end of the Civil War and continued until the last boarding schools closed in 1973.[102] Native languages and religious customs were prohibited. The schools were abusive emotionally and physically. Education contradicted culture and enforced assimilation.

These children were even taught to stand like whites: with backs straight, heads up, and eyes straight ahead—when their own culture taught them that the respectful stance towards another human being was to stand slightly aside, and to keep one's eyes downcast. Children were not just taken from their homes, they were encouraged to completely repudiate their parents' ways . . . their parents' principles, religion, and way of life.[103]

These were acts of genocide, part of the history of attempts to completely annihilate Native Americans.[104] "The trauma of shame, fear and anger has passed from one generation to the next, and manifests itself in the rampant alcoholism, drug abuse, and domestic violence that plague Indian country."[105] While these policies have been to some extent reversed, including recent efforts to revive Native languages, Native American educational achievement remains abysmally low.

There has not been apology, repair, or reparations for this harm. The Native American boarding schools are a unique example of everything that is wrong and unequal about segregated schools, including the utter failure to remedy the harm once this policy was abandoned. Native American education presents unique issues of language, culture and development that are integral to Radical *Brown*.

For Chinese children, segregation was tied to immigration policy, which limited immigration and citizenship beginning in 1790 to "free white persons."[106] In the post-Reconstruction era racial hierarchy, African Americans were to be segregated, and Chinese completely excluded.[107] Instead of being expelled, the Chinese were to register, which many did not do out of fear of deportation. Demonization of the Chinese was based on the myth that they were the "Yellow Peril" who could overwhelm Whites and that, because of their race, they were permanently foreign.[108]

From 1850 to 1930 the largest concentration of Chinese was in San Francisco, where the school board excluded Chinese children from school, then admitted but segregated them, then reverted to exclusion.[109] The community organized private Chinese language schools, with the goal of teaching Chinese language and culture. Japanese immigrants, with the strong backing of their embassy, were more successful in educating their children in the public schools, eventually being excluded from the segregation requirements due to successful political pressure.[110]

The Mexican-American experience of segregation particularly centered around language.[111] Education was geared to subordinated status,[112] and the subsequent assimilation model of integration perpetuated that goal. Language policies included "Spanish detention," for speaking Spanish on school grounds, and devaluing bilingualism.[113] "The purpose of the educational system was to reproduce the caste society of the southwest, with Anglos at the top and Mexicans, Indians, and Blacks at the bottom."[114]

Mexican American parents litigated over the issue of whether their children were "White."[115] Tejanos (Texas residents of Mexican origin) were classified as White but still segregated.[116] Ironically, sometimes their claimed "Whiteness" was later used to argue that their presence in combination with African American students constituted desegregation.[117] Not until the 1970s were Mexican Americans declared an identifiable ethnic group separately considered for purposes of school desegregation.[118] Distinctive to Mexican Americans was this pattern of extralegal segregation, legal Whiteness, and the racialization of language.[119]

Conclusion

Understanding the scope of segregation is essential to define and implement systemic equality. Understanding segregation's connection to slavery, as well as its origin in the violent systemic reaction to Radical Reconstruction, is also essential. Segregation defines the harm to be remedied by *Brown* and the affirmative, comprehensive, systemic, equality necessary to take its place. Segregation layered upon the foundation of slavery exposes the depth of the chronosystem that enfolds White and Black racial identities and the complex developmental needs to recognize common humanity.

What was the impact of segregation on individuals, piling on top of 250 years of slavery, contradicting emancipation, the rewriting of the Constitution, and Radical Reconstruction? The intensity and micromanagement of every aspect of life, the construction of physical separation, the communication of Black inferiority and White supremacy geographically, architecturally, culturally, by custom and by law, reinforced by the threat of violence for deviation from the "rules" no matter how small, all impacted individual identity and development in a context that defined Blackness and Whiteness. Black identity and everyday life were bound by what W. E. B. Du Bois called double consciousness: on the one hand celebrating Black identity, resilience, and worth and, on the other hand, knowing Blackness was the target of violence, dehumanization, and oppression. One hundred years of segregation meant that another three to five generations stood on the shoulders of their ancestors of the prior 250 years, experiencing the intensification of racial hierarchy to replicate slavery. Those new generations included World War I and World War II soldiers who answered the call to defend democracy and freedom for a society and government that did not recognize their humanity and equality. The dissonance of professed principles and everyday reality was exacerbated. The scope of what was needed when *Brown* was decided requires grappling with the meaning-making and identities of Whites and Blacks during segregation. *Brown's* radical vision can only be realized by a clear-eyed understanding of segregation. *Brown* unmistakably requires the embrace of common humanity in place of racial hierarchy, requiring repair and the new construction of identities. That is what *Brown* meant.

CHAPTER 4

Radical Comprehensive Equality Found and Lost

WE HAVE EXPLORED THE RADICAL MEANING of *Brown* based on the scope of the inequality, racial hierarchy, and inhumanity of slavery and segregation. In this chapter we turn from this negative definition of the scope of the Court's mandate to the Court's affirmative embrace of equality. The *Brown* Court envisioned equality as defined by the radical equality mandate of the Reconstruction Amendments and the Court's earliest decisions on the scope of those amendments. It did so by its primary reliance on *Strauder v. West Virginia* as the precedent that defines equality in *Brown*. In the early post-*Brown* cases the Court reaffirmed radical, comprehensive equality by requiring the elimination of segregation "root and branch." The Court was clear about *Brown's* mandate. Radical *Brown* is supported not only by reference to the scope and depth of the system it was to replace, but also by this clear articulation of the vision of equality.

Thus, we focus in this chapter on how the Court defined what equality means. The Court's use of case law in *Brown*, what it relies on, confirms that the definition of equality is broad, comprehensive, and all-encompassing. The *Brown* decision constitutes the equivalent of a Third Founding, a call to complete the unfinished Second Founding of the Reconstruction Amendments and Radical Reconstruction, to embrace common humanity, requiring tearing down three and a half centuries of inhumanity and hierarchy, after a hundred years of rebuilding inequality. In this chapter we elaborate on *Strauder* as well as the early post-*Brown* decisions that ratify this definition of equality. We also review implementation after the early post-*Brown* cases, which severely undermined *Brown*. More recently there has emerged some continued foundation for radical equality in the development and diversity cases that support all children's humanity.

Strauder v. West Virginia: Comprehensive Equality

Brown adopts a definition of what equality means that is not just "formal" or public equality, but equality in every aspect of life. The central case cited and quoted in *Brown* as its definition of "equality" is *Strauder v. West Virginia*.[1] *Strauder*, one of the earliest cases to interpret the meaning of the Equal Protection Clause of the Fourteenth Amendment, defines equality as inclusive of all public and private aspects of equal personhood. Implicitly, equality means equal humanity, opportunity, and freedom as that enjoyed by White males, a definition linked to the beliefs of its historical context but unmistakable in its meaning: full and equal personhood. *Strauder* articulates equality as including positive rights, so not merely "freedom from" discrimination but "rights to" equal personhood. *Strauder*, as the legal foundation for understanding "equality" as antisubordination and affirmative rights, and common humanity, supports the reading of *Brown* as Radical *Brown*. Translated to contemporary language, it supports equality free of gender and racial exclusion and hierarchy and therefore reconstructs both male and White identities, and as well as their intersectionality.

In the course of the *Brown* decision the Court claimed that the history of the drafting of the Equal Protection Clause was inconclusive regarding the definition of equality. Similarly, the status of public education at the time the amendments were drafted was declared irrelevant because education was not widespread as a presumed responsibility of the state to the people. Indeed, under the slave codes, education was criminally punishable if provided to the enslaved and outright denied or provided only in segregated settings for free Blacks. Thus, in *Brown* the Court used a different source to define equality.

Strauder is primary, because it is language from *Strauder* that the Court uses to flesh out the meaning of equality. The *Brown* Court states, "In the first cases in this Court construing the Fourteenth Amendment, decided shortly after its adoption, the Court interpreted it as *proscribing all state-imposed discriminations against the Negro race.*"[2] This textual statement is supported by footnote 5 of *Brown*, where the Court quotes the following language from *Strauder* on the meaning of the Equal Protection Clause:

[The Equal Protection Clause] ordains that no State shall deprive any person of life, liberty or property without due process of law, or deny to any person within its jurisdiction the equal protection of the laws. What is this but declaring the law in the States shall be the same for the black as for the white; that all persons, whether colored or white, shall stand equal before the laws of the States, and in regard to the colored race, for whose protection the amendment was primarily designed, that no discrimination shall be made against them by law because of their color? The words of the amendment, it is true, are prohibitory, but they contain *a necessary implication of a positive immunity or right*, most valuable to the colored race,—the right to exemption from unfriendly legislation against them distinctively as colored,—exemption from legal discriminations *implying inferiority in civil society*, lessening the security of their enjoyment of *the rights which others enjoy*, and discriminations which are *steps toward reducing them to the condition of a subject race.*[3]

This critical language from *Strauder* states that the status of Blacks will be the same as Whites in *all* respects, that they will be protected from discrimination, that there is an *affirmative duty* to ensure their equality; and this requires preventing any actions that would return them to *any* aspect of slavery. The scope of "*all* state-imposed discriminations" reaches political, civil, and social equality. The standard employed that underscores comprehensive equality is the status of White men. Along with the positive command of the Fourteenth Amendment, this requires the state to support those formerly enslaved in achieving full equality. Equality with the scope and substance of White male citizenship equals comprehensive equality. Equality to replace slavery equals comprehensive equality. Segregation's linkage to slavery, systemically designed to reestablish slavery, even to worsen the subordination of slavery, means that the clear message and definition of *Strauder* extends to the specific system of segregation at issue in *Brown*. Segregation violates the equality principle and demands the completion of the comprehensive, systemic equality defined in *Strauder* as constitutionally mandated.

Strauder involved the murder trial of a Black defendant indicted in 1874, a mere six years after the Fourteenth Amendment was ratified. At trial the defendant asked that the case be removed to federal court, arguing he would not have a fair trial in the state courts of West Virginia since state statute limited jury service to White males. The claim was not that the defendant was entitled to a jury of Black men, or of some proportion of Black men, but rather that he had a right to a jury selected from a pool that did not exclude all Black jurors because of their race. Removal was denied and he was tried and convicted.

The Supreme Court rendered its opinion in favor of the defendant in 1880, only twelve years after the Fourteenth Amendment was enacted. The Court's understanding of the meaning and purpose of the Amendment could not have been clearer:

> [The Fourteenth Amendment] is one of a series of constitutional provisions having a common purpose—namely, securing to a race recently emancipated, a race that, through generations, had been held in slavery, *all the civil rights that the superior race enjoy.*[4]

The standard set is explicitly racial; the Court viewed Whiteness as a badge of superiority but also as the comprehensive definition of full personhood. There is no self-examination in this statement of the contradiction between equality and the Court's ongoing assumed White racial superiority. This lack of interrogation of White identity persists in *Brown*, where the Court limits its analysis of the developmental impact of segregation to Black children. The evident racism in both *Strauder* and *Brown* nevertheless does not diminish the meaning of equality; it merely exposes the unexplored racial identity of the Court, the transparency of their own race.[5] Even if inartful, the Court's understanding is clear: the Fourteenth Amendment confers equality in *all* respects. The purpose, vision, and goal of the Amendment was to equalize Blacks to the status of Whites. *By definition, that would alter the status of Whites as well.* All rights were included, not a limited set of rights or a compromised definition of equality or a racial hierarchy within equality, which would be completely untenable.

To reinforce this definition of equality, the *Strauder* Court references the opinion in the *Slaughterhouse Cases,* decided even closer in time to the ratification of the Fourteenth Amendment.

The true spirit and meaning of the amendment, as we said in the Slaughterhouse Cases, 16 Wall. 36, cannot be understood without keeping in view the history of the times when they were adopted and general objects they plainly sought to accomplish. *At the time when they were incorporated into the Constitution, it required little knowledge of human nature to anticipate that those who had long been regarded as an inferior and subject race would, when suddenly raised to the rank of citizenship, be looked upon with jealousy and positive dislike, and that State laws might be enacted or enforced to perpetuate the distinctions that had before existed, discriminations against them had been habitual.*[6]

The Court recognizes the challenge to Whites to embrace equal humanity and personhood. The goal of absolute, comprehensive equality would generate resistance, but *the scope of equality was clear:* the rights conferred were inclusive of all those enjoyed by Whites. White supremacy was at an end if Blacks' equality encompassed the status and humanity understood to be the natural rights of White males. At the same time, given the historical context, equality was likely to generate resistance, violence, and discrimination contrary to equality. The Court saw the necessity of protection due to the impact of slavery, expressed in its own racist views of inferiority even as the Court paternalistically recognized the need for affirmative state action:

> It was well known that, in some States, laws making such discrimination then existed [meaning the Black Codes, but it could as well mean discriminatory laws in the North], and others might well be expected [due to emancipation]. The colored race, as a race, was abject and ignorant, and in that condition was unfitted to command the respect of those who had superior intelligence. Their training had left them mere children, and as such, they needed the protection which a wise government extend to those who are unable to protect themselves. They especially needed protection against unfriendly action in the States where they were resident.[7]

While accurately reflecting the conditions of slavery, the Court hardly acknowledges the state's responsibility for nearly three centuries of subordination of an entire race of human beings and the failure of the federal government to provide the necessary economic and educational support for this most massive transition. The Court's statement can certainly be read as re-creating inferiority. Their embedded expression of racial hierarchy to describe the amendment that dismantles hierarchy, nevertheless, should not undermine the definition of equality in the Fourteenth Amendment. That definition was comprehensive and radical.

Strauder underscores the necessity of affirmative attention to significant needs for comprehensive equality to be realized:

> It was in view of these considerations that the Fourteenth Amendment was framed and adopted. *It was designed to assure to the colored race the enjoyment of all the civil rights that, under the law, are enjoyed by white persons* and to give that race the protection of the general government in that enjoyment whenever it should be denied by the states. It not only gave citizenship and the privileges of citizenship to persons of color, but it denied to any State the power to withhold from them the equal protection of the laws, and authorized Congress to enforce its provisions by appropriate legislation.[8]

The Court circles back to the *Slaughterhouse Cases* to reinforce this interpretation of the definition of equality and the purpose of the Fourteenth Amendment:

> No one can fail to be impressed with the one pervading purpose found in all the [Reconstruction] amendments, lying at the foundation of each, and without which none of them would have been suggested—we mean the *freedom of the slave race, the security and firm establishment of that freedom, and the protection of the newly made freeman and citizen from the oppressions of those who had formerly exercised unlimited dominion over them.*[9]

Reaffirming this comprehensive, radical meaning, the *Strauder* Court concludes:

> If this is the spirit and meaning of the amendment, whether it means more or not, it is to be construed liberally to carry out the purposes of its framers. . . . What is [equal protection] but declaring that the law in the States shall be the same for the black as for the white; that all persons, whether colored or white, shall stand equal before the laws of the States . . . [10]

With this definition of equality in hand, the Court makes short shrift of the West Virginia statute limiting jury service to White males. The exclusion of Black men "is practically a brand upon them affixed by the law, an assertion of their inferiority, and a stimulant to that race prejudice which is an impediment to securing to individuals of the race that equal justice which the law aims to secure to all others."[11] Among the rights secured by equal protection, equal justice secures a right to a jury of one's peers, what the Court describes in the gendered understanding of its day as "a body of men composed of the *peers or equal* of the person whose rights it is selected or summoned to determine."[12] The Court then upholds the exercise of congressional power to permit removal of a case to federal court as a legitimate means to accomplish the ends of the Fourteenth Amendment.

Throughout the opinion, the Court is aware of the likely persistence of White prejudice, assumptions of Black inferiority, efforts to

reestablish the attributes of slavery, racial hierarchy, and White supremacy and construes the amendment as being designed to prevent *all* of
these things. It is a bulwark to prevent subordination and an affirmative duty to accomplish real, substantive equality. *Strauder*, therefore, is
a powerful statement of equality as comprehensive, radical, and systemic. The primary reliance of the *Brown* Court on *Strauder* to reach its
judgment and explain its reasoning pulls on the chronosystem to define
equality, endorsing a broad comprehensive definition of equality and
the meaning of the Reconstruction Amendments.

Thus, *Strauder* is a significant key to unlock our rereading of *Brown*.
Other scholars have recognized its power and scope as well. Sanford
Levinson calls *Strauder* "the most illuminating single case ever decided
by the Supreme Court regarding the doctrinal implications of the Equal
Protection Clause for the ever-controversial topics of race, and in our
own time, ethnicity."[13] Benno Schmidt characterizes *Strauder* as an opinion of "lost promise,[14] characterizing it "as corrosively frank as it was
doctrinally forceful."[15]

The radical scope of equality defined in *Strauder* and the necessity
for strong, lengthy federal action to ensure that it was achieved is only
reinforced by the Court's acknowledgment in *Brown* that segregation
had unconstitutionally destroyed the goal of Radical Reconstruction.
In 2019 *Strauder* was again cited as standing for the broad scope of liberty intended by the Fourteenth Amendment in *Flowers v. Mississippi*, a
case that held unconstitutional the removal of Black jurors through
peremptory challenges.[16] Recounting in detail the history of persisting
jury discrimination despite *Strauder* and linking contemporary discrimination using "neutral" rules to these historic patterns, the Court
clearly identified the linkage from past to present while embracing
Strauder as setting the constitutional standard of equality.

While *Strauder* was the primary case cited by the *Brown* Court in
footnote 5 of the *Brown* opinion, it was not the only one. The other cases
also articulate a broad, comprehensive definition of equality. Equality
and freedom, comprehensive and radical, were the opposite of slavery. As
comprehensive as the system of slavery had been, so then must be the
system of equality. Each case reinforces this definition of equality.

The first additional citation is the *Slaughterhouse Cases*,[17] referenced in the *Strauder* opinion as noted earlier. The case reinforces the concept of comprehensive equality as the core meaning of the Equal Protection Clause. This was the first case decided by the Court (1873) after the enactment of the Reconstruction Amendments. It underscores the "unity of purpose" of the amendments: the comprehensive freedom "of all the human race" by virtue of the Thirteenth Amendment and the reaffirmation and universality of freedom by the added protection of the Fourteenth Amendment.

In any fair and just construction of any section or phrase of these amendments, it is necessary to look to the purpose which we have said was the pervading spirit of them all, the evil which they were designed to remedy, and the process of continued addition to the Constitution, until that purpose was supposed to be accomplished as far as constitutional law can accomplish it.[18]

The specific purpose of equal protection was to respond to any state effort to undermine the equal status, humanity, and personhood of former slaves or free Blacks:

The existence of laws in the States where the newly emancipated negroes resided, which discriminated with gross injustice and hardship against them as a class, was the evil to be remedied by this clause, and by it such laws are forbidden.[19]

The *Slaughterhouse Cases* opinion articulates the purpose of the Reconstruction Amendments only five years after the Fourteenth Amendment was ratified. The elimination of slavery was presumed to establish conditions just as comprehensive as its opposite; slavery was the "evil" to be eliminated, and a new multiracial society was to take its place.

The two remaining cases cited in footnote 5 were decided simultaneously with *Strauder* and also involved claims of jury discrimination. *Virginia v. Rives*, a murder case involving several Black defendants accused of killing a White man, challenged the composition of the grand jury and the venire for jury selection, both entirely composed of White men.[20] The Court determined that the defendants might indeed have constitutional claims of denial of equal protection but that these claims must be pursued though state appeals. In the course of rendering its decision, the Court explored the meaning of the Fourteenth Amendment and the laws enacted under its authority, specifically, the 1866 Civil Rights Act conferring specific rights upon *all* persons *to the same extent "as is enjoyed by white citizens."*[21] The Court finds this language as well as the language of the Amendment to be clear and comprehensive:

> The plain object of these statutes, as of the Constitution which authorized them, was *to place the colored race, in respect of civil rights, upon a level with whites.* They made the rights and responsibilities, civil and criminal, of the two races *exactly the same.*[22]

By this racial language in the statute (conferring rights equal to those "enjoyed by white citizens"), the Court illuminates the underlying parallel constitutional command of equality to dismantle systemic White supremacy and establish systemic racial equality, by measuring that equality in comprehensive egalitarian racial terms previously exclusively reserved to Whites.[23]

The second case decided with *Strauder, Ex Parte Commonwealth of Virginia,*[24] similarly affirms the broad meaning of the Reconstruction Amendments. A Virginia state judge was indicted under a federal statute in federal district court for violating the rights of Black defendants by excluding all Blacks from the jury pool. Judges had the responsibility under Virginia law to draw up jury pool lists. Because of the judge's total exclusion of Blacks from the jury pool, the judge was charged with violation of the Civil Rights Act of 1875, which provides that "no citizen . . . shall be disqualified for service as grand or petit juror in any court of the States, or of any State, on account of race, color, or previous condition of servitude."[25] The issue to be resolved by the Supreme Court was whether this federal statute was constitutional. The Court, after citing the language of the Thirteenth and Fourteenth Amendments, states their purpose and meaning:

> One great purpose of these amendments was to raise the colored race from that condition of inferiority and servitude in which most

of them had previously stood into *perfect equality* of civil rights with all other persons within the jurisdiction of the States. They were intended to take away all possibility of oppression by law because of race or color.[26]

The Thirteenth and Fourteenth Amendments expand congressional power by expressly conferring the power to enact legislation to achieve the ends of the amendments "to secure to all persons the enjoyment of *perfect equality* of civil rights and equal protection of the laws."[27] The Civil Rights Act of 1875 was held constitutional, and therefore the indictment of the judge was proper.[28] Equality was defined in breathtaking simplicity and comprehensive scope: "perfect equality".

These two cases, *Rives* and *Ex Parte Virginia*, are braided with *Strauder*, all standing for the same broad definition of equality as full, comprehensive, and "perfect." All three do so in the context of the criminal justice system, one of the interlocking systems of subordination that were components of racial subordination under slavery and post-emancipation. By citing and choosing the language from *Strauder*, as well as the citation of powerful language in *Rives* and *Ex Parte Virginia*, the *Brown* Court stood on the foundation of its earliest cases construing the meaning of the Reconstruction Amendments as comprehensive, radical equality. This grounding, then, is the basis for the Court's definition of equality in *Brown*. Segregation, a system of inequality intended to replicate racial hierarchy, sustain White supremacy, and intensify the oppression of Blacks, was clearly unconstitutional.

These cases stand for a broad statement of the scope of rights as equivalent to those of White men. The language of *Strauder* quoted in *Brown* is a frank acknowledgment of the historical context and the likelihood of prejudice and discrimination which rendered Blacks, particularly Black men, in need of "protection" because they otherwise would only have the presumed maturity of "children." This language, debasing and subordinating even as it endorses a broad, deep, robust vision of equality, is striking. It exposes the unexamined racial identity and beliefs of the justices.

Strauder and the accompanying cases in footnote 5 are critical to rereading *Brown* as a radical definition of equality. But they do not stand alone. There are several other components of the *Brown* decision that further support this conclusion.

First, the Court condemns *Plessy v. Ferguson*,[29] the infamous case upholding the constitutionality of the "separate but equal" doctrine. In *Plessy* the Court found a Louisiana law mandating the separation of railroad passengers by race constitutional, and therefore the arrest and conviction of Homer Plessy for boarding a "Whites only" car was not constitutionally defective. *Plessy* infamously held that any interpretation of "separate but equal" as communicating inferiority or racial hierarchy was unfounded. As the Court had stated in *Plessy*,

> We consider the underlying fallacy of the plaintiff's argument to consist in the assumption that the enforced separation of the two races stamps the colored race with a badge of inferiority. If this be so, it is not by reason of anything found in the act, but solely because the colored race chooses to put that construction upon it.[30]

Justice Harlan, in his famous *Plessy* dissent, argued to the contrary, that the social meaning of segregation was clearly understood:

> Everyone knows that the statute in question had its origin in the purpose, not so much to exclude white persons from railroad cars occupied by blacks, as to exclude colored people from coaches occupied by or assigned to white persons. . . . The fundamental objection, therefore, to the statute, is that it interferes with the personal freedom of citizens.[31]

Justice Harlan, while arguing against segregation, was very clear that finding segregation unconstitutional would in no way undermine racial hierarchy. His assumption of White superiority and supremacy as an objective reality, another instance of the justices' unexplored racial identity, was clear in the most famous passage of his dissent arguing for the value of color blindness as a means to sustain hierarchy:

The white race deems itself to be the dominant race in this country. And so it is, in prestige, in achievements, in education, in wealth, and in power. So, I doubt not, it will continue to be for all time, if it remains true to its great heritage, and holds fast to the principles of constitutional liberty. But in view of the constitution, in the eye of the law, there is in this country no superior, dominant, ruling class of citizens. There is no caste here. Our constitution is colorblind, and neither knows nor tolerates classes among citizens. In respect of civil rights, all citizens are equal before the law.[32]

In *Brown*, the Court effectively overruled *Plessy*. The Court implicitly recognized its own powerful role in support of racial hierarchy. At the core of the Court's reversal is an acknowledgment that the underlying foundation of segregation is a belief system, a norm, a culture; it is a philosophy, grounded in racial inferiority, racial inhumanity, and racial hierarchy. The rejection of "separate but equal" fatally undermined segregation as a comprehensive system, not solely limited to education. The basis for that rejection was its incompatibility with equality. The paternalistic language of *Brown* may echo the racism of Harlan's dissent, but the unmistakable embrace of unmitigated, complete equality upends that reflexive racist expression, leaving in place the meaning of equality as shared, equal humanity.

A second aspect of *Brown* that reinforces a comprehensive radical definition of equality is the Court's focus on the "intangible" aspects of equality. As we have argued throughout, this focus zeroes in on the essential embrace of common humanity and equal development that energizes "equality." The Court was not satisfied to consider tangible factors, such as buildings, books, number of teachers, etc. Even if those factors were equal, the Court reasoned, it was essential to look to intangible factors, "those qualities which are incapable of objective measurement but which make for greatness," those factors that impact the "ability to study, to engage in discussions and exchange views with other students," in other words, the intellectual, developmental, and psychological aspects of education.[33] Separation, according to the

Court, was not neutral; it had an intended, racially hierarchical meaning, a meaning intended to undermine the equal personhood of each child.[34] Equal personhood was denied both Black and White children. The meaning of equality is just the opposite.

The Court's focus on the intangibles did not displace the record of highly unequal schools under segregation. Prior litigation, mostly at the graduate school level, had demonstrated that separation had often meant no school at all, or highly unequal schools based on objective measures. The *Brown* Court's insistence on focusing on the *intangibles* added a powerful meaning to "equality" that was incompatible with "separation." It reoriented the comprehensiveness of equality to the underlying assumptions of race and humanity and a vision of systematic equality as the heart of the Fourteenth Amendment. This definition of equality in education, and by implication, throughout all the interlocking systems and beliefs of segregation, was truly radical in its return to the promise and vision of the Reconstruction Amendments.

One final additional ratification of this definition of equality is the Court's decision in the companion case to *Brown* of *Bolling v. Sharpe*.[35] *Bolling* was the school segregation case from Washington DC. The Fourteenth Amendment did not apply, as the amendment only applies to the states. Instead, the grounding for the constitutional claim was a violation of the Fifth Amendment, which applies to the federal government and thus to the District of Columbia.[36] The language of the Fifth Amendment provides protection for due process of law but contains no explicit language similar to the Fourteenth Amendment's Equal Protection Clause.[37] Nevertheless, the Court interpreted due process as including equal protection: "The concepts of equal protection and due process, both stemming from our American idea of process, both stemming from our American idea of fairness, are not mutually exclusive."[38] Although the Court recognized that the concepts were not interchangeable, it concluded, "Discrimination may be so unjustifiable as to be violative of due process."[39] Racial classifications are contrary to constitutional tradition and suspect.[40] Segregation, the Court holds, is a deprivation of liberty, rendering segregation unconstitutional under the Fifth Amendment:

Liberty under law extends to the *full range of conduct* which the individual is free to pursue, and it cannot be restricted except for a proper governmental objective. Segregation in public education is not reasonably related to any proper governmental objective, and thus it imposed on Negro children of the District of Columbia a burden that constitutes an arbitrary deprivation of their liberty in violation of the Due Process Clause.[41]

Our analysis thus recaptures the strong, deep, comprehensive definition of equality present in *Brown*. Present inequality reflects the failure to heed *Brown*'s mandate. Our view does not stand alone. One of the most compelling analyses endorsing *Brown*'s powerful scope and radical meaning is the 1960 defense of the opinion by Charles Black,[42] written in the language of his day:

> The basic scheme of reasoning on which these cases can be justified is *awkwardly simple*. First, the equal protection clause of the fourteenth amendment should be read as saying that the Negro race, as such, is not to be significantly disadvantaged by the laws of the states. Secondly, *segregation is a massive intentional disadvantaging of the Negro race, as such, by state law. No subtlety at all.*[43]

Black rests his argument on the strength of the *Slaughterhouse Cases* and *Strauder* and even goes so far as to say *Plessy* does not contradict those cases; rather, "the fault of *Plessy* is in the psychology and sociology of its minor premise."[44] The purpose of the Fourteenth Amendment is comprehensive equality; segregation cannot be excluded or allowed as "equal." To argue otherwise is preposterous:

> But if a whole race of people finds itself confined within a system which is set up and continued for the very purpose of keeping it in an inferior station, and if the question is then solemnly propounded whether such a race is being treated "equal," I think we ought to exercise one of the sovereign prerogatives of philosophers—that of laughter. The only question remaining (after we get our laughter under control) is whether the segregation system answers to this

description. Here I must confess to a tendency to start laughing all over again.[45]

Black, a White southerner, is clear about the meaning of segregation: inferiority.[46] But he does not simply say "because I said so":

> Rather, history links segregation to slavery and like slavery was imposed and reinforced tightly both legally and extralegally. The social meaning of segregation is the putting of the Negro in a position of walled-off inferiority—or the other equally plain fact that such treatment is hurtful to human beings. Southern courts, on the basis of just such a judgment, have held that the placing of a white person in a Negro railroad car is an actionable humiliation; must a court pretend not to know that the Negro's situation there is humiliating?[47]

Black concludes that the harm of segregation is not limited to its victims but also encompasses its perpetrators:

> I can heartily concur in the judgment that *segregation harms the white as much as it does the Negro*. Sadism rots the policeman; the suppressor of thought loses lights; the community that forms into a mob, and goes down and dominates a trial, may wound itself beyond healing. Can this reciprocity of hurt, this fated mutuality that inheres in all inflicted wrong, serve to validate the wrong itself?[48]

Black's essay, written in the language of his day to refer to African Americans, affirms two of the basic points of Radical *Brown*: the critical link between slavery and segregation that informs the meaning and impact of segregation and the broad, comprehensive, radical meaning of equality guaranteed by the Constitution.

How would full, equal humanity be implemented? Imagine, given the Court's total rejection of segregation as well as its radical definition of equality, that equality required full comprehensive substantive equality grounded in common humanity. Humanity equivalent to the segregation ideal is White humanity; by definition it is comprehensive.

Common humanity is transformative of Whiteness as well, as humanity is no longer White-defined. With that in mind, imagine the implementation of the vision of common humanity; what would that look like? What would it require in the contexts in which Whites and Blacks stand and develop?

Post-*Brown*: Radical *Brown* . . . or Not?

The earliest cases decided after *Brown* confirm the scope of equality as comprehensive radical equality. The Court insisted that segregation must be eliminated "root and branch."[49] A return to the early post-*Brown* decisions to understand *Brown*'s radical scope is warranted not only because they accurately reflect what the Court meant but also because it is what equality demands and must be.

The immediate effect of *Brown* was wrenching: "At a stroke, the Justices had severed the remaining chords of de facto slavery."[50] This second emancipation disrupted the formalized, legalized system of segregation.[51] Paul Finkelman argues that *Brown* is the most radical constitutional case ever, or at least for its century.[52] Yet as one Southern judge noted, "The cancer of segregation will never be cured by the sedative of gradualism."[53] This prediction proved all too true: the Court's command for implementation "with all deliberate speed" invited delay, and the overwhelming pattern was resistance for decades.[54] Removing formal, facial rules left neutral rules and underlying belief systems in White supremacy and Black inhumanity intact. The vehemence and strength of resistance testifies to the depth of commitment to Whiteness as White supremacy and to the distance to be travelled to achieve equality. *Brown* as icon, if limited to a deradicalized, emaciated meaning, not only fails to achieve its mandate, but also becomes a weapon to continue and rationalize dehumanization.

Emblematic of the initial massive resistance was the challenge to the Court's very authority to decide the case. In *Cooper v. Aaron*,[55] the Court reaffirmed its authority and the obligation of the states to respect the constitutional rights of children.[56] This constitutional obligation could not be nullified directly or indirectly.

The right of a student not to be segregated on racial grounds in schools so maintained is indeed so fundamental and pervasive that it is embraced in the concept of due process of law.... [*Brown*] is now unanimously reaffirmed. The principles announced in that decision and the obedience of the states to them, according to the command of the Constitution, are *indispensable* for the protection of the freedoms guaranteed by our fundamental charter for all of us. *Our constitutional ideal of equal justice under law is thus made a living truth.*[57]

Resistance nevertheless continued, including the closing of all public schools in Prince Edward County, Virginia.[58] The Court decried the incessant delays and insisted on implementation: "Delays in desegregating school systems are no longer tolerable."[59]

The Court moved quickly to use *Brown* in areas other than education and rejected the idea of gradual change.[60] "The rights asserted here are, like all such rights, present rights; they are not merely hopes to some future enjoyment of some formalistic constitutional promise. The basic guarantees of our Constitution are warrants for the here and now."[61] Claims of potential unrest or hostility were not allowed to justify continuing segregation.[62] "*Brown* never contemplated that the concept of "deliberate speed" would countenance indefinite delay in elimination of racial barriers in schools, let alone other public facilities not involving the same physical problems or comparable conditions."[63] The range of decisions that followed *Brown* included striking down segregation in beaches and bathhouses, golf courses, swimming pools, and parks.[64] Other areas where desegregation was immediate included state colleges and universities, transportation, racial zoning, employment rights, and union representation.[65]

In these cases involving other aspects of segregation, the Court clearly saw the links between slavery and segregation.[66]

Just as the Black Codes, enacted after the Civil War to restrict the free exercise of [property] rights, were substitutes for the slave system, so the exclusion of Negroes from white communities became a substitute for the Black Codes. And when racial discrimination herds men into ghettos and makes their ability to buy property turn on the color of their skin, then it too is a relic of slavery.[67]

Justice Douglas identified the injury of discrimination as falling on both Whites and Blacks:

> *The true curse of slavery is not what it did to the black man, but what it has done to the white man.* For the existence of the institution produced the notion that the white man was of superior character, intelligence, and morality. The blacks were little more than livestock—to be fed and fattened for the economic benefits they could bestow through their labors, and to be subjected to authority, often with cruelty, to make clear who was master and who slave.[68]

He adds that slavery continues: "While the institution has been outlawed, it has remained in the minds and hearts of many white men. Cases which have come to this Court depict a spectacle of slavery unwilling to die."[69] Segregation is understood as a system of slavery. Its end demands its opposite.

The Court powerfully reaffirmed the radical scope of *Brown* in 1971, declaring that it required the elimination of racial discrimination *"root and branch."*[70] Simplistic steps to formally open the door of White schools to Black students and Black schools to White students were not enough. *What was required was the opposite of segregation in every respect.* This reaffirmed the comprehensive scope of *Brown*, versus merely a formal obligation for schools to "look" different.

> The objective today remains to eliminate from the public schools all vestiges of state-imposed segregation. Segregation was the evil struck down by *Brown I*. . . . That was the violation sought to be corrected by the remedial measures of *Brown II*. That was the basis for the holding in *Green* that school authorities are "clearly charged with the affirmative duty to take whatever steps might be necessary to convert to a unitary school system in which racial discrimination would be eliminated root and branch."[71]

This meant strong remedies.[72] "A school desegregation case does not differ fundamentally from other cases involving the framing of equitable remedies to repair the denial of a constitutional right."[73]

Radical Equality Disavowed

The early reaffirmation of radical comprehensive equality was not sustained. A first critical step was the Court's treatment of de facto segregation as legally and constitutionally distinctive from de jure segregation. This cut deeply into the Court's definition of the scope of segregation, making proof of a constitutional violation far more difficult for de facto systems.[74] This distinction was exacerbated by the view that private choices, unreachable under Fourteenth Amendment doctrine, which only reaches state action, were the cause of education and housing patterns, and that schools could not be held responsible for racially identifiable schools created by private prejudice. A second limitation was the Court's separation of urban and suburban schools, making it difficult if not impossible to order metropolitan integration to combat segregated housing patterns.[75] A third limitation that emerged was a constrained sense of time and the depth of the challenge involved in destroying the underlying system of segregation.[76] The Court accepted the idea that the elimination of segregation at one point in time was sufficient to achieve *Brown*'s mandate. "Root and branch" was hardly recognizable under this watered-down view of *Brown*.[77]

There were justices who strongly disagreed with these limitations. Justice Powell viewed segregation as national whether de jure or de facto.[78] "We should abandon a distinction which long since has outlived its time and formulate constitutional principles of national rather than merely regional application."[79] Justice Marshall characterized persisting racial disparities in education as "manifestations of economic, cultural, and political hegemony; the promise of *Brown* . . . was to end this dominance."[80] Justice Ginsburg criticized the misunderstanding of time as well as of the scope of *Brown*'s mandate: "The Court stresses that the present remedial programs have been in place for seven years. But compared to more than two centuries of firmly entrenched official discrimination, the experience with the desegregation remedies . . . has been evanescent."[81]

One attempted use of *Brown* that might have sustained its radical scope would have been to recognize it as the basis for a constitutionally guaranteed fundamental right to education. But that possibility was seemingly foreclosed in 1972 by the Court's decision in *San Antonio Independent School District v Rodriguez*.[82] Only when confronted with a total deprivation of education did the Court find a constitutional violation.[83]

Serious efforts to integrate even under a limited definition of what that meant were only undertaken in many areas once the federal government used the incentive of federal funding under Title VI of the 1964 Civil Rights Act[84] and the Elementary and Secondary Education Act (ESEA).[85] Integration defined primarily as student assignment and the racial composition of the student body occurred through the use of both voluntary and court-ordered plans and policies that used freedom of choice, magnet schools, transfer programs, zoning lines, pairing, and clustering. Most court orders ended in the 1990s. Some recent efforts have focused on socioeconomic diversity and teacher diversity. These efforts also focus on bodies and numbers.

Teachers and administrators from Black schools were shifted only to a limited degree, and in the years since *Brown* was decided, the ranks of teachers of color shrank dramatically.[86] In 1954, 82,000 African American teachers taught two million Black students.[87] "By 1972, more than 41,600 African-American educators in the southern states had been displaced or lost their jobs." Currently, Black teachers account for only 7 percent of the teaching workforce.[88]

The lengthy focus on prying the door open to single-race White schools while no other implementation occurred constrained the legal development of doctrine to elaborate the meaning of the opposite of segregation. This continued to be the focus when "neutral" efforts continued to keep the door shut and to deny quality education in majority or exclusively Black schools. Evaluation of districts during this long period of resistance, as well as how we measure "school equality or equity" today, has focused strongly on the tangibles, particularly the mix of race and ethnicity in the student body.[89] Whatever the underlying beliefs regarding mixing students, we have not even accomplished *the mixing of bodies* in many schools. We argue that this definition of integration is a parched, limited read of *Brown* that ignores the meaning of comprehensive systemic equality.

In the most recent case interpreting *Brown*, the Court continued its limitation of *Brown*'s meaning. "'Full compliance' with Brown I required school districts 'to achieve a system of determining admission to the public schools *on a nonracial basis.*'"[90] The message is clear: "The way to stop discrimination on the basis of race is to stop discriminating on the basis of race."[91] Colorblindness, sanctified by a misreading of *Brown*, now justifies and reconstructs inequality. Justice Breyer in dissent viewed *Brown*'s mandate quite differently: race consciousness is essential to remedy race hierarchy essential to achieve race equality.[92] Justice Breyer disputes what segregation meant:

> But segregation policies did not simply tell schoolchildren "where they could and could not go to school based on the color of their skin,"; *they perpetuated a caste system rooted in the institutions of slavery and 80 years of legalized subordination.*[93]

He finds the interest in racial diversity to be compelling because it rights a wrong, because it is educationally valuable, and because it contributes to democratic values.[94]

The Development and Diversity Cases

Despite the evisceration of *Brown*'s radical mandate over the past seventy years, there are some affirmative threads of support in the post-*Brown* era for Radical *Brown*. First, the Supreme Court has embraced the value of developmental research to evaluate children's rights. Developmental knowledge underscores the comprehensive ecology of the child's environment as critical to their growth. Cases support the developmental principles at the heart of *Brown* and the infusion of contemporary critical developmental research in support of children's equality. Second, the Court has recognized the compelling value of diversity, supporting the importance of the inclusion of all children in an equal system designed to foster and value their shared humanity. Diversity triggers a complex range of developmental benefits coupled with serving the specific needs of each child. Countervailing pressure challenging diversity admittedly persists, and the Court's most recent decision on affirmative action suggests a betrayal of that concept, but in principle, diversity supports common equal humanity.

The Supreme Court embraced interdisciplinary research on adolescent development to inform constitutional analysis of youth decision-making and juvenile criminal liability, as well as youths' potential for rehabilitation, in a series of juvenile justice cases decided from 2005 to 2012. These cases add a robust interdisciplinary perspective and substantive content to the unique constitutional rights of children and youths. They suggest affirmative rights to equal developmental support, or developmental equality, which is at the core of Radical *Brown*.

In *Roper v. Simmons*,[95] where the Court decided that execution of a child of any age was unconstitutional, the Court rested its opinion on developmental science in support of the concept that "children are different."[96] In two subsequent cases on life imprisonment without the possibility of parole, the Court again turned to developmental research.[97]

Developments in psychology and brain science continue to show fundamental differences between juvenile and adult minds. For example, parts of the brain involved in behavior control continue to mature through late adolescence. Juveniles are more capable of change than are adults, and their actions are less likely to be evidence of "irretrievably depraved character" than are the actions of adults.'[98]

Developmental research substantiates that *youth matters*.[99] Furthermore, the developmental characteristics of *each* youth, related to home and community, elements over which youth have no control, are also relevant. Development is not a neutral process but, rather, is affected significantly by context. Finally, in a case evaluating the questioning of a teenager at school,[100] the Court found that age mattered to the youth's perception of the situation. Age is an objective characteristic that affects a person's perception of their freedom to leave a situation where the only other people in the room are adults.[101] This embrace of developmental science is not limited to the juvenile justice cases. In a line of cases regarding minor's reproductive rights, the Court similarly drew on developmental research, emphasizing the affirmative competence, capacity and capability of many teenagers when making decisions in contexts that allow for time and deliberation.[102]

The developmental cases are important not only in the spheres in which they have been applied but also as further support for Radical *Brown*. Not only is developmental science relevant to issues of judgment and decision-making, but it is also foundational to issues of identity and learning. Developmental insights have implications for every system that supports children and youths' developmental trajectories. This includes identifying systemic barriers to healthy development but also enhancing and supporting the positive structures to maximize developmental well-being and growth. The developmental cases bring further insights into legal concepts of equality.[103] The constitutional basis for that support is children's unique combination of dependency and emerging autonomy.[104] This is a claim of positive rights essential to liberty which must be attentive to differences in circumstances as well as individual differences. This is where Radical *Brown* and the developmental cases meet: at the crossroads of comprehensive, systemic equality. The means both to attain systemic equality and to sustain that reality require developmental insights that are anchored in the realities of children of color and White children.

A second set of Supreme Court cases that reinforce Radical *Brown* are the cases on educational diversity. Fundamentally, these cases reflect a central constitutional vision of a nonhierarchical, multidimensional society. Diversity values intangibles and identities, exactly the kind of intangibles central to *Brown*. By identifying differential benefits for White students and students of color, it incorporates critical contemporary differences among racial groups and complementary identity challenges. Diversity adds complexity and richness to the culture of education and what goes on in the classroom, and is essential to transform education to achieve systemic educational equality. Diversity imagines the elimination of the domination of one perspective and presumed superiority linked to self-learning, as well as learning about and with others.

The initial case in which the concept of diversity was embraced, *Regents of University of California v. Bakke*,[105] recognized diversity as a *compelling* state interest meeting the most rigorous constitutional standard of strict scrutiny.[106] In a pair of cases twenty-five years after *Bakke*,[107] the Court not only reaffirmed the value of racial diversity, but also strengthened its foundation. Diversity scholarship demonstrated the contribution of a diverse student body to learning outcomes, preparation for a diverse society and clients, leadership, and good citizenship.[108] Diversity "promote[s] cross racial understanding," by helping to break down racial stereotypes and "enable[s] [students] to better understand persons of different races."[109] Diversity as requiring critical mass is linked not to presumed point of view but, instead, to the idea than the goals of diversity cannot be achieved by mere tokenism.[110]

In the one of the more recent cases involving diversity, race was a minimized express factor in the admissions process but was strongly present in the implementation of a neutral policy with known racial consequences,[111] the policy of admitting students who graduated in the top ten percent of their high school class. With known housing discrimination and education discrimination patterns, the ten-percent policy was a formula that achieved considerable racial diversity without expressly taking account of race.[112] The Court, approvingly citing the rationales for racial diversity as a compelling state interest, upheld the admissions policy.[113]

On June 29, 2023, after the manuscript for this book was completed, the Supreme Court issued its opinion on the use of race as a factor in college admissions, finding the admissions policies of Harvard College and the University of North Carolina unconstitutional under the Equal Protection Clause.[114] In the decision, split 6–3, the majority articulated continued support for the value of diversity as a compelling reason to deviate from strict colorblindness, but severely limited both its use as a goal and the means to accomplish it, as well as signaling that the acceptability of using the diversity principle itself was time limited. Rather than endorsing diversity as a tool to engage with inequality, the majority insisted that it be used rarely and narrowly, and it must end—implicitly, soon. Central to the majority's judgment is the insistence on *colorblindness* as the constitutional command of the Equal Protection Clause of the Fourteenth Amendment.[115] Colorblindness as the Court defines it requires sameness with respect to all persons, ignoring racial context, history, and current realities. Its sole command is *nondiscrimination*. The dissenters, on the other hand, point to an entirely different meaning of the Fourteenth Amendment: the "guarantee of *racial equality*."[116] *Equality* as the goal requires color consciousness, not colorblindness (or an understanding of colorblindness that requires race consciousness), because of an "endemically segregated society where race has always and continues to matter."[117] Colorblindness is perverse in this context: "Our country has never been colorblind."[118] In that context, a contemporary rule of colorblindness would reify inequality and embedded discrimination. To the contrary, "Equality requires acknowledgment of inequality."[119] *Brown* is read completely differently by the majority and the dissenters. Based on our rereading of *Brown*, we unequivocally argue that *Brown* mandates comprehensive *radical equality* based on the design and vision of the Reconstruction Amendments.

Race matters. The diversity principle, articulated in *Bakke* and strongly supported until this most recent case, is still begrudgingly recognized albeit arguably gutted by the constraints imposed by the majority. Diversity, and more importantly comprehensive equality, is powerfully articulated by the dissenters. The diversity principle supports Radical *Brown*'s core concentration on humanity and development for all. Radical *Brown* enhances the diversity principle because Radical *Brown* articulates the central necessity of comprehensive equality.

Conclusion

The radical vision of comprehensive equality is clearly articulated in *Brown*, resting particularly but not exclusively on *Strauder*. The early post-*Brown* cases affirm this, that the goal is equality root and branch. The post-*Brown* development and diversity cases (with the exception of the majority opinion in the most recent case) also support this vision of children's needs and serving *all* children's humanity. This vision realizes the unfinished business of Reconstruction.

The countercurrent is certainly present in the record of failed implementation for seventy years. Radical equality was resisted, cabined, denied, and limited in a host of ways. Perhaps it was too much for one case to carry. Yet *Brown* continues to hold a powerful place, as evidenced by the recent misreading and misuse of *Brown* to reverse constitutional support for affirmative action as contradictory to "colorblindness." *Brown* does not stand for ignoring racial inequality; rather, as we have demonstrated, it mandates comprehensive equality. It requires deep commitment and elaboration to achieve.

Integration has been seen as a one-way process, with no focus on issues of White identity, White supremacy, White privilege, and White claims of raceless-ness even as Whites remain highly race conscious. Whites were not challenged to explore their racial identity or the consequences of accepted inequality and false superiority for their well-being or how they valued others. Peggy McIntosh captured the everydayness of those consequences by identifying the "invisible knapsack" of White privilege along with the constant disincentive to see privilege.[120] Unearned privilege is a significant aspect of White identity, but privilege alone does not capture the lack of self-recognition of White racial identity or the virulence of ongoing racism toward others.

Time and intergenerational connections continue to challenge a consciousness that wants to forget, to relegate to the past, to claim that a solution has been achieved, that racial progression has occurred and that equality exists. Inequality is then personal, not systemic, structural and state supported. The length of the delay adds to the chronosystem of sustained, systemic inequality and the multiple ecologies of developmental inequality.

We now stand at four hundred years and counting. Since *Brown* was decided, we have encompassed three generations. The dissonance is enormous. The lack of awareness and denial is huge. Again, we must ask, What does that mean for us individually and, thus, collectively? We explore this in depth in part II, articulating what implementation would require to actually follow the mandate of Radical *Brown*.

Embedded in the *Brown* decision is a transformative understanding of the developmental makeup and capacities of children. Although expressed in the decision and framed as exclusively a concern about the negative impact of segregation on Black children, and thus by extension a concern for all subordinated children, inherently, this principle of the unfair and unconstitutional impact of structural inequality encompasses the impact on all children. This includes the construction of White supremacy and its derivative privilege—and costs of privilege—for White children. Recognition of developmental implications as the radical message of *Brown* mandates a close, critical, and differentiated understanding of the human developmental process itself. Developmental knowledge must be used to radically change education to equitably support the common humanity of all children.

PART II

Humanity

CHAPTER 5

Necessary Perspectives for Rereading *Brown*

THE AMERICAN CONTEXT DESCRIBED in part I—slavery, emancipation, segregation, and Radical Reconstruction—is the foundation for the contemporary lived situations of America's Blacks and Whites. The nation suffers from and is haunted by a viewpoint of its history that avoids fundamental and difficult truths. The long-term, intergenerationally transmitted, and calamitous proclivity for the historical invisibility of Black people's mistreatment has consequences. It is associated with contemporary policies and practices around the core theme of race. It distorts the past and provides as substantive practices engrained traditions of Black dehumanization, hegemony, and the conscious structuring of conditions for sustaining a state of racial hierarchy.

Brown as implemented for seventy years mirrors this dilemma. Our core principles are contradicted by their continued betrayal, yet these contradictions are rendered invisible, repeating a pattern since our Founding. *Brown*'s mandate is clear: it is comprehensive equality expressive of the recognition and lived reality of common humanity. That mandate is *radical* because it requires disengaging from, healing from, and coming to grips with inhumanity embedded practices and beliefs grounded on Black inferiority and White supremacy. The change required by *Brown*'s mandate is *radical* because inhumanity has been fostered, hidden, and justified for so long, it seems as if common humanity cannot be imagined. *Brown*'s mandate is not, and should not, be radical if we truly believe and live our foundational principles as a democracy of free and equal people *all* included in "We the People." Thus, perhaps the *Brown* remedy assumed that the effects would remain unnoticed by "assumed under-educated non-humans" as well as those authentically voicing objections to conditions of inequality. However, we suggest a different explanation. We hazard the existence across ecology settings—broadly disseminated intersubjectively transmitted and embraced—*a functional Black Inhumanity Perspective* (fBIP). Its positionality in American life is deliberately under-interrogated. More accurately, it remains unrecognized as part of America's embraced fabric of democracy. Governor Ron DeSantis's recently enacted policies guarantee that such assumed dissonance-producing information remains invisible and, thus, unavailable for interrogation. fBIP is exemplified by preferences for the selective framing of the nation's history. Currently and most frequently politicized as rejections of critical race theory, in fact, it represents resistance to broad discourse about race and racism.[1]

As we have reread *Brown*, its mandate is Radical *Brown*—common humanity. Why is that so? As we set forth in part I, it is because the text of the decision establishes the scope of the harm (segregation, comprehensively, resting on slavery, comprehensively) and condemns it systemically. The vision of equality rests on equal humanity (a new system "root and branch"). Common humanity as *Brown*'s mandate is both a legal, constitutional judgment and a developmental framework. Why is that so? As we have argued, it is because *the legal recognition of harm was developmentally based, and its remedy is therefore developmentally defined.* It requires developmental framing for its implementation. A clear understanding of the developmental harm and the developmental vision to achieve common humanity requires developmental framing and definition. Otherwise, a full understanding of the scope of the vision and its implementation is rendered invisible.

We began this volume using PVEST as our scaffolding device because it is our best tool to interpret this radical mandate as well as understand its demands. PVEST tells us that within a recursive and inclusive system (or its linked multisystemic representations)—in addition to complex interactions between components of the system, cultural traditions, and individuals of varied levels of vulnerability—the overall ecology is powerfully affected by social and cultural values and ideas (the macrosystem) and history (the chronosystem). Unfolding the radical rereading of *Brown*, we provide a particular scaffolding organization demonstrating the many impacts of fBIP, thus, affording a heuristic device for analysis. In part I, we examined in detail the core values and ideas of the chronosystem, including the interconnected periods of slavery, emancipation, Radical Reconstruction, and segregation; the multiple cases making up *Brown*; and the post-*Brown* cases. The links and connections in the four-hundred-year chronosystem between slavery, segregation, and present de facto inequalities remain unbroken because of the failure to break core beliefs in inhumanity and hierarchy. Those deeply embedded beliefs and principles define the legal, constitutional, foundational harm recognized and condemned in *Brown* that require the implementation of common humanity. In demonstrating the long-term scaffolding of fBIP, they simultaneously invite and expose the developmental meaning and consequences intergenerationally, individually, and contemporarily.

Our developmental PVEST scaffolding gives real meaning to the radical command and the egregious failed implementation of *Brown*. The deep chronosystem described in part I is an essential pervasive ecology that enfolds our individual location in inequality. In part II we continue the use of fBIP to elaborate the mandate of common humanity by understanding where we are seventy years post-*Brown* due to the failure to achieve this radical mandate. It concretely sets forth what is required to accomplish that essential goal.

Following the scaffolding function of chapter 1, and the chronosystem emphasized in part I, in part II the next steps of rereading *Brown* add unavoidable human meaning-making into the mix.[2] As inferred from individuals' everyday sense-making, the inclusion further demonstrates the ever-presence and significance of fBIP. We expose the role of *context* as an "individual-context" explanatory device for interrogating contemporary relational and human development processes and outcomes.[3] A PVEST-informed framing and strategy affords insights about contemporary life and resiliency-facilitating requirements (e.g., well-being, life course competencies, and thriving) desired for all children. PVEST demonstrates the bidirectionality of human processes and represents a helpful conceptual device. Our rereading strategy also facilitates interrogation of the sustaining contributions of particular social science practices, assumptions about race differences, research methods, and conceptual traditions—all susceptible to fBIP, as well as consequences of it given its four hundred-year "invisibilized" status(!). We argue and identify contributors to (1) the societal tensions referenced, (2) the fueling of hegemony itself, and (3) the scaffolding character for the system's sustainability. Absent the radical rereading we advocate, negative outcomes are predictable. Rigorous interrogation reduces significant shortcomings and has benefits. Positive conceptual strategies (1) curtail inauthentic examination of contemporary life, (2) limit decontextualized policy considerations, (3) prevent habitual ignoring of longstanding social ills, and (4) emphasize context-linked, identity-focused, development status-sensitive, and shared-humanity-framing race quandaries. Demonstrated is not just the "what" or outcome focus of human experience, but also the "how."[4] Those answers aid in designing effective remedies, which take into account the ever-presence of fBIP.

The institution of slavery, the Civil War, the character of emancipation, and Radical Reconstruction represent individual and collective conscious misrepresentations. As framed by Adam I. P. Smith, memory shortcomings vis-à-vis historical truths contribute intergenerational tensions and deter the dissonance essential for authentic and rooted social change. As Smith notes:

> Despite decades of work by historians, many Americans remain determined to see the Civil War as a struggle among noble white folk with little or no implications for the state of race relations today. Like Queen Victoria dressing up in tartan, they have clothed themselves in rebel garb. As long as they continue to do so, American history will be inseparable from the politics of the present.[5]

Smith critiques conceptual shortcomings and memory distortions as consequential to the policies, practices, and scholarly traditions in place three generations post-*Brown*.

As suggested by Karl Marx, this analysis is not new. Marx's 1852 assessment of Louis Napoleon's (Napoleon III) 1851 coup underscores the critical role of history:

> Men make their own history, but they do not make it as they please; they do not make it under self-selected circumstances, but under circumstances existing already, given and transmitted from the past. The tradition of all dead generations weighs like a nightmare on the brains of the living."[6]

In our radical reading of *Brown,* the incentivized memory lapses communicate intergenerational tensions as well as *unexamined* motivations for distortions. Our rereading embraces the perspective that vulnerability is a globally shared and unavoidably human status irrespective of resource level, skin color, and other social demographics and historical factors, including the situation of chattel slavery status.[7] This aids in the explanation for long-term uninterrogated fBIP.

Overview: The Problem

Common humanity and vulnerability accompany navigating diverse environments in pursuit of individual well-being and collective thriving. Thriving efforts attempt to meet and address the fulfillment of life-course-specific developmental tasks, respond to competence needs, and require coping reactions and responses.[8] Navigating the life course and responding to necessary developmental tasks is not free of potholes; challenges are rampant and represent humanity as raw and unapologetic messiness.

As suggested in part I, history serves as scaffolding and context for unfolding humanity and is a shared reality. Its inclusion and integration serve to increase clarity about a priori status, engage unavoidable human processes, and communicate the "how" of individual and collective outcomes for "We the People." Individual and collective thriving efforts—given variability—occur at different levels of vulnerability (i.e., the balance or imbalance between variously sourced risks and the presence and access to protective factors).[9]

We place at center-stage the significance of ignoring Blacks' humanity. The implications for successful practice and policy matter. For example, functionally making White lives and meaning-making processes the "standard of humanity" remains in vogue but is problematic for *Blacks and Whites*. When life course processes for people of color are ignored as well as the enveloping role of history, unavoidably, hierarchical, unequal outcomes persist.[10] Regarding developmental status, not only is Black child "adultification" an issue, but also, assumptions of Black psychopathology persist. Context features produce reactive coping and identities at the individual and collective levels. Viewpoints that ignore history and context produce policy limitations that matter.[11]

Our rereading of *Brown* takes as foundational, operational, and substantive a commitment to assumptions of shared humanity considered within historical context.[12] It appreciates that an interrogation of the failure to do so is impactful and problematic for Whites. The invisibility of the historically buttressed racial dilemma generates "inequality presence denial."[13] Because of variation within and between groups employing "inequality presence denial" as a reactive coping pattern, interrogating contributors to historical invisibility as well as resistance to invisibility requires examination.

Resisting Sustained Inhumanity

A cognition- and phenomenology-framed interrogation of a four-hundred-year-old system of race and color discrimination aids with explanations for the problem of sustained relational tensions.[14] fBIP as systems of beliefs—unchallenged, untoward attitudes and assumptions—remains underinterrogated. Informal operationalization refuels systems of oppression, linking intergenerational trauma aligned with reactive coping requirements, Whites' fears of Black bodies, and White identity processes, including uninterrogated beliefs of White superiority (i.e., Whiteness as the standard for humanity and all positive attributes). Considered from a PVEST framing—given centuries of unacknowledged violence perpetrated on Black people—evident is unacknowledged, untoward, and maladaptive White reactive coping, expressed and lived as normalizing the (mis)treatment of Blacks.

The lack of endogenous and character-relevant incentives such as guilt and of structured disconnections with exogenous factors such as the recognition of human oppression is sustaining and impactful. Rendered invisible are oppressive and dehumanizing systems.[15] Such traditions make inaccessible an identification with individuals generally considered "the other."[16] Accordingly, a lack of empathy and recognition of others' human status stifles authentic and intended change. America's long-term race dilemma scaffolds and supports the continuation of a Whiteness-privileged status quo over 150 years following slavery's formal end. The tradition prevents the acknowledgement, diagnosis, and treatment of the highly fragile and intergenerationally transmitted social malaise resistant to change. Resisting or forgetting that *Black Lives Matter* represents the persistent American race quandary.

Continuing under-interrogated—and impacting racial groups differently—are huge and morally questionable human and economic capital losses spanning centuries of American life. Equally salient from a human development perspective is the failure to consider the interconnectedness of the multiple domains of human functioning (i.e., neuro-physical-biological, socio-emotional, and cognitive). Considered collectively, the myriad deficiencies raise questions about nationally touted values of shared liberty and everyday practiced justice.

Inequality Presence Denial, Coping, and Resiliency

Assisted by PVEST's vulnerability/resiliency framing, the need to thrive while meeting developmental tasks and needs raises multiple under-interrogated themes. For example, irrespective of being underacknowledged in the social, developmental, and behavioral sciences, there are psychological, contextual, and neuro-physical-biological correlates impacting vulnerability status for Whites. Such shortcomings have implications for stress level and the need for ego-involved reactive coping.[17] For example, "inequality/racism presence denial" is a reactive coping strategy.[18] Its impact is made worse by, and has consequences for, the nature of ego developmental processes and outcomes, that is, unaddressed repressed identities and ego compensation, including hege-mony behavioral traditions.[19] It aids in the explanation for the long-term presence and seeming imperviousness of fBIP. There are unique patterns for those privileged by skin color (Whiteness) compared to those assumed to represent high vulnerability status (i.e., the latter sit-uation is viewed as synonymous with risks and challenges only). Minor-ity children and communities of color are frequently resilient. Their access and use of protective factors and supports produce resiliency and thriving often linked to cultural socialization practices and an own-group reference orientation.[20] This resiliency is frequently ignored—thus maintaining its invisibility in developmental science, published scholarship, and policy decisions.

The many everyday and copious cases of Black resiliency are made invisible; psychopathology and misadventure are researched as "the norm" in research questions and methodologies that are employed.[21] Acknowledging Black resiliency and the efficacy of successful coping in the design of authentic supports makes sense. The lack of resiliency recognition for Blacks and the imposition of continued invisibility of their humanity hinder the design and utilization of supportive strate-gies, thus further hindering responses to structured inequality and persistent inequities, and reinforcing the problematic status of "per-sistent inequality denial."[22] Consistent with any malady in need of treatment, a diagnosis is needed for determining a solution to long-term fBIP.

Racial socialization traditions and cultural reframing, including creative and impactful use of the arts, provide critical resources fre-quently used by Black individuals, families, and immigrant commu-nities, thus serving as resiliency-promoting resources. Frequently overlooked, they function as still present but are missed past opportu-nities for diminishing stereotypes and fomenting positive and authentic change.[23] For Black and Brown individuals, a status of thriving, healthy intra- and interpsychic developmental processes as well as resilient out-comes are infrequently assumed or researched; the fact limits the design of culturally consonant, contextually linked, and developmen-tally effective life course supports.

Black resiliency remains as unacknowledged today as it was in the *Brown* decision.[24] That shortsightedness encourages fBIP. Memory suppression of harm imposed on others (e.g., racism presence denial) is therefore overlooked as identity-relevant suppression traditions remain under-interrogated and rendered invisible. Negative stereotype proliferation across ecologies of development, and an absence of intergenerational exemplars of collective thriving and Black resiliency, reinforces stereotyping.[25] Historical factors impactful for both Blacks *and* Whites require careful investigation and society-wide dissemination.

New Directions for White Resiliency Efforts

Despite patterns of historical suppression of Black humanity, there are examples of White resistance to hegemony.[26] Magnifying that fact also suggests strategies for abating fBIP. Studies of White resiliency would benefit from understanding White traditions of racial socialization, successful and positive coping for managing guilt, and the developmental processes for Whites who successfully resist structured inequality presence denial. Interrogation and replication of individual and collective coping strategies of the character described have implications for authentic social change.[27] An emphasis on successful socialization efforts is needed for resisting and recovering from racial hierarchy beliefs and identities as contributors to fBIP.

This perspective of needed White resilience from fBIP largely remains absent from human development and social science texts.[28] It was certainly not present in the consideration of *Brown*. The assumption was that Black children's interaction with Whites was a requirement for offsetting assumed Black self-disparagement. The ego maladies challenging Whites, including fBIP, were not a consideration and, thus, remained generally unacknowledged as a psychological health hazard for Whites with consequences for Blacks as well. Ecological psychology was just gaining traction in the social sciences regarding the importance of children's contexts. However, *Brown* and its implementation suggest a level of obliviousness: the "change strategy" was limited to the assumed necessity to improve Black children's "sense of self" through sharing learning contexts with Whites.

Urie Bronfenbrenner's ecological systems theory inclusion and conceptualization of the chronosystem afforded a critical potential asset. It laid a foundation for acknowledging historical contributions and interpreting processes and individual outcomes. Too few social science efforts have taken advantage of and benefited from Bronfenbrenner's chronosystem conceptual contributions.[29]

Continuing into the twenty-first century from twentieth century research efforts, the conceptual shortcomings noted here continue and are consequential.[30] Abetted by social science scholarship in economics, sociology, and particularly, psychology—in addition to health fields—structured systems and ecologies determinative of polices, practices, and "aspirational supports" are persistent. Lacking humanity insights about Black lives, the impact of "scientific efforts" functions quite distinctly from the articulated need and intent. As experienced by Black children, it was deeply flawed and—seventy years later, post-*Brown*—continues to be highly negative for the three domains of Black children's development (socio-emotional, cognitive and neuro-physical, and biological levels). In essence, the implementation of *Brown* as a *"humanity-thin"* conceptualization of Black children remains deeply deficient. It ignores the humanity of Black children and their cross-domain developmental needs, which are particularly significant in learning contexts requiring intellectual risk-taking.

Opposite from a human development-embracing perspective, the implementation of *Brown* ignored children's humanity and, thus, socio-emotional and cognition-relevant developmental needs. Specifically, its character and operationalization (1) provided contexts without culturally consonant role models (i.e., Black schools were closed and Black teachers let go); (2) required forcibly shared hostility-imbued spaces, (3) assigned and organized school leadership and faculty presence, preventing opportunities and conditions for bidirectional identifications, and (4) precipitated psychologically heinous conditions for children and adults. Teachers are hesitant to embrace the learning and development of "others" with whom they lack identification and cultural knowledge, and instead continue to present and imbue curriculum with uninterrogated fears, particularly with respect to Black boys. At the same time, Black children's cross-domain coping strategies may compromise intellectual risk-taking and achievement goals. In sum, operationalizing racism presence denial, the "remedy as constructed policy," itself, suggested fBIP and clearly indicated significant shortsightedness because it ignored the mandate of common humanity and, instead, reconstructed hierarchy.

We argue that lacking an appreciation of humanity and context-linked life course development relational experiences and needs, developmental task successes are compromised. The daily context-specific assets and coping processes required of Blacks (but generally absent as protective factors and supports) too frequently have significant and intergenerational consequences when basic humanity needs are ignored. The a priori assumptions and frequent deficit science orientations regarding people of color represent inherent difficulties to authentic progress. They prevent the design, support, and implementation of policies actually experienced by youth as authentic. They are necessary for achieving thriving processes and resiliency outcomes as linked to developmental status, context character, and cultural traditions that are maximally beneficial for healthy coping.[31] Too frequently, practices serve to compare Black-White outcomes but miss the preliminary, context-dependent and culturally relevant opportunity to understand and make use of insights concerning the "how" of human development processes of thriving, as opposed to the traditional focus on racial outcome differences or the "what." Inequality of conditions including both separate and unequal educational opportunities for children of color, restricted work opportunities, and housing inequities undermines thriving. All represent contextual factors contributing to outcomes emphasized in Black-White comparison studies and produce—not surprisingly—disparate findings favoring the unacknowledged privileged. The programmatic and research demonstration patterns, then, serve to further stigmatize rather than to recognize the absence of a humanity perspective inclusive of Black and Brown children. Accordingly, the match (or not) between Black children's characteristics and context matters.

Significantly, those linkages become progressively complex when demographics suggest multiple sources of stigma based on intersectionality analysis.

Scaffolding and Exacerbating Intersectionality Factors

Throughout, we have made clear that phenomenology is a field of philosophy that enjoys a long and nuanced history and use. The incorporation of phenomenology through the PVEST framing makes clear the foundational importance of human development theorizing for interrogating human behavioral processes and interpreting outcomes. The inclusive and novel PVEST theoretical representation of human development processes (i.e., inclusive of marginalized individuals) provides interrogation prowess. It provides nuanced ways of incorporating perception, meaning-making, non-pathologizing normal human processes, context variation and coping explanations, and identity formation-processing opportunities.[32]

The salience and value of PVEST framing has to do with its focus on *the individual's subjective experience*. Because there are conscious processes involved, which are associated with an individual's meaning-making or first-person experience, the perspective is particularly sensitive to biology-based maturation processes, which unavoidably link with affective and cognitive processes. Relatedly, those processes vary as a function of bidirectional and recursive links with context character. Together, it is the combination of attributes that has made PVEST foundational to interpreting life course processes inclusive of diverse humans.

The experience of intersectionality further explicates the need to accommodate the combination and variation of risks and privileges requiring accommodation in the conduct of social science for an authentic representation of everyday experiences and diverse lives unfolding in highly varied contexts. Described in detail in chapter 8, intersectionality was originally defined as the experience of subordination along multiple and simultaneous categorical axes. It occurs in such a way that is "greater than the sum of [for example] racism and sexism [alone]."[33] Its focus provides a significant contribution to Spencer's PVEST framing given the virtually infinite possibilities provided by intersectionality analysis for representing the broad variations of human vulnerability. This includes the under-exploration and acknowledgement of the many forms of privilege. Since its delineation by Crenshaw, intersectionality has opened researchers' eyes to before-unseen experiences of people at the intersections of multiple systems of oppression.[34]

The aligning of intersectionality strengths with the theoretical power of PVEST provides important insights. It affords opportunities for the design of programming and policies that consider an inclusive approach as remedies to contemporary Black bodies' risks, challenges, and coping given four hundred years of dehumanization. We argue Radical *Brown* requires attention to race—as well as intersecting attributes—and this focus opens the door to conceptual innovation when considered from a human vulnerability, context-sensitive, and resiliency promotion strategy. The potential for recognizing developmentally appropriate, culturally consonant, and context-acknowledging supports and protective factors is possible when intersectionality and inclusive human development framing are aligned. The strategy is effective for maximizing the life course human development of Black and Brown bodies.

The Facilitating Role of Social Science for Black Inhumanity Assumptions

We argue that the contributions of "science" to the dehumanization of Black bodies represents a long tradition in the social sciences that requires consistent contesting.[35] As one of the first American social scientists and the premier scholar of race in the twentieth century, W. E. B. Du Bois's scholarly contributions laid the foundation for the serious examination of race within American society. A significant portion of his work focused on the role of *racial embodiment* in the development of personal identity; he delineated the role of race for self-processes. Du Bois's insights evolved, shifted, and adapted as he bore witness to significant social change, political events, and his own search for understanding through continued intellectual engagement.[36]

Du Bois' insights on racial embodiment remain relevant in examining the unique dimensions of identity development for Black youth, and diverse youths more broadly, in the twenty-first century. In *The Souls of Black Folk*, Du Bois centers a racialized Black self by introducing the concept of *double consciousness*, which urged readers to consider how "the color line" affects the individual's sense of self, the very core of one's personal identity.[37] Du Bois articulates the heaviness of the psychological burden to be seen as, but perhaps even more importantly, to "feel" like, a problem. Not only is it the unique burden of the racialized Black self to wear "the veil," but it prevents the wearer from being fully seen, thus, never having one's humanity affirmed by those who exist beyond it. As Itzigsohn and Brown succinctly note, "the theory of Double Consciousness is a phenomenological description of self-formation under conditions of racialization."[38] For Du Bois, the primary project of *Souls* is to foster understanding of how the individual Black person makes sense of an all-encompassing racialized world that affects all aspects of one's life.[39] Racialization is fundamentally the dilemma of race-linked adverse experiences shared by all Black people. As suggested by Itzigsohn and Brown, double consciousness provides a vehicle for considering how "the color line" affects the sense of self.

Du Bois's *Souls* affords a second major benefit, which demonstrates that context matters. The ecological salience is not only for those racialized by the social embodiment of the color line. It operates as well for those having created, continually gained from, and sustained the system of racial embodiment. In other words, Du Bois, within the PVEST framework, explains White identity as well. As a systems theory and given its conceptual capacity, PVEST not only illustrates the "what," or impact, of racial embodiment functioning as a context for all humans but also demonstrates the "how" as a mechanism for the sustenance and continuation of the system described in *Souls*. Framed here, it prevailed as fBIP. As an enveloping context for shared "everyday experience," racial embodiment functions as the ecology of development and experience for all, but with variously scaffolded levels of human vulnerability. Du Bois centered a racialized Black self by introducing the concept of double consciousness. However, for those (1) incentivized by hundreds of years of economic gain (i.e., low human vulnerability given disproportional access to protective factors, assets, and supports), (2) motivated by identity-based power-maintaining traditions (i.e., protected and structured reactive coping strategies [e.g., potential loss or inferred fear]), and (3) emboldened by the embodiment of internalized personal identity beliefs of Whiteness-linked superiority (i.e., stable identity processes), Du Bois's *Souls* provides another major contribution and primary outcome. The PVEST system analysis affords a human development-relevant explanation for "racism/inequality presence denial." It represents one form of reactive coping utilized for maintaining racialized traditions.[40] Avoiding an acknowledgement of the reactive coping practice hinders critical examination of racial embodiment for those determining the color line.

For Du Bois, the primary project of *Souls* is to further understand how the individual Black person makes sense of an all-encompassing racialized world that affects all aspects of one's life. From a PVEST perspective, the role of racial embodiment in the development of personal identity provided by *Souls* is another primary outcome. As an additional benefit, its incorporation affords an under-interrogated additional color line emphasis. Specifically, in making use of Spencer's PVEST theory, Du Bois's *The Souls of Black Folk* specifies the salience of social context for a life course analysis of the color line impact.[41] This helps to unpack and scaffold personal identity processes and vulnerability status not only to unpack Black identity and consciousness, but also White identity and consciousness of Whites historically and intergenerationally reinforced to produce racism/inequality presence denial.

Conclusion

We conclude by reinforcing seminal observations in preparation for the subsequent chapters in part II. The persistence and life course depth of fBIP and the lack of an appreciation of Black children's humanity led to the misuse and misreading of *Brown*. Thus, its status as a decision is merely aspirational, rather than serving as a blueprint for change that acknowledges the significant impact of ecological considerations and the role of history. Colorism and an imposed inhumanity status imposed on Blacks and superiority status inferred for Whites allows for everyday de jure and de facto traditions to endure. The lived and under-interrogated beliefs aid a particular identity process. They provide a comfortable and uncritical thriving situation for Whites (i.e., shielding them from shame, blame, and opportunities for authentic change). At the same time, for Blacks, practices suggest their inhumanity as well as persistent unaddressed conditions of chattel slavery given the many examples of structured inequalities and inequities. The questions commonly posed by social science assist and perpetuate inhumanity assumptions.[42] Questions about slavery and imbued superiority identity processes (assumed) for Whites are ignored. Additionally, the maladaptive coping suggested by racism presence denial and long-term fBIP, as well as "scholarship" dissemination strategies of the social sciences, continue to demonstrate the great human vulnerability of Blacks accompanied by explanations for and the framing of differences that further fuel beliefs of Black inferiority. Underemphasized is the humanity of Black people, their use of creative coping strategies for thriving and resilience (e.g., long-term creative use of the arts for socio-emotional well-being), and the necessary protection of their humanity. For most, effective management of conditions of persistent dehumanization has resulted in innovative and creative reactive and stable coping processes.

The following chapters further explore the dehumanization, historical context, and developmental implications of Radical *Brown*. Chapter 6 addresses the doll studies cited in *Brown* with a perspective that interrogates alternative interpretations. Had the nation practiced different inferred identities for Whites (i.e., their "assumed superiority") and resisted the imposed inhumanity status for Blacks, the decision might have been conceptualized and implemented differently. Chapter 7 interrogates identity processes given the long-term historical context of inequality beliefs. Chapter 8 focuses on intersectionality and intersubjectivity. Intersectionality provides a critical race perspective of the complex interaction of identity factors. Intersubjectivity reminds us of the fluid dynamic of identity. These chapters elaborate and support movement from *Brown*'s limitations as implemented thus far toward executing real, comprehensive equality based on its true meaning as a radical mandate for authentic change based on the core command of equality as shared humanity.

CHAPTER 6

Colorism

Interpreting and Reframing the Doll Studies

IN THIS CHAPTER WE INTERROGATE the use and interpreta-
tion of the Clarks' doll studies cited in the *Brown* decision and particularly the decision's claims of identity injury. We analyze post-*Brown*
developmental science on identity and children's development from an
ecological, developmental, and phenomenology-acknowledging framework. Our conceptual strategy explains why the Court's failure to incorporate developmental sensitivity in its remedy failed to support those
for whom it was intended as well as those youngsters privileged (White)
by race and the missed theoretical shortcoming.

We begin with a critical passage in *Brown*. It is the Court's core reasoning, where the Court adopts language from the Kansas federal district court that had decided in favor of Linda Brown and her parents.
The Court follows that language with a clear statement that rejects the
justification for segregation, relying on social science as its authority:

"Segregation of white and colored children in public schools has a
detrimental effect upon the colored children. The impact is greater
when it has the sanction of the law; for the policy of separating the
races is usually interpreted as denoting the inferiority of the Negro
group. A sense of inferiority affects the motivation of a child to
learn. Segregation with the sanction of law, therefore, has a tendency
to (retard) the educational and mental development of Negro
children and to deprive them of some of the benefits they would

receive in a racial(ly) integrated school system." Whatever may have been the extent of psychological knowledge at the time of Plessy v. Ferguson, this finding is amply supported by modern authority. [footnote 11][1]

Footnote 11, reproduced here, provides authority for the Court's statement of modern "psychological knowledge" (as of 1954) of the impact of segregation:

11. K.B. Clark, Effect of Prejudice and Discrimination on Personality Development (Midcentury White House Conference on Children and Youth, 1950; Witmer and Kotinsky, Personality in the Making (1952), c. VI; Deutscher and Chein, The Psychological Effects of Enforced Segregation: A Survey of Social Science Opinion, 26 J.Psychol 259 (1948); Chein, What Are the Psychological Effects of Segregation Under Conditions of Equal Facilities?, 3 Int. J. Opinion and Attitude Res. 229 (1949); Brameld, Educational Costs, in Discrimination and National Welfare (MacIver, ed., 1949), 44–48; Frazier, The Negro in the United States (1949), 674–681. And see generally Myrdal, An American Dilemma (1944).[2]

While Footnote 11 contains a multitude of citations, it is the very first reference, to the Clarks' doll studies, which has drawn the most attention, and their work has stood as the representative for social science/developmental science as authority for the Court's judgement.

We critique the Clarks' doll studies considered in *Brown* and particularly the claims of identity injury. It is significant that the social science research relied upon triggered faulty interpretations of the research data provided on Black children. Specifically, youngsters' *humanity expressed as child status individuals was not considered.* We analyze post-*Brown* developmental science on identity and children's development from an ecological, developmental, and phenomenological framework. Our conceptual strategy reveals why the Court's failure to incorporate developmental sensitivity in its remedy failed to assist and support those for whom it was intended. Specifically, the Court's remedy failed both privileged youngsters and those subjected to a subordinate status. Radical *Brown* requires an understanding and critique of this failure as well as the necessary developmental framework to achieve *Brown*'s common humanity mandate. Young children's development involves constantly taking in information, including structured and organized *mis*communications about others (e.g., minorities and immigrants). We argue that these processes occur across contexts that vary in risk and challenge and require coping, which may appear problematic if perceived from an adult's perspective. The Court failed to understand that children repeat when asked what they hear and "know." For young children's developmentally appropriate less mature and less developed inference-making ability, appropriate interpretations are necessarily more complex for both children in subordinate social positions and others in race-defined privileged circumstances. Radical *Brown* considers that the Court, and subsequent interpreters of the opinion, made adult interpretations and inferences about injury and remedy from data reflecting children's cognitive functioning without an understanding of its developmental context and, thus, nuance. The limited implementation strategy post-*Brown* failed to consider the varied meanings inferred as a function of the child's developmental status and racial group membership and the implications for coping during later periods of development.

Colorism: The Doll Studies

A frequent assumption is that the Court based its core judgment in part on research findings that suggested that segregation produced feelings of inadequacy in Black children that were inimical to their education and development. As Chief Justice Warren stated in the opinion, "To separate [schoolchildren] from others of similar age and qualifications solely because of their race generates a feeling of inferiority as to their status in the community that may affect their hearts and minds in a way unlikely ever to be undone." This statement was followed by footnote 11. The Court went on to conclude, "Any language in *Plessy v. Ferguson* contrary to this finding is rejected." In *Plessy*, decided in 1896, the Court had upheld segregation under the infamous doctrine of "separate but equal," claiming that segregation had no negative meaning and did not signify or communicate racial hierarchy. It was not so intended by Whites; therefore, any inference to the contrary had to be trumped up by Blacks: "We consider the underlying fallacy of the plaintiff's argument to consist in the assumption that the enforced separation of the two races stamps the colored race with a badge of inferiority. If this be so, it is not by reason of anything found in the act, but solely because the colored race chooses to put that construction upon it."[3] The Court in *Brown* rejects this view, and rather than doing so in equally conclusory language without authority other than the justices' (White) view of the world, the Court in *Brown* cites the research contained in footnote 11, most importantly, the Clarks' research.

Footnote 11 has had outsized significance in the enormous outpouring of analysis of the *Brown* decision. Heise notes two principal critiques of footnote 11: (1) a technical critique of the quality of the research cited and (2) a theoretical critique questioning the extent to which footnote 11 shaped the decision in *Brown*.[4] Some scholars praised the Court's use of scientific findings as a basis for considering constitutional matters.[5] Others expressed skepticism about the value of the social and behavioral sciences given their nascent development at the time, suggesting that it could just as easily be used in support of segregation should academic fancies shift.[6] Benjamin and Crouse explore the presentation of evidence by Kenneth Clark, suggesting that racial segregation contributed to mental and emotional stress.[7] They criticize the American Psychological Association for its lack of a response to the decision as well as the decision's ultimate limitations in bringing about racial equality. Others suggest that based on the logic of *Brown*, had scientific evidence not pointed toward emotional distress, then segregation might still have been justified.

Others have suggested that the social science evidence played no part at all in reaching a final decision but, rather, was used as a rhetorical device to persuade others, given the justices' fears regarding the potential implications of their decision. Edwards argues that, in fact, the Court did not rely on the social science scholarship cited in footnote 11 to inform their ruling on the unconstitutionality of public-school segregation.[8] He suggests that the discussion over whether or not the

Court should have relied upon social science findings obscures the question of whether they actually did rely upon it. The opinion contains very little in the way of discussion or analysis of the findings and merely cites them as authority. Edwards additionally notes that there was little evidence to suggest that either Warren, his clerks, or fellow justices spoke in any detail about the scientific literature. He argues that this scholarship was cited in anticipation of the fallout from the Court's decision in an effort to maintain legitimacy. By grounding itself in the objective authority of social science (then on the ascendancy), the Court could insulate itself from the expected furor over the implications of its decision. Edwards does not go as far as others in applying intentional designs to this but, rather, suggests that it was a background effort to maintain authority in the face of expected reaction.[9]

The classic Clark Doll Studies began in 1939. The American psychologists Kenneth and Mamie Phipps Clark conducted a series of studies that purported to show that Black children in Northern and Southern cities as early as three years old could distinguish between different color dolls (White, Black, Brown) and identify which dolls represented their own racial group and that Black and White children demonstrated a consistent preference for White dolls over Black ones. A review and summary of some of these studies and others that followed were cited in the infamous footnote 11 in *Brown*.[10]

Controversially, one of the conclusions drawn out of this research was the assumption that the Clarks' findings indicated a sense of inferiority or low self-esteem among Black children. Critics of the doll studies point out the theoretical limitation of the Clarks' work: notably, there were experimental and methodological issues involved, but also the absence of a developmental perspective in the interpretation of findings of very young children. Subsequent reevaluations of this work found greater variation within groups, with older Black children demonstrating a preference for the Black dolls. This is significant given that subsequent research has further illustrated the distinction between self-esteem, identity, and racial attitudes/preferences. Lacking this developmental perspective, the work of the Clarks and other researchers, as well as the views espoused in the Warren Court's opinion in *Brown*,

erroneously attributed feelings of inferiority and low self-esteem to
Black children as the explanation for their preference for White dolls.
Rejecting this position, other researchers have shown that Black children
can maintain high self-esteem while also changing their preferences for
skin tone/race over time.[11]

Other post-*Brown* research has continued to show that children
demonstrate an awareness of racial difference and skin-tone preference
and that both Black and White children consistently attribute more
positive qualities to White dolls over Black dolls. More recent treatments
have expanded, revised, and altered aspects of the original doll studies,
with some exploring how such preferences might be altered through
incentives, as well as utilizing greater technological sophistication. Jordan and Hernandez-Reif utilized computer-generated images in place of
dolls and added several different shades of skin color (rather than
black/white) in their study of 40 Black and White children (age three
to five) living in Alabama. The researchers believed children were more
familiar with computer-generated images and that this would better
serve the research rather than using dolls, while also allowing for a
greater range of options. Additionally, they examined whether hearing a
story about a dark-skinned character saving a baby duck changed the
children's original answers. This particular study was also careful to
account for demand and experimenter bias, which they believed may
have plagued previous work in this area, such as informing children
there were no right or wrong answers while also allowing for "both/
neither" answers and utilizing a monotone voice in the presentation
of the choices. The results indicated that with the inclusion of a
greater variety of skin shades, children showed no preference; however, the children continued to prefer White to Black in the traditional
model. The story depicting a Black character positively was shown to
have a greater effect upon Black children than White children, with
the former being less likely to identify a Black character as one who
looks bad.[12]

Critical to acknowledge is that the nation's historical imbuing of
humanity and power with Whiteness is deeply engrained. Its unconscious power is enhanced given the acceptability of ignoring the fact

both socially as everyday practice and by knowledge producers. Spawned by the presence of skin color differences, the penchant for the acceptability of "racism presence denial" in the practices of systems including research (i.e., except when pathologizing Blacks and Black life), its persistence is omnipresent as functional Black Inhumanity Perception (fBIP). More recently, researchers of skin tone have suggested the need to better incorporate research design options for Asian, Hispanic, and multiracial children, as well as looking at international examples for comparison. Researchers exploring bias among Hispanic children also found a bias toward lighter skin. Kaufman and Wiese observed a sample of fifty-two Hispanic children age five to seven (twenty-eight female, twenty-four male), and their work confirmed many of the observations found in the Clarks' study, particularly with regard to the children's self-reported preference for skin colors lighter than their own. Their research was designed to be more sensitive to factors mediating the influence of skin color by integrating the relationship between the children's skin color preferences and their own skin color into the process. With this in mind, the majority of the children selected lighter skin types as their idealized skin tone. In contrast to this work, Stokes-Guinan conducted a revised doll test of 116 Hispanic children (age three to ten). The Hispanic children did not demonstrate pro-Hispanic and anti-other preferences but continued to show preference for White dolls over Black and Asian ones.[13]

Studies have also shown that Black children are more likely to remember narratives which depict darker-skinned African Americans in a negative or stereotypical light. Averhart and Bigler studied 56 African American children in kindergarten and first grade and assessed their ability to recall different narrative representations of people with various shades of skin. Generally, the children were more likely to identify stereotyped portrayals over counter-stereotyped ones. This included children more often remembering the stories that depicted darker-skinned characters in a negative (stereotypical) light, with younger children identifying lighter-skinned characters as potential teachers, neighbors, and friends more often than older ones. Overall, these studies have tended to reinforce the original results of the Clarks' study, with

incentives and technological changes having limited impact on changing child and adolescent attitudes toward skin color.[14]

Colorism is a social ideology bound up with the institutions of public life, such as school and the workplace. While the family would seem
to serve as a place of refuge from which its members might contest dominant racial narratives, some research has shown that Black families
often reinforce colorism by privileging their lighter-skinned members.
Russell et al. suggest that a Black family's preoccupation with skin color
begins at the time of the child's birth and note the frequency with which
Black families adopt children with lighter skin. McDonald explores a
case study where a woman born with darker skin than her mother and
siblings was abused and neglected as a result of her mother believing
that she had "lowered" the family's status. Wilder and Cain interviewed
twenty-six Black women (ages eighteen to forty) in five focus groups and
showed that among Black women, maternal figures often play a central
role in shaping Black children's attitudes about skin tone. Many of these
women claim that they learned at a young age to associate darker skin
with ugliness and lighter skin with beauty.[15]

One area of research that remains particularly voluminous is the
impact of colorism on the social mobility of African Americans. Many
investigators examine the relationship between skin color and educational attainment and economic success in both contemporary and
historical contexts. Numerous studies have found that even when
accounting for parental variables, lighter-skinned Blacks are more likely
to obtain higher levels of education and pursue more prestigious and
lucrative professions than those who have darker skin. Black males and
females with lighter skin tones are generally more likely to find employment, and lighter-skinned males were more likely to attend post-
secondary educational institutions than darker-skinned peers.[16]

Another area linked to academic and life outcomes is punitive
measures such as school discipline and interactions with the criminal
justice system. Researchers have found that despite controlling for socioeconomic status (SES), delinquent behavior, and academic performance,
the odds of suspension were about three times greater for darker-
skinned Black females than for those with lighter skin. Compared to

their White female peers, African American female adolescents with darker complexions were almost twice as likely to be suspended from their schools. This has been observed in encounters with the police, suggesting that darker-skinned Blacks and Latinos are stopped and arrested more often than their lighter-skinned peers. This can be further observed within the criminal justice system, where among first-time offenders, on average, Whites receive similar sentences to light-skinned Blacks but lower sentences than darker-skinned Blacks.[17] The pattern of findings suggests that Whiteness privileging conditions persist, as does the prevalence of racism presence denial. The functional Black inhumanity perspective (fBIP) functions to scaffold and maintain particular traditions as sources of challenge in need of responsive coping and remedying. The failure to deny its existence leaves strategies for change "thin" if the need is acknowledged at or goes beyond traditional diversity, ethnicity, and inclusion efforts.

The implications for colorism are particularly concerning in the areas of health care and health-related effects. The global prevalence and deleterious effects of skin bleaching/lightening have been documented by researchers for several years. In the realm of mental health, although some find that Black Americans have better mental health outcomes than Whites, others suggest that darker-skinned Blacks have worse rates of depression and that the disparities in the rates of depression between light- and dark-skinned African Americans might exceed the disparities between Blacks and Whites overall.[18]

Some researchers have focused on more subjective evaluations such as personal attractiveness. Drawing from the National Survey of Black Americans (NSBA), Hill found that skin color has a greater impact upon the perceived attractiveness of women than men, with lighter skin being seen as a more attractive quality. Wade and Bielitz examined perceptions across gender and race and found that African American women with lighter skin were rated higher than lighter-skinned African American men on intelligence and parenting. Women generally rated dark-skinned individuals higher than men did on intelligence. Self-esteem and self-efficacy have been important topics within the literature of colorism, with some exploring the differences affecting male and females.

Thompson and Keith demonstrate that skin color remains an important indicator for self-esteem in women but not men and for self-efficacy
in men but not women. They also maintain that for women, the power
of colorism is strongly associated with the individual's social class,
with working class darker-skinned women having lower self-esteem
than dark-skinned women in higher social classes. Elmore explores
the relationship between self-perceptions of skin tone and the processes of identity formation in adolescents. Other scholars have
shown that young women who embrace an African American standard of beauty (reflecting a higher level of self-esteem) exhibit lower
levels of substance use than those who embrace White standards of
beauty. This preoccupation has also been reported among White
women in what some have labeled a "reverse colorism" with these
women seeking to enhance the exoticness of their appearance via tan-
ning, injections, and implants.[19]

Colorism is not unique to the United States, and there have been a
number of efforts to explore the implications of colorism around the
world. Ferguson and Cramer show that rural Jamaican children who
self-identify and idealize skin type as white exhibited higher levels
of self-esteem.[20] Some scholars have taken up the idea of "economies of
color" in examining the pigmentocracy underlying racial liberalism
globally. Charles studied how Jamaicans have historically practiced skin
bleaching in order to enhance sexual attractiveness. In a survey of
self-reported health and racial categories in selected Canadian cities,
Veenstra found that darker-skinned Blacks were more likely than lighter-
skinned ones to report poorer health outcomes.[21]

The doll studies and colorism research attest to the persisting presence of colorism but a far more complex picture of its developmental
consequences than that of the nine US Supreme Court justices, all
White men, who viewed the research from their own context, consciousness, and subordinating perspective. Patriarchal Whiteness wrapped a
powerful humanity insight in patronizing language of deficit and inferiority. Our rereading of *Brown* recaptures the core message of shared
humanity in the Clarks' research along with its revelations of colorism
for both White and Black children. It is essential to pay attention to

the task of stripping away the inhumanity of colorism by acknowledging and exposing it, as well as identifying the challenges to creating identity grounded in shared humanity rather than racial hierarchy. It is an essential task of our developmental perspective and insight to describe and unravel this dynamic.

We situate the doll studies first by reference to W. E. B. Du Bois and Frantz Fanon and their articulation of color consciousness. Next, we challenge the perspective from which the studies were characterized in *Brown* through the lens of decolonization. Finally, we connect them to the chronosystem of racial hierarchy, in terms of developmental stress and the coping mechanism of collective memory.

DuBois and Fanon: Color and Consciousness

The Court's opinion minimizes an articulation of Black humanity. This may suggest an inherent view that Whites represent the status quo of how humanity is envisioned as the "default" permeating perspective. Any colloquial definition of humanity assumes a common relatedness to all—characteristics that belong to humans rather than animals. Features unique to human beings include kindness, mercy, and sympathy. Thus—at baseline—an example of humanity is treating someone with kindness.

Critical to acknowledge is that race is defining. The experiences of Blacks have been devoid of assumptions of humanity. Our rereading of *Brown* is based upon that core assumption. The implications for everyone's core vulnerability statuses—both Blacks' and Whites'—is profound. The stable positionality for Black Americans vis-à-vis White's evaluative dehumanizing stance regarding non-Whites is scaffolded by, at minimum, four hundred years of coping with difference and relational traditions. On par with the centuries of oppression and destruction of the nation's Native Americans, there are few more horrific periods than America's slave history and its systematic dehumanization of a people totally without an effort at recrimination for the act, reconciliation as a response, or reparations for the intergenerational damage committed. Slavery remains in the nation's memory but lacks any apparent remorse. The unapologetic "ghost of slavery" continues to weigh more like a nightmare from which the country remains ensnared with continuing consequences for the present. Its violence, dehumanization, and unrepentant character make it decidedly different from other places also yoked to Black enslavement.

As noted earlier, W. E. B. Du Bois's analysis frames this as the problem of racial embodiment and the development of double consciousness to describe how "the color line" affects an individuals' sense of self as the core of personal identity.[22] Double consciousness is a phenomenological description of self-formation under conditions of racialization. Color-based skin color beliefs foment positionality supporting subordination for Blacks and humanity status and superiority for those "living outside the veil."[23]

Little has changed in foundational ways regarding the untoward impact of America's racial pecking order for people of color, generally, and Black Americans, specifically. Historically overlapping with the Clarks' efforts—and like W. E. B. Du Bois's influence—Frantz Omar Fanon's insights, as well, have inspired generations. Informing postcolonial studies as well as critical race theory, Fanon's context-sensitive focus is informed by a particular psychiatric perspective. Fanon emphasizes the psychopathology of colonization and its untoward influences on human, social, and cultural outcomes. Fanon's best-known work, *Black Skin, White Masks,* is consistent with Du Bois's concept about the "wearing of the veil." Fanon underscores the role of color, describing the problem of the oppressed Black person's challenges navigating the world as a "white-ness" performance.[24]

Du Bois's scholarship on racial embodiment and the implications of the wearing of the veil and Fanon's insights on colonialization together make clear racialization pathology as a decisive, deep, and problematic tradition. The Clarks' rendering of the doll studies with its emphasis on "physical identifiability" judgements provides prescience to any discussion of "color." These combined insights explore the question of skin color and the psychology of the individual differently from the colonialist version of the "White standard" of humanity status. Critical is that Du Bois' emphasis examines the phenomenology of the individual, or "how it feels to be a problem," while Fanon focuses on the consequences of the colonial context and the psychological implications for person-hood. The Clarks' approach to research explores the meanings of Black–White difference categorizations for revealing children's assumptions about the self and their awareness of the humanity (and inhumanity) messages of their context. Color consciousness in the Clarks' research reflects not only awareness of the deep cultural and systemic effort to impose racial hierarchy but also the presence of resilience and self-esteem that resist that hierarchy in children of color.

Decoloniality: A Perspective to Evaluate the Doll Studies

Unpacking the Clarks' work to reveal its reflection of racial hierarchy and its embeddedness and harm to all children, not the developmental inferiority of Black children, is aided by using the perspective of *decoloniality*. This provides *chronosystem context* as an explanation for the continuing salience of skin color. Critically, it is a necessary acknowledgement given the long-term and cumulative problem we identify as the lack of a humanity perspective when it comes to Black and Brown bodies. The perspective supports the problem of racism presence denial and thus the power and persistency of fBIP. We aim to decolonize the Clarks' research as well as to underscore that it is foundational to substantiate our rereading of *Brown* by using contemporary social science as a guide for implementation. The studies command ongoing critical knowledge, dissembling and destruction of racial hierarchy, and the implementation of shared humanity.

Coloniality is defined as ways of being, ideologies, and patterns of power that originate during colonial periods and remain following formal decolonization. "Decoloniality" refers to the political and epistemological movement that seeks to confront, delink, and dismantle the relations of the colonial matrix of power. Maldonado-Torres describes decoloniality as "the dismantling of relations of power and conceptions of knowledge that foment the reproduction of racial, gender, and geopolitical hierarchies that came into being or found new and more powerful forms of expression in the modern/colonial world."[25] The application of this perspective to the study of psychology is relatively recent. Some suggest that the field of mainstream psychology as practiced in

"WEIRD" (Western, educated, industrialized, rich, and [supposedly] democratic) countries is complicit in coloniality. Some claim that a decolonial approach to psychology would turn away from treating the individual as the central unit of analysis and instead incorporate social, economic and political contexts. The recent critique of WEIRD psychology posits the discipline's inability to see the diversity of human-kind. Drawing from Frantz Fanon's call to decolonize knowledge production, they position a decolonial approach to psychology as one that might empower and emancipate those outside of the Euro-American-centric global order. Mainstream practices, the decolonial-ists argue, detach people from their contexts and assume levels of shared human experience that do not necessarily apply to those in the major-ity global south. These "epistemologies of ignorance" or methodolo-gies of unknowing insulate psychologists in WEIRD countries from understanding the experiences of those who do not fit their assumed standards.[26]

One area of inquiry in the decolonial approaches to psychology is the principle of "accompaniment." This approach shares similarities with culturally sensitive approaches to evaluation where the research-ers maintain a position of humility with regard to the communities they are working with instead of assuming the role of an expert with solu-tions to their population's "problems." Emphasis is placed on centering the narratives of the marginalized communities rather than engaging with traditional topics that dominate mainstream psychology and which problematize those considered other.[27]

The decolonial approach to psychology emphasizes the "denatural-izing" of hegemonic practices and ideologies viewed as central to the mainstream practice of psychology. Direct engagement with marginal-ized communities and an engagement with everyday life are prominent approaches aiming to decolonize and struggle against epistemic vio-lence or the penchant to silence marginalized groups.[28]

We embrace the need for decolonialized approaches in the social sci-ences. Consistent with our humanity-requiring perspective, human development processes unfold in multiply layered contexts of develop-ment. This includes awareness of and reactions to skin color differences.

However, ways of thinking about "skin color" differences have been conceptually limited given (1) a lack of awareness of the multiply layered contexts of learning and development, (2) their character, and (3) normative human processes. The multiply layered context of development made popular by Bronfenbrenner includes, most significantly, the chronosystem, or a historical perspective. This is in addition to the amorphous but all-enveloping *macro-system* (beliefs, attitudes, assumptions, and preferences), the *exo-level* (where policy-relevant decisions are made), the *meso-level* (bringing together systems of "intended supports," such as church and school), and most proximal for individuals, the *micro-level* (direct contact, hands-on impact for individuals). It is essential to include and acknowledge the significant value of the decoloniality viewpoint in all of these ecologies and therefore to pay close attention to collective cultural traditions.[29] Ontological components of our epistemics concerning skin color include cultural context considerations and human development process acknowledgement (i.e., neuro-physical-biological, affective, and cognition processes), as well as historical context in the multiple levels of humans' navigated ecologies of development and learning.[30] The colonialist perspective implicit in WEIRD psychology assumes power-scaffolded "Whiteness" as the standard for human experience. Part of the dehumanizing orientation encountered by Brown and Black bodies, as a WEIRD conceptual orientation, is that the character of one's relatedness to one's own skin color is treated not as a "problem," but the accepted "norm" accompanied by expectations for health, beauty, and all realms of acceptability.[31]

Acknowledging the impact of WEIRD, our position goes beyond the accompaniment strategy, which acknowledges the importance of cultural identification. The strategy we propose in examining the role of color from a decolonialized perspective additionally acknowledges the intersectional role of socio-emotional, cognitive, and biologically based maturation processes when interrogating colorism. It is most important to do so when there is dissonance, or a lack of "fit," between perspectives about one's social characteristics and power. Also noticeable by very young children, everyday experiences are fraught with experiences of "non-fit" between self and the spaces one navigates when engaging in everyday development and learning. Whiteness precipitates "normative experiences" assumed to represent "the standard" with regard to behavioral expectations, treatment, and inferred value; there are consistent and consonant interactions with contexts (a sense of "fittedness"). For people of color there is dissonance (or inferred "lack of fit") with this White frame. Du Bois captures this in his classic question, "How does it feel to be a problem?" That is, most interactions with context statuses for Black and Brown bodies—highly different from the "consonance" enjoyed as a function of Whiteness—most frequently are rife with "misfittedness,"[32] with being "a problem."

We highlight and interrogate normal and linked everyday human processes. Acknowledging differences in the stages of developing and expressing our humanity with an appreciation of maturation changes and processes is essential. It is problematic to assume that the capacities of an infant, toddler, or young child are the same as those of middle childhood (primary grade/middle school), adolescence, emerging adulthood, or middle/late adulthood individuals. The absence of such sensitivity "adultifies" and assumes a sameness of capacities, potential, responsibilities, judgements, and meanings of language. Inferring "sameness" in expected competencies disregards maturation-based and context-linked variations and limitations that instead require differentiated supports. In other words, "adultifying expectations" may serve to problematize individuals due to a failure to recognize the special placement of childhood and youth statuses. We emphasize that both culturally sensitive and context-acknowledging strategies must incorporate individual-level maturation-based human processes. Before moving to the role of the Clarks' research and its implications for the positionality of humanity in *Brown*, there should be some acknowledgement of the role of memory in the consideration of the "facts" reviewed and prior cases considered given the chronosystem's role in 350 years of Black and White individuals' shared ecologies in North America.[33]

History, Collective Memory, and Colorism

Another developmental implication essential to understanding colorism research is the impact of the chronosystem—historical context—on identity both as a stress factor and in the use of collective memory as a coping mechanism. In Radical *Brown* history is a defining consideration of developmental consequences and solutions, or implementation of shared humanity. History is also essential to a legal argument not only of the core meaning of *Brown* as shared humanity, but also of the legal, constitutional obligation to remedy the very system law historically helped to construct and continues to sustain. Here, we consider some of the developmental consequences of four centuries of sustained definition, and social, cultural, and multisystemic support for, the idea of Black inhumanity.

As the historian David Davis points out, slavery had at least three major consequences.[34] First, he concurs with a growing body of historical research that maintains that at the time of emancipation, slavery was not a backward inefficient economic system destined to die a natural death. Indeed, it anticipated and incorporated many aspects of modern commercial systems and buttressed enormously profitable enterprises. Second, he argues that the Emancipation Proclamation, along with the Thirteenth, Fourteenth, and Fifteenth Amendments, represented the climax of what he calls the Age of Emancipation, with four million people being liberated in a short space of time that grossly outpaced previous efforts at abolition in the United States and elsewhere. Finally, although Davis acknowledges the economic ramifications of slavery and abolition, he nevertheless suggests that the debates over slavery were fundamentally tied to *a moral contradiction which sought to treat slaves as both humans and property.* This "problem of slavery" played out in subsequent issues relating to abolition in regard to the compensation of former slaveholders as well as what was perceived as the problems of what to do with newly liberated slaves. Given the dehumanization and animalization that justified and characterized slavery, *both pro and antislavery advocates alike struggled with how these former slaves could transition into being property-holding and responsible citizens while still facing prejudice from their neighbors.* It was for these reasons that colonization schemes were crafted and implemented with various degrees of success. With the passing of Thirteenth, Fourteenth, and Fifteenth Amendments, the United States embraced a legalistic approach that codified the illegality of slavery as well as the citizenship and civil rights of former slaves.[35]

Davis's concept of the "problem of slavery" recognizes dehumanization as a lasting aspect of the system. His analysis also describes the scope and paleness of the Thirteenth, Fourteenth, and Fifteenth Amendments as codifications to actually alter beliefs that literally hundreds of years stoked and internalized as a major source of conflict and resistance to authentic change. Our conceptual strategy represents a human vulnerability and resiliency perspective which acknowledges the critical balance or imbalance between protective factors as assets versus structured risks and traumatic conditions. No matter the historical period, the fact of developmental tasks to be met and positively responded to as a set of life course tasks required for health and well-being remains as a necessity. Meeting those tasks with varied levels of vulnerability results in stress, which requires managing. Davis's historical review of slavery makes clear that both Whites and Blacks were burdened by huge challenges to be mastered. Managing the stress requires coping, which can be adaptive or maladaptive. There is evidence of significant resiliency outcomes achieved by Blacks brought about by particular coping strategies and evolved traditions at the individual and community levels, such as the creation of self-help associations, Black business creation, and the building of Black schools. Except for documented exemplars of White violence on individual Blacks, such as lynching and the burning of communities, other psychological strategies attempted for coping processes by Whites are less well known. Thus, beyond the systematic killing of Blacks that continues into the present day, there is little known about the coping practices of Whites in response to the Emancipation Proclamation and passage of the Thirteenth, Fourteenth, and Fifteenth Amendments without specific strategies for addressing the dilemma the immorality of slavery beyond these legalistic codifications. The task for Whites to maintain a sense of superiority without conscious introspection of inherited character (morality) attributes given an intergenerationally transmitted history of unacknowledged violence as well as the habit of racism presence denial has implications for identity processes for everyone. Consistent with the PVEST framing, dealing with the stress of the chronosystem triggers coping. Among the coping mechanisms is collective memory, constructing the past in a way that renders the moral contradiction invisible or simply past.[36] In *Brown*, the Court does this by rendering history inconclusive on the subject of segregation, in order to avoid the consequences and inherent contradiction of claimed equality with the inequality and inhumanity of slavery present at the founding, in the Declaration of Independence, and in the Constitution. The moral contradiction, the problem, is resolved by history denial and false memory.

Although impossible to review here, the memory literature is a rich field, and its review would provide additional insights and analysis opportunities. It is important to acknowledge that collective memory as a coping mechanism for colorism is a way to resolve the stress of the deep contradiction between American principles and the realities of inequality. Detaching the present from the past, or rendering the past less violent and inhumane, or treating that past as no longer relevant ignores the persistence of the chronosystem and structural, systemic racial inequality. Engaging in collective memory ignoring dehumanization and refusing to challenge false memory leaves powerful developmental stress and maladaptive coping in place. The Clarks' research and colorism work generally expose both the stress of history and the power of collective memory to deny it. Of course, doing so perpetuates inhumanity.

Memory is distinct from history but nevertheless overlaps with it. Topics such as self, race, and nation can draw from the same sources and materials as historical narrative and can be subject to the same bias, interpretation, and presentation while competing with and contesting other narratives. If political and cultural memory are based on the selection and exclusion of memories, ordered and mediated toward a particular end, then collective memory is "as much a result of conscious manipulation as unconscious absorption and it is always mediated." The character of *Brown* may have been mediated by collective memory to ignore the depth of the impact of generations of Black dehumanization, resulting in a "remedy" that never had an opportunity for success.[37]

Conclusion

Reading the doll studies with these development insights in mind is critical for appreciating enduring fBIP when considering the remedy provided by the Court in response to the harm endured. Understanding what coping mechanisms must be addressed is essential. In our analysis of the doll studies, consideration of basic human development processes for children's choice behavior needed for interpreting and understanding Black children's reactions to long-term conditions of inequality is essential. What was reflected was the basic fact of colorism as the "allocation of privilege and disadvantage according to the lightness or darkness of one's skin" that defined the socialization of children whether White or Black.[38] It is understood as the process that Whiteness privileges Whites *period*. In addition, it privileges light- over dark-skinned people of color in areas such as income, education, housing, and the marriage market. The scope of colorism is huge, and children become increasingly conscious of it with age. Not seeing color is pure fiction. However, understanding its nuanced impact and undergirding inhumanity stance increases with maturational processes for all. The work of Kenneth and Mamie Clark should be credited with an abiding focus on its consequences for equality.[39]

CHAPTER 7

Identity Complexity

Evolving "Self" in a Fictitious "We the People" Constitutional Context

Our rereading of *Brown* acknowledges the noble constitutional framing in the Preamble to the Constitution, but "We the People" serves an unintended purpose. It is inherently contradictory yet encapsulates a vision of shared humanity inclusive of all as "people." In fact, "We the People" framing permits ignoring both the nation's stable racial inequality practices as well as institutional traditions of Black dehumanization. In other words, it ignores the persistence and everyday presence of fBIP as an unabated status in American life for everyone. The language use distortions contribute to individual and collective cultural practices and coping traditions. The failure to acknowledge active practices of inequality renders the language a tradition that assists collective memory distortions. Long-term use of "We the People" phrasing suggests shared benefits of citizenship status and the overall achievement of equivalent social and economic benefits; it implies acquisition of a collectively experienced national identity and attendant accrued benefits. This is opposed to the many experienced challenges and hegemony-reinforcing social traditions—requiring life course coping—that continue the historical context of American life for communities of color.[1] Enslavement history differences suggest greater complexity of identity processes for both those privileged by Whiteness and individuals dehumanized due to the nation's historical use of slavery as its economic anchor.

Adaptive and maladaptive coping reinforce stereotypes of racial dominance as well as the legitimacy of dehumanization practices. For people of color, in response to the many challenges encountered (i.e., under-acknowledged daily experiences of structured inequality), psychological *dissonance reigns*. We have suggested that dissonance reflects the lack of fit between interests pursued and expected juxtaposed against available and accessible supports, or their utter absence. For the nation's diverse "People," as an ontological reality for everyday developmental tasks pursued and myriad traditions encountered, the character of coping needs varies immensely. Inhumane conditions precipitate dissonance or uncomfortably experienced situations and, thus, coping needs. Collectively, context quality and daily experience differences matter for everyone.[2] Richard Lerner posits the importance of "best fit" between contextual conditions and human thriving; however, generally, developmentalists fail to operationalize America's stable racial hierarchy. The shortcoming ignores consequent myriad coping needs; it contributes both to particular collective identifications and individual identity processes for the nation's diverse citizens.[3]

Jamelle Bouie points out that "among the ironies of American history [is] that both opponents and defenders of hierarchy cast their views and their struggles in terms of freedom and liberty."[4] Omitted is clarity regarding *whose* freedom and liberty are intended. Bouie offers as an example the views of early American settlers who spoke of their "inalienable rights" to claim lands they coveted that had been long occupied by Native peoples. Bouie also notes that apologists for segregation framed federal action as threatening Southerners' freedom, as Americans' right to do as they please. He cites historian Tyler Stovall, who suggests that to its defenders, hierarchy is a matter of freedom and liberty. This constructs freedom as the freedom *from* domination and the freedom *to* dominate.[5]

Freedom to dominate is a key component of White supremacy and critical for identity processes for Whites and Blacks. Increasing levels of Whiteness communicates one's greater freedom. Bouie underscores the past as descriptive of the present—the imprint of the chronosystem on contemporary inequality. As he notes, "The more white one was . . .

the more free one was."[6] His analysis of the power of context is compelling: "'White freedom' is not named as such because it is somehow intrinsic to people of European descent, but took its shape under conditions of explicit racial hierarchy, where colonialism and chattel slavery made clear who was free and who was not. For the men who dominated, this informed their view of what freedom was."[7] Tradition reinforced this view of freedom. As Bouie states, "As an ideology, Stovall writes, white freedom meant both 'control of one's destiny' and the freedom to dominate and exclude. And the two moved hand in hand through the modern era."[8] Critical to appreciate is the continuation of racism and colorism as vehicles for the differentiation of treatment.

Memory suppression practices such as using "We the People" language when addressing America's stable state of inequality serve to further facilitate the persistent need to cope with "dissonance" for Blacks and people of color. The fact further burdens and increases the high vulnerability status of individuals not included in an assumed hierarchy of Whiteness. At the same time, assisted by collective memory traditions as well as everyday privileges, beliefs are reinforced of the "sameness of conditions and equity of supports" as well as constitutional linguistic and reaffirming metaphors denoting shared liberty, freedom, and democratic ideals.[9] Assumptions that opportunities are enjoyed by all and are included in "We the People" language have implications for how outcomes, supports, and traditions are packaged as policies and how efficacy is evaluated. Traditional hegemonic connotations concerning White freedom and Black dehumanization are reinforced both nationally and intergenerationally, both formally in history and civics classrooms as well as informally in myriad contexts as White hegemony socialization and supports.

The context of under-acknowledged differences in challenges confronted and coping is a critical source of impact for identity processes. The Clarks' research was important in demonstrating that racial messages are a deep part of American culture to which all children are unavoidably exposed.[10] Given the lack of a human development perspective regarding the human life course experience of Black people, however, particular inhumanity assumptions are part of *Brown's* foundational grounding. Scholars have consistently described the foundational role of Black communities for children's learning and thriving.[11] However, *Brown*, to the contrary, inferred that Black communities possess no inherent positive attributes for human flourishing. The assumption continues to be that Black families and communities fail to serve as positive representations for the healthy identity formation of Black children. Thus, the *Brown* decision reinforced the undergirding assumption that healthy identity for Black children is impossible except in situations guaranteeing interactions with White children who provide models of competence, thriving, physical health, and psychological well-being. We counter that perspective by noting that *Brown* resource-supporting policies and practices inequitably favor settings frequented by and reserved for White children. Thus, race-defined patterned gap findings have more to do with inequality and inequities of supports.

Rereading *Brown* requires implementing its core message of shared humanity. As outlined, PVEST is an identity-focused cultural ecological systems framework emphasizing human meaning-making.[12] It accentuates the continual presence of shared human vulnerability, critically impacted by the balance or imbalance between risks present and the accessibility of protective factors. Uneven coping requirements, given varied experiences of liberty, freedom, and the promises of democracy, foment various adaptive or maladaptive responses.[13] PVEST theorizes that it is the redundancy of patterned responses as coping strategies, given challenges, that creates stable ego identity processes associated with particular periods of the life course.[14] A hegemonic belief system of Black dehumanization and inferred White superiority is a primary identity socialization factor. It is present from family- and media-communicated messages as well as "missed" school-based curriculum and teaching that, if present, would counter and resist hegemonic belief system-embraced identifications. In other words, the presence of fBIP matters.

Evaluating and comparing life course developmental task success by race—ignoring context considerations, the chronosystem, and abetted by "traditional" social science representations—narrowly reinforces hegemonic beliefs of White superiority.[15] In parallel, assumptions of equality prevail without constructive analysis of dehumanizing practices and contributions of challenging life course contexts. What emerges is an inherent "lack of fit" between individuals of color and America's context character.[16]

Ignored, as well, are the individual and collective costs of demonstrated Black resiliency, that is, achieving resilience and good outcomes either individually or collectively but at significant costs. Competence-pursuing efforts occur in settings where everyday freedom, liberty, and democracy—experienced for Blacks as language displays only—are, in fact, traditions of freedom and support for Whites that further function to dominate non-White others. The facilitating social structures upholding disparate experiences and levels of vulnerability between racial groups are "contested" primarily as words of aspiration. Maintained are inequitable conditions and undergirding hegemony beliefs that impact all aspects of American life; in fact, outcomes include unequal learning contexts more dire than those in existence prior to *Brown.*

Frequently ignored are constitutionally imbued meanings of "freedom" as dual language interpretations for Whites versus Blacks that influence different levels of human vulnerability. The notion of freedom to "do what one pleases" and the freedom from domination and linked everyday experiences of Blacks and Whites is instructive for identity processes.[17] Varied normative levels of stress explain diverse coping needs that result in more challenging and complex life course ego processes for people of color. PVEST scaffolding links vulnerability status, stress, and coping processes to life course outcomes and demonstrates the impact of stereotyping and contexts of high risk and stress. Thus, the linkages between components of PVEST precipitate the need for more coping, and thus, the systemic process continues to heighten psychic energy needs and unavoidable ego processes.[18]

The presence of fBIP defines the reason for divergent lives and identity processes for Whites and people of color, which necessitate acknowledging and chronicling the multiple layered contexts of socialization and learning and include contributions from the chronosystem.

Critical to consider is the contrast between Blacks' ongoing sojourn in America and Whites' chronosystem support in constitutional language self-protecting hegemonic beliefs regarding "the self" as well as systemic supports of Whites' developmental successes. Referred to and baked into social theory communicated in various ways are opinions about group superiority and uninterrogated assumptions of Blacks' inhumanity. Persistent colorism associated with historical contributions functions as the "air" linking all levels of the ecologies of development.[19]

Identity formation represents similar overlapping biopsychosocial human developmental processes (links between socio-emotional, cognitive, and neuro-physical-biological status). Context variations are experienced differently. The dual meanings and associated experiences of freedom suggest varied levels of effort.[20] They are impacted by access to opportunity and produce varied and consequent ego processes. Not surprisingly, the experiences yield mixed life course trajectories. As individuals address normative thriving needs given expected developmental task completion, they are evaluated against "standards." These standards have the potential to either defame or glorify outcomes as affirming hierarchically determined self- and group evaluations without ever acknowledging inequities. Identity formation was inadequately explored in *Brown*. Radical *Brown* requires that identity formation be comprehensively understood in order to achieve, not simply aspire to, shared humanity. "We the People" should reflect a reality of equality based upon authentic conditions of shared humanity.[21]

Group Identity Contributions to Self Identity

The long-term experience of dissonance for Blacks, the lack of "good-fit" between individual experiences and context—as fBIP—impacts everyday individual efforts.[22] At the group level, the lack of "fit" is represented as collective resistance movements and messages in response to domination efforts. Organized efforts and protective factors against the risks of daily assaults and oppression reduce Black human vulnerability and attendant stress levels. Thus, consistent with PVEST theorizing, they play a positive role for human coping and contribute to individual-level identity processes.

For example, in response to fBIP requiring resistance, at the group level, systems of coping have included *political movements* (e.g., slave rebellions, Underground Railroad, Marcus Garvey's Niagara or Back to Africa Movement, the Nation of Islam, Black Power movements [e.g., the Black Panthers, the Revolutionary Action Movement], the Student Non-Violent Coordinating Committee, contemporary "Black Lives Matter" groups), *artistic depictions* (e.g., jazz music, the blues, hip-hop, rock and roll, myriad dance genres, quilting bees, the Black Arts Movement, spoken word), and *morality-linked belief systems of faith and hope* (e.g., spirituality, faith groups/religious organizations, faith-based civil rights activism). All signify the power and beauty of Blackness. The contemporary refrain that "Black Lives Matter" represents positive reference group orientation, and as described by William E. Cross in *Shades of Black*, ameliorates the myth of Black self-hatred, demonstrates the diversity of Black self-processes, and undercuts erroneous self-deprecatory assumptions.[23]

Group identity efforts that represent and provide Black psychological processes that scaffold and contribute to thriving have been evident as intragroup socialization processes for fostering well-being in reaction to everyday experienced fBIP. At the same time—even though problematized from a White dominant lens and resisted—Black collective efforts have functioned between subordinate and dominant groups. Serving as instruments of protest and models of resistance to White hegemony for hundreds of years, they are infrequently recognized as such. Nonetheless, individually and collectively, such efforts serve to support Blacks' individual and collective identity, provide contexts of socialization and formal teaching opportunities, assist responsive and adaptive coping as resistance messages, and inculcate positive values even when it was illegal to do so (e.g., teaching Blacks to read).[24] Inclusive human development links and coping with life course human development responses are culturally patterned, represent adaptive practices, and become "rote" responses expressed across time as life stage-specific ego processes.

To name a few exemplars of selfhood—identification as a learner, a civic minded member of society, a parental role provider, or a member of a group—all suggest "habits" of coping. Identities are scaffolded by context-specific conditions and are influenced by historical events.[25] As a component of a consistently dynamic system, habits of coping suggest and contribute to vulnerability and evolve into stable identity patterns. The unavoidable sense-making contributes to socio-emotional awareness, evokes feelings, arouses cognitive handling of precipitated feelings, and is associated with the social experiences at the various levels of context. All are bi-directionally influenced by psychophysiology and, particularly, maturation.

The "best fit" seamlessness and supportive conditions more frequently experienced for Whites are different from the often stable conditions of dissonance and trauma experienced by Blacks. Not surprisingly, different levels of reactive coping efforts and trauma were experienced by Blacks and Whites during the attempts to end segregation. Candid awareness of the dual meanings of liberty, justice, and freedom for Blacks and Whites was not reflected in the implementation of the *Brown* decision. Moreover, shortcomings are more complex when developmental factors are considered. For preschoolers, the character of coping, opportunities for learning, and meanings made of linguistic labels are different from those at middle childhood, adolescence, emergent adulthood, and later periods across the life course. Thus, the policy-relevant strategies required must be different. This is essential to the implementation of Radical *Brown* going forward.

1. Preschoolers' Race Choices and Identity: Reflections of Context

How a preschooler expresses a valuing of things "White" and a parallel lack of interest in those items and individuals that are "dark," represent behavioral exposures observed particularly during malleable periods of life when the modes of learning are very much influenced by imitation.[26] They may not represent internalized belief systems about self and others. Thus, *context matters.*

This developmental insight is clear in the following exchanges between an experimenter and preschool-age participants (four to six years old), demonstrating exposures to "modelled" bias. These verbal data were collected by Spencer in 1969–1970 for a sample of White children in the Midwest.[27] The preschooler responses are parallel to comments of young children in research conducted by Spencer twenty years later at the request of producers of the 1989 ABC special *Black in White America*.[28]

The following are selected responses of preschool children in Spencer's 1970 project, which was closely based on the Clarks' research cited in *Brown*. Bracketed comments are those of the same-race experimenter as the child respondent; she asks questions and makes references to posters of identical pictures of children or animals, differing from each other only by color for animals (black or white animals) or by skin color for identically depicted children in a play context (artist-drawn pictures of individuals either pinkish white or medium brown in skin tone).[29] Each Black- or White-skin-toned child was depicted very similarly except for hair, skin, and eye color.

For the initial phase of the research, the study called for all of the Black and White preschoolers to be "trained" by a same-skin-color mechanized puppet. Puppet feedback "communicated" to children was that all "white colored" animals (horses, ducks, dogs) or light-colored or White persons (individuals shown in a "play context") should be provided *negative* evaluative feedback; in parallel form, the puppet instructions to children to be provided about the black or brown animals or individuals was to be positive. The goal was to determine if the puppets were effective in maintaining or changing young children's verbalized beliefs, attitudes, or preferences about particularly colored animals and children. The methods used stimulus language mirroring the research strategy provided by the Clarks. In addition to the group analyses, individual findings were recorded. The comments reproduced below were reported for the White preschool participants.[30]

First, individually, a same-race experimenter (designated by the letter E) asked for each child's color/race value judgements. The experimenter then either affirmed the child's response (i.e., E's agreement) or communicated disagreement to the child's verbalized judgement. Thus, following "feedback from the mechanized puppet," which consistently provided positive evaluation of the color black or dark-skinned child at play, the experimenter posed questions of each child. The preschool participant provided judgments of the black- versus white-colored animal stimuli or the Black versus White child in a play context followed by the question posed by the experimenter. The quotation marks indicate audiotaped responses from the preschool child. All of the following sample responses are from White children.

SAMPLE I

(E asks, "Which is the dirty duck?" Child chooses the black duck and is corrected.) "Well, no, she doesn't look clean to me." (E asks, "Which is the stupid horse?" Child chooses the black horse and is corrected.) "Well, I don't think so." (E asks, "Which is the ugly horse?" Child indicates the black horse and is corrected. "Well, the other horse with the dirt on it looks kind of ugly."

SAMPLE 2

(E asks, "Who would you ask to be your friend?" Child chooses the White child and is corrected.) "I don't like Black—I don't like Black people." ("You don't like Black people—why?") Pause. "Because of their icky shoes." ("Is there any other reason?") "No." (E asks, "Which girl would you ask to play with you?" Child chooses the White child and is corrected.) "That's because I don't like Black girls." ("And why don't you like Black girls?") "Because of the clothes they wear."

SAMPLE 3

(E asks, "Which girl would you choose to be your friend?" Subject gives the incorrect response and is corrected.) "But I hate Brown girls." ("You hate Brown girls?") "They look ugly to look at." ("Why do they look ugly to look at?") "Because they look like they are kind of dumb." ("How do kind of dumb people look?") "Kind of brown."

SAMPLE 4

(E asks, "Which is the dirty girl. Child chooses incorrectly and is corrected.) "She doesn't look dirty to me." ("Why?") "Because people who are sort of orange—that means they are clean!" ("Oh, like you.") "Yes."

SAMPLE 5

(E asks, "Which is the naughty girl?" Child gives incorrect response and is corrected.) "She doesn't look naughty to me. When people are mad they turn that brown color." ("Oh?") "Yes" ("Why?") "Because that's what they are supposed to do when they are mad." ("Oh, are they?") "Huh huh. And then they turn back to their color again."

The White "valuing responses" in the data were consistent with those obtained twenty years later in 1989 and recorded for Black children in the ABC special *Black in White America* and forty years later for White and Black children on a CNN special.[31] Kenneth and Mamie Clark reported similar findings for White children (data not referenced in *Brown*). Like Spencer's 1970 findings, the response patterns suggest early and consistent devaluing of all things dark.[32] There was no mention of the early adverse impact of segregation and unchallenged stereotyping of dehumanizing conditions for Blacks having untoward impact on White children in *Brown*. Instead, the framing of *Brown*, an assumed primary and solo impact on Black children's psychological function-ing, failed to acknowledge the adverse, unfiltered consequences of rac-ist evaluative judgements internalized early on by *White* children. *Brown* made invisible strategies for interrogating early racism verbiage of White children. By limiting its focus to Black children, the decision inferred that the assumed psychopathology of Black children would be offset by removing them from their under-resourced Black schools to well-appointed, non-neighborhood White schools. Thus, unac-knowledged, uninterrogated, and ignored were long-term, racist and dehumanizing assumptions about Blackness and, we suggest, fBIP as "the accepted standard" for between-group relationships and intra-individual self-processes.

For Black children, subsequent replications of the research with both preschool-aged and middle childhood youths have documented that with cognitive maturation and broadening social relationships, Black children understand the bias of "White centeredness," or Euro-centric beliefs, and may hold sentiments that are Afro-centered, or positive Black-valuing perspectives.[33] Both the ability to take the per-spective of others and more general cognitive maturation result in Black youths' positive personal identity. Positive African American group valuing shows linkages with youths' personal identity or self-esteem.[34] The valuing of dark objects and Black bodies bodes well for youths of color given maturation and social experiences; their identity development shows "consonance," or a sameness, between intrapsychic beliefs and the valuing of Black group membership.[35] Critical to appreciate is that the "sameness" of personal identity and group identity have positive implications for youths' coping with developmental tasks and the securing of competencies.

Thus, contrary to *Brown*'s reporting of the Clarks' research, for young children of color, the exposure to and verbal imitation of anti-Black sentiments, in fact, are not internalized because of normal levels of cognitive egocentrism (i.e., appropriate self-centeredness). Instead, the Clarks' research reflects the fact that young children reproduce language and labels to which they are exposed and that are widely disseminated but that psychologically they do not internalize, given their normal status of cognitive egocentrism (self-centeredness). With cognitive maturation, exposure to models and messages of positive group identities, and consequent experiences of dissonance between internal self-constructions and "own-group" reference group orientations, the dissonance between the two perspectives generates "uncomfortableness." Thus, entering middle childhood and beyond, there is movement by children away from repeating and potentially internalizing negative stereotypes and identifications.[36] Thus, an embracing of Black culture is probable.

It is the combination of positive personal identity, group identity-consonant identification, and social cognition awareness that collectively correlates with self-valuing.[37] Given cognitive maturation and its links with socio-emotional functioning, there is a shift to an own-group-accepting racial attitude pattern for Black children. Critical to acknowledge is a lack of similar age shifts for White children from anti-Black verbal patterns to neutral or random racial attitudes and preference behaviors given maturation changes. Interestingly, the White community may have an important function for supporting change.[38] White experimenters in Spencer's research were more effective at reinforcing attitude change than were Black experimenters in teaching White children that the color white and White individuals are "bad!"[39] In sum, as is potentially the case in the Clarks' studies footnoted in *Brown*, race and color biases are learned by Black and White children given contexts that communicate messages fomenting discrimination and bias. At the same time, however, language labels can be effectively unlearned in the case of young children.

2. Middle Childhood and Adolescence

Socio-emotional and cognition patterns shift given subsequent norma-tive changes from middle childhood into adolescence. Major biological differences matter as well as influential social cognition-based capaci-ties to take the other's perspective as a function of youths' penchant to navigate broader spaces and interact in broader places with multiple others. The responsive affective processes, collectively, impact cognition-linked ways of understanding.[40]

Unavoidably, human ontology is a basic part of the process. It is also necessarily epistemic given the meanings that evolve from interactions that occur in cultural contexts, including those designed for learning and development. The insights from maturation-associated changes are taken for granted when there is consonance between individual char-acteristics, as associated with Whiteness, and the nature of the context. Unacknowledged dissonance, on the other hand, between individual characteristics and the basic assumption of humanity is the experience of people of color. Most acutely, adolescents are aware of this dissonance given cognitive maturation and their broader navigation of contexts explored independently from parents. By "dissonance," we refer to a con-sistent state of uncomfortableness between the self and real-world experiences in myriad contexts. fBIP precipitates a lack of experienced seamlessness, or "goodness of fit," between the self and the outside world.[41]

Inequality contributes to ongoing, stable experiences of dissonance for people of color. Four hundred years of unequal experiences and inhu-manity beliefs associated with skin color virtually guarantee the need for the development of "coping muscle" to fBIP. As framed from a

PVEST standpoint, patterned reactive coping experiences are important. Associated with dissonance conditions, reactive coping may take many forms.[42] Certainly for Whites, direct interventions such as more authentic representations of four hundred years of history are resisted and/or intergenerationally repressed as memories and therefore continue to be needed.

In many ways, *Brown* as implemented was strictly aspirational and inadequate given that the real challenge is the design of policy, practices, and historical teaching in schools, to contribute to needed change for securing equity given hundreds of years of inhumane treatment that remains unaddressed. Essential to acknowledge is that inhumanity assumptions about people of color remain impactful for identity-based individual processes and interpersonal practices and interactions. Beginning in early childhood, a shift in perspective has to occur for Black children given the pervasiveness of inhumanity messages about Black lives and hegemony assumptions concerning Whites. Thus data suggest a middle-childhood shift for young children of color who, when queried during early stages, verbalize Black stereotypes as beliefs, attitudes, values, and preferences; however, self-concept assessments show an independence from color and racial stereotype knowledge. However, middle childhood demonstrates fewer color- and race-stereotyped responses, with those children maintaining positive assessments of self-worth, value, and esteem.[43] No such middle-childhood shift is reported for White children. Underexamined is the greater role of schooling for older children, given both the content of the curriculum, the cognitive capabilities of older children, and youths' greater cognizance of the broader environment and messages of power and opportunity.

Black Racial Identity and Self-Esteem

An equally important body of developmental research is the self-esteem literature focused on Black children and youths, which demonstrates the high self-esteem of Black children. One of the pieces in the chronosystem that has contributed to this consistent finding is the affirmative role of Black education historically and currently. There has been a

growing body of literature on the subject of the positive contributions
and unique advancements that segregated Black schools make in regard
to African American's social and educational improvement. These works
have often taken critical aim at the findings and rationale of *Brown*.
Scholars in this vein have examined the history of Black schools and
their educational leaders and advocates,[44] noting the decimation of
Black schools and education in the wake of the *Brown* decision.[45]
Research on the leaders of these institutions emphasizes the subtle
public and private tactics employed to advance the cause of Black education while protecting themselves, their students, and their communities.[46] The institutional leadership functioned as "double agents,"
having to appease White authorities while advocating for their Black
neighbors.[47]

Within the realm of Black identity, the research results have been
consistent, with racial identity affirmation positively predicting levels
of self-esteem in African-Americans adolescents and college students.[48]
This has been particularly true in recent years as models of racial identity have become increasingly more nuanced in assessing the degree and
quality of racial identity.[49] In the first decades following school integration, research on self-esteem and race showed that in contrast to some
widely held conceptions, Black children generally displayed higher levels of self-esteem than White children and that they did not suffer from
the presumed "self-esteem deficit."[50] Subsequent work continues to support these findings.[51] Absent from this research, however, was how
racial identity might predict or influence self-esteem levels in African-
American adolescents. Toomey and Umana-Taylor conceptualized two
different ways in which racial/ethnic identity is linked to self-esteem.[52]
Racial identity can either promote self-esteem via pride in one's self/
collective or protect by minimizing the negative effects of stressors via
racial discrimination.[53]

Phinney et al.[54] found that neither gender nor socio-economic status was a strong predicator of self-esteem in African-American youths
but that ethnic identity was a significant predictor of self-esteem across
racial groups. Yasui et al. found that self-esteem was associated with
adolescent adjustment for both White and Black youths.[55] They focused

on students who were considered both successful and at-risk. Harris-Britt examined how racial socialization messages can protect African-American adolescents from perceived racial discrimination.[56] They found that although racial pride did not predict self-esteem, other forms of racial socialization (i.e., understanding of cultural history, expectations of possible bias/discrimination) could positively predict higher levels of self-esteem.

One area of recent interest is the mediating/moderating influences of racial identity on self-esteem. Multiple studies have found a positive correlation or impact of Black racial identity on self-esteem and academic achievement.[57] Black racial identity also has been found to counter adverse race discrimination experiences,[58] minimize anxiety and depression,[59] and counter negative body image.[60]

Generally, the literature seems to point toward an overall positive association between racial identity and self-esteem at least in regard to African-American youths. Disagreements between researchers focus on conceptual differences relating to how one measures racial identity (i.e., pride of the group or affirmation of oneself) and whether this identity promotes/protects minority youths from stressors or whether this identity serves as a positive asset in and of itself. An important part of the complexity of the identity processes described for middle-childhood and adolescence/young adulthood is the role of human maturation and unavoidable malleability and change in the domains of human *cognition, socio-emotional, and neuro-physico-biological* functioning as core aspects of human development. Thus, recent brain studies, although limiting in regard to attention to context considerations, nevertheless also provide insights.

Early research on the adolescent brain emphasized the heightened intensity and volatility of emotions experienced during that developmental period.[61] This "sturm und drang" model emphasized tumultuous relationships (with peers and parents), moodiness (emotionality), and risky behavioral traits (crime, suicide), with the media reporting a generalized stereotype of adolescents as lacking self-control due to their underdeveloped prefrontal cortex. This perspective was introduced at the same time that adolescence was defined as a distinct period.[62] Critics have pointed out that their own research contradicted the idea that adolescence was inherently "stormy."[63] In recent years, developments in neurobiological research and magnetic resonance imaging (MRI) brain imaging techniques have led scholars to further challenge this model. MRI brain imaging has revealed major structural changes occurring in brains of adolescents that have particular significance for their social interactions. Well into late childhood, the prefrontal cortex continues to develop new synapses, becoming more complex and efficient. The sources of the heightened emotionality and erratic behavior are uncertain, as an underdeveloped prefrontal cortex is present for younger children, who do not display the same behavior, suggesting nonlinear development. More recent research has revealed that the adolescent brain is more vulnerable to stress than children or adults. These developments have led some to suggest that this period is better characterized as one of increased vulnerability as well as opportunity.[64] The sensitivity of the adolescent brain is a risk factor, but environmental influences can assist in mediating positive outcomes.

Casey and Caudle highlight three major misconceptions about the adolescent brain and its relation to self-control and social interaction.[65] These include the notions (1) that adolescent behavior is irrational or deviant, (2) that adolescents are incapable of making rational decisions because of their immature prefrontal cortex, and (3) that all adolescents experience "sturm und drang." Their work suggests that adolescents can demonstrate rational motivation and self-control, notably in emotionally neutral contexts but less so in emotionally taxing ones. They found that the increased emotionality in adolescence is the product of an imbalance in the development of subcortical limbic (e.g., amygdala) relative to prefrontal cortical regions.[66]

Another stereotype concerning adolescent behavior is in the capacity and tendency toward risk-taking behavior. Research has revealed that adolescents are much more nuanced in their assessments of risk. For example, risks associated with social interactions are often mediated by their perceptions of how their peers have assessed the particular risk behavior.[67] With regard to impulsive behavior, the cognitive processes involved in regulating behavior are complex and evolving during adolescence. MRI studies have shown that the adolescent brain is inefficient in processing inhibitory tasks. Despite great effort, it does not adequately interact with the neural structures and can result in inappropriate behavior and poor self-control compared to adults.[68]

Long-term assumptions of inhumanity have consistently been an aspect of the chronosystem level of contextual experiences for people of color.[69] Considering the fBIP high-stress experiences of youth of color, their responses may well suggest socio-emotional resilience and cognitive precocity given the productive outcomes achieved by many. The latter are evident in spite of stressful experiences, significant and enduring colorism, and stereotypic identifiability practices.

Chronosystem Intergenerational Contributions to American Identity

A chronosystem-level acknowledgement of the dehumanization of enslaved people marked solely by skin color is essential for its impact regarding identity processes for Blacks *and Whites*. The successful coping strategies engineered by Blacks and used for collective survival and human thriving in spite of fBIP were never considered as building blocks to an authentic foundation for social change. The evidence of self-esteem research suggests strongly that they should be.

A sensitivity to developmental differences is critical. Recent identity research suggests that youths labeled or identified in some way as "other" (e.g., Black, Latino, female, poor) have markedly different context-relevant societal experiences as they increasingly become aware of their social positions.[70] Addressing a variety of domains, the work has made strides in framing the complexities of racial identity, civic identity, becoming an "adult," and sexuality.[71] When identity processes are discussed in the myriad contexts of development for Blacks and Whites, it is evident why too infrequently there is dissonance about the continuation of Black dehumanization, whether observed as everyday practices (and the need for coping and adaptation to the same), and the racialized contexts of learning and development.

Identity-focused scholarship has tended to concentrate on the construction of different social labels as isolated and homogeneous categories or as additive forms of marginalization.[72] Unfortunately, this perspective backgrounds interlocking systems of oppression, as well as the role of phenomenological interpretation. Research that focuses only on the role of race and racial identity in relation to school outcomes may ignore nuances and heterogeneity by gender. Furthermore, many dominant frameworks in developmental literature do not address how power structures and personal experience intersect in identity formation processes. While identity research has added greater complexity and awareness to particular marginalized categories in adolescent development, the prevailing theories still lack critical nuance that addresses the joint simultaneity of factors and complexity of human experience and identity formation. This area is ripe for interpretation and is the subject of the next chapter on intersubjectivity and intersectionality.[73]

Intersubjectivity and Intersectionality

Humanity Framing for Rereading Brown

We live in a society that is uniquely afraid of Black children.... Americans become anxious—if not outright terrified—at the sight of a Black child ringing the doorbell, riding in a car with white women or walking too close in a convenience store. Americans think of Black children as predatory, sexually deviant and immoral.... There is something particularly efficient about treating Black children like criminals in adolescence. Black youth are dehumanized, exploited and even killed to establish the boundaries of Whiteness before they reach adulthood and assert their rights and independence.

—KRISTIN HENNING, *The Rage of Innocence: How America Criminalizes Black Youth* (New York: Pantheon, 2021) (xv)

OUR PAST CONTINUES TO INFORM OUR PRESENT. The objectification of Black bodies and the dehumanization of Black lives continue to permeate our reality. Kristin Henning's compelling statement about Black children reminds us that the imposition begins in the case of children who are "adultified" and rendered threatening to Whites. Imposed perceptions of danger and their endangerment are multiple and intersectional. The fact is experienced intersubjectively, by Whites and some Blacks, as an expression of confirmed inhumanity.

Radical *Brown* demands the upending of this recursive inequality and its consequences.

In this chapter, we discuss intersubjectivity and intersectionality and their relationship in constructing persistent Black *inhumanity*, and thus their critical role in fostering shared *humanity*. *Intersubjectivity* communicates the fact of stable systems of oppression grounded in Black inhumanity beliefs as shared social meaning. There is an unavoidable and cognition-linked awareness of these stable systems. Individuals' exposure to the uncontested "facts" of these systems serve as behavioral traditions. Human social cognition makes their reality an unescapable fact. Functioning as uncontested and critical "intangibles," they propagate shared social meanings, and function osmosis-like in transmission through the processes of socialization and social learning. This happens in myriad contexts such as settings of development, identity formation, and "intended support," including home, school, religious settings, and the media.

Intersectionality theory interfaces with intersubjectivity. Intersectionality highlights overlapping *identity categories as systems of challenge or support*. We argue why and how PVEST incorporates the focus of this work, which has been largely omitted from developmental literature. PVEST shows us why interacting identities matter by demonstrating "the how" and linked processes. Particularly relevant are meanings made by diverse children and youths' sense-making at critical points of intersection. The phenomenology emphasizing perspective provided by PVEST emphasizes that socialization, developmental factors, context character, and the person's own "sense-making" matter for coping.[1]

Like the context-linked and scaffolding biological system of our human bodies, the psycho-social-emotional and bio-systems perspective of PVEST serves a critical heuristic purpose.[2] It acknowledges biological, socio-emotional, and cognitive human processes and accrued insights linked to context and developmental status. Thus, it affords complementary and linked conceptual strategies for the humanity and human development perspective that scaffolds our framing for Radical *Brown*.

An embraced humanity viewpoint is central to our radical rereading of Brown.[3]

The Interaction of Intersubjectivity and Intersectionality

Intersubjectivity is critical to identity because this is how we "make meaning" of things. How individuals infer meanings early on may protect the psyche by impeding young egocentric children's social understanding of negative messages such as racism.[4] At adolescence, given major shifts in cognition, more differentiating levels of cognitive function provide unavoidable awareness of negative messages. Exacerbating stress occurs when the potential for positive selfhood is challenged or thwarted. The context and dehumanizing messages, including the failure to acknowledge hegemony as broadly structured inequality, are traumatizing and impactful. We see this in the relational patterns between police and minority communities, particularly male minority youths. Intersubjectivity communicating inhumanity is present in systems of oppression entrenched and evident across ecologies of human development, contributed to by historical traditions represented in the ecology by the chronosystem.

Intersubjectivity scaffolds interpersonal character between and within groups. Intersubjectivity functions and provides sources of emotional content—including stable trauma—given unavoidable cognition-based awareness. It influences variations in the stress level produced by schooling and learning. Without a racist or sexist word necessarily spoken—particularly salient in contexts of racial inequality and exclusion—schooling contexts represent and contribute to very different levels of vulnerability for White children versus youths of color. For the latter, it may generate traumatizing feelings of hatred and fear. Any youth finds it difficult to embrace learning settings that represent and spew hatred, generate unacknowledged fear for selfhood, and prevent the foundational need for demonstrating effective motivation or personal causation.[5]

Human processes such as learning and memory aid the ability of humans to make sense of things. Their level of social cognition, that is, their ability to infer the perspectives of others, makes awareness of shared social meanings a "given." Intersubjectivity, then, is an undeniable aspect of human life and social interactions. Intersubjective awareness is inferred and contributed to by a social "fittedness" or "nonfit" as individuals navigate spaces in pursuit of successful completion of developmental tasks.[6] Success and competence of developmental task pursuit are linked with individual characteristics that function intersectionally together with developmentally related social "sense-making." This takes place in social ecologies that include the role of historical context as the chronosystem.[7] Intersecting with context, such as unacknowledged and underinterrogated school settings, particular patterned outcomes are not unexpected. These interacting complex factors of development are essential to interrogate; if we fail to do so, the patterns that emerge are treated as deficits that continue to reinforce beliefs of Black inhumanity.

Intersectionality is critical to existing intersubjective meaning and reframing social meaning. It requires the consideration of the undermining or privileging experiences associated with race, gender, economic status, sexual orientation, disability, developmental stage, and immigration status. Intersectionality describes the interaction, complexity, and mutual reinforcement between systems of oppression. It requires us to critically unpack and confront our context and identities. We focus on the developmental impact of a context of (intersectional) inequality. For example, being an adolescent and Black, as individual characteristics, fails to represent the interaction of these identity factors, and others including gender and class, to create the highly vulnerable status of Black youths growing up in America. The message from intersectionality insights is that any one demographic factor may be fraught with potential untoward stressors and unique systems of oppression. A major intersectional insight is that the impact of the combinations of the categories is synergistic, far exceeding the consequences of simply viewing them as additive.

Intersubjectivity and intersectionality interact, with implications for stress level, coping processes, and vulnerability. These relationships, however, are generally overlooked in social science work that guides key occupations. This includes K–12 and higher education teaching professionals,

criminal justice employees, and the health care professions. Unacknowledged and untoward intangibles as relational shortcomings continue
unabated and repetitively reproduced. Training settings too often serve
as sources of hegemonic intersubjectively communicated beliefs. Particularly communicated in predominately White institutions as experienced
by Black students (versus affirmations of hegemony for Whites), its socio-
emotionally relevant content compromises cognitive performance and
represents missed positive learning opportunities.[8]

Not surprising, as evidence of individual and collective coping, is
the persistent statistic that the majority of the nation's Black doctoral
degree and professional school graduates earned a portion of their training in historically Black colleges and universities [HBCUs]).[9] The context of inequality and racially linked traditions matters. Tyler Stovall
reminds us that White freedom means that the more White, the more
free.[10] Given the varied definitions in place for "freedom" and the actual
operational opportunity for freedom, freedom from segregation and
oppression have remained fundamentally aspirational. Our dispute
with the crafters and implementers of *Brown* focuses on and acknowledges the salience of context representing four hundred years of Blacks'
sojourns within and across America's ecologies, frequently linked to the
lack of opportunities for the sharing of the nation's economic benefits
promised to all as encapsulated in the Constitutional promise of "We
the People."

A focus on context, especially the ecologies of development and
learning, has the potential for interrogating the myriad situations of
socialization. It acknowledges everyday experiences as human development and as a scholarly focus.[11] Ecological approaches remain simplis-
tically represented in the social and health sciences, if referenced at
all. The specifics of what happens when individuals experience a lack
of "fit" are not explicitly considered. In fact, much of social science
assumes a seamlessness between the character of context and individuals' experience. The "degree of fittedness issue" is infrequently included
in the design of research and the interpretation of data. Equally absent
are historical contributions to contemporary context features. Interrogation of the chronosystem's contributions to everyday experiences

remains invisible, if acknowledged as relevant at all. Specifically underacknowledged or entirely absent are context attributes such as stereotypic beliefs about Blacks, specifically, and minority children more generally. In parallel, cultural socialization efforts in minority communities linked to resiliency outcomes are too infrequent as well. Further, historical circumstances that would aid in interpreting the degree or character of individual-context fit and vulnerability are ignored.

Intersectionality is critical within these conceptual shortcomings.[12] Socializing occasions and structured experiences of adolescent traditions (e.g., navigating settings and preparing for adulthood tasks and responsibilities) are experienced intersectionally. Intersectionality provides helpful insights for youths' resiliency promotion and the design of policies that are authentically impactful for all youths' positive change. It explains the variations of stress level experienced and coping levels required in activities such as "driving while Black" as a teenager or the social consonance anticipated by White youths.

Youth experiences—differentially inferred as intersubjective processes—are evident and communicated throughout ecologies from the micro, meso, and exo to the macro level. The expectations are affirmed through uninterrogated chronosystem-contributing assumptions concerning expected human development youth supports. White youths expect to have access to summer jobs, safe and well-attended recreational facilities, academic enriching opportunities, and classes with teachers who wish to be there as sources of support and learning. The dilemma is the lack of policies and practices authentically supportive of Black, youthful, low-resourced humans living in underresourced and blighted urban communities. This persistent, uniquely American, and broadly segregated "democracy" is normatively exacerbated by inequalities. The failure to appreciate shared humanity characterizes multiple levels of social ecology and limits post-*Brown* remedies. This context continues in place, now seventy years after *Brown*.

Intersubjectivity and the Persistence of fBIP

Intersubjectivity makes evident why America's continuing racial inequality and inequitable conditions continue seventy years after

Brown. The stable social phenomenon is that the human development needs of those historically dehumanized and objectified remain unsupported today. They lack a priority status, suggested by an apparent lack of awareness of dehumanization as a definition and association with non-White status. Thus, there is a failure to meet the requisite human development needs of people of color generally, but Black youths' flourishing requirements in particular. Worse yet, ignoring the shared human process of intersubjectivity given intersectionality exacerbates developmental inequality. Policies and intended practices introduced in a normalized trauma context as remedies (e.g., affirmative action language but inequality traditions) are racialized and unsuccessful. They are insufficient for offsetting the implicit and explicit effect of systematic dehumanization and objectification. They are present irrespective of disciplinarity identification.

As described, the centrality of fBIP's positionality and effectiveness is deeply ingrained in the sciences as well as represented in literary scholarship and the humanities. These disciplines function to disseminate assumptions and permeate all contexts. Ecologies include knowledge creation systems, data interpretation efforts impacting policies, and cross-context effects as practices for professional training, student learning vehicles (e.g., curricular and programming), and information dissemination across settings. Particularly in the social sciences, "following the science" means internalizing the outcomes of fBIP. The perspective's representation in federally funded research—as well as philanthropy-defining efforts—especially matter. It is impactful in the training of professionals as "intended supports," as well as in the scaffolding of policies effective in maintaining systems of inequality. The persistence of inequality of conditions and inequities of shared freedom, liberty, and justice suggests that the Constitution's "We the People" language utilization, in fact, remains infused with fBIP.

As we have emphasized from our PVEST framing—given the shared fact of diverse levels of human vulnerability and resiliency potential, and the core role of identity[13]—an unacknowledged fBIP and resistance to interrogation of this perspective interferes with *all* Americans' flourishing and human development. The absence of acknowledging long-term and persistent fBIP as dehumanizing systems matters. Considered in myriad operational contexts, this invisibility dissuades consideration, prohibits interrogation, prevents productive recommendations, and dilutes remedies to reduce inequality. In sum, the absence of fBIP discourse undermines the design of authentically structured supports.

The situation of strategically limited fBIP recognition is the polar opposite of supporting shared humanity as intersubjective meaning. The fBIP in shared human processes occurs in socially constructed contexts, which makes the fact of inhumanity definitions and linked treatment impossible to ignore. PVEST framing and analyses demonstrate the consequences in the form of varied levels of stress and trauma, including physical and psychological uncomfortableness given uneven challenges and supports.[14] Also consequential are maladaptive coping traditions both for those victimized by fBIP and for recipients of its inferred power. Given fBIP considerations, this exposes the humanity consequences and the needs of children/youth for ecology-linked supports that are essential to *Brown*'s mandate but not delivered by *Brown* as implemented.

We suggest that an ecological emphasis and confrontation of fBIP provides lucidity in multiple ways. It makes clear the "what" and "why" of collective cultural traditions, including their persistence regarding inhumanity assumptions. Additionally, it provides explanations for individual coping reactions as adaptive or maladaptive responses as well as interrogating etiologies for "how" different meanings are created.[15] This is especially important during adolescence given adulthood preparation requirements and increased behavioral expectations.[16] Young people respond to the requirements and expectations during a period of significantly increased and rapid cognitive, socioemotional, and biological maturation changes. They occur most frequently as youth pursue developmental tasks more broadly and independently while navigating their own and others' communities.

We have suggested that human identity processes for those intergenerationally privileged by long-term inequities simply due to Whiteness have not been well understood. For those with a "knapsack of privilege," a downside of privilege and linked behavioral orientations may be that

it limits experiences and consciousness. The concept of structured affor-
dances would suggest that privilege may dictate or limit. It provides or
furnishes a frame for assuming the world acts in a certain way.[17] Problem behavior for White youth may be due to the absence of positive,
adaptive coping skill development practice opportunities due to
socially structured and maximized (White) individual-context best fit
and conditions of consonance. This is different from a positionality of
dissonance. Dissonance accompanies the unrecognized trauma of
intersubjectivity awareness given the persistent youth-experienced intersectionality effects of race, adolescence, gender, and economic status.

The contemporary pushback from the inclusion of critical race
theory–relevant content in K–12 curriculum materials is an example of
fBIP. Clearly not understood is that the critical race curricula contro-
versy represents—on the one hand—critiques of and resistance to the
inclusion of accurate historical records concerning the role of slavery
in the nation's global profit margin and level of perpetrated violence for
maintaining slavery as a system of oppression. Those who would exclude
critical race theory prefer to maintain the position that Blacks' contributions remain unremarkable or invisible, thus rationalizing hegemony
and inhumanity status. On the other hand, insistence on the dissemination of critical race theory insights through social studies curricular
content provides a vehicle for an informed electorate and social justice.
Accurate history textbooks, curricular options, and opportunities for
discourse aid in stopping the dissemination of historical fiction. Accurate portrayals of America's history and practices have positive and
important implications for the nation's social fabric, its race dilemma,
and the inability to cope with human difference.

Too frequently, inaccuracies include failing to acknowledge the
nation's violent slavery traditions (continuing as policing practices) and
its Black-body, free-labor, chattel slavery–dependent economic past.
Uninterrogated, this continues to have implications for economic and
social inequities. Necessary for inclusion are the long-term role of slavery
for the nation's agricultural markets, the physical building of the nation's
cities' infrastructure, and major contributions to the arts, to name a few.
Also essential to acknowledge are the many service sector roles. Black

bodies remain foundational to America's gross domestic profit schemes and economic successes enjoyed at the local and global levels.[18]

Just as important, although stereotypic assumptions prevail for those burdened by four hundred years of well-organized oppressive conditions of inequality, Blacks' human resiliency prevails. Individual and collective sense-making, coping processes, and cultural traditions as major American contributions must be recognized and celebrated. Emanating from within diverse ecologies impactful for both relational and developmental patterns, upon threats of death for their creation and persistent denied opportunity, nonetheless, effective coping traditions and resiliency continue, including the creation of learning opportunities and civic engagement.[19] However, consistent with the limits of *Brown* remedies, resilience—and strength-based acknowledgments—are still ignored. This compromises effective policy and practice.

Intersectionality and Inhumanity

Intersubjective means of inhumanity are intersectional. As Elisabeth Spelman famously argued, "identity" is not like pop-beads: people cannot separate the "woman part" from the "African-American part" or from the "middle-class part."[20] To the contrary, identities connect and function as a synergistic whole: "As opposed to examining gender, race, class and nation, as separate systems of oppression, intersectionality explores how these systems mutually construct one another."[21]

So, for example, we cannot characterize African American women's experiences as being "more of" White women's experiences or as being basically the same, only worse.[22] Nor can we add the problems of African American men and White women, as the discourse of "double oppression" suggests, in order to understand the Black female experience. The structures of race and gender *intersect* to create a matrix of domination in which each cell defines a position in the race and gender hierarchy.[23] There is no gender apart from race; there are no raceless women. For *all* women, not just women of color, race shapes the experience and meaning of femininity. Moreover, race and gender are not the only systems of oppression that intersect: race, gender, class, disability, nation, sexual orientation, and age (among others) are all intersecting systems of oppression that further interact to position a person in the hierarchies of personhood and humanity.[24]

Every social position is defined by an interaction between these hierarchical systems. Speaking of gender apart from race, class, ethnicity, and other divisions is inaccurate and distorting: there is no such thing as gender apart from race and class, no such thing as race apart from gender, no such thing as class apart from gender or race.[25] Ignoring the intersectional nature of these systems means we systematically overlook the experiences of many different groups and, by default, focus only on the most privileged, on whom most of our theorizing and research are based. So, for example, feminist theory has disproportionately focused on the issues and concerns of White women, presumed heterosexual, middle class, and able-bodied. This privileges some while marginalizing others, as well as excluding interrogation of disfavored masculinities (e.g., men of color, gay men, anti-hegemonic masculinities). It also fails to expose the interaction of White privilege with gender disadvantage. However, in particular situations, the privilege of Whiteness continues to trump the intersectionality described. Thus, for the intersection of gender and race in particular employment situations, White femininity advantages still trump Black masculinity and Black femininity hiring. Silicon Valley may have a dearth of Black bodies, while White women still represent a significant presence.

It is important to underscore that intersectionality is not just a concept that applies to marginalized groups. Rather, intersectionality is an aspect of social organization that shapes all of our lives. Gender structures shape the lives of both women and men, and everyone has a race/ethnicity. Privilege combines and interacts with oppression, just as multiple oppressive systems interact and are not merely additive. Groups may be advantaged or disadvantaged by structures of oppression: they may be intersectionally marginalized (Black working-class women), intersectionally privileged (White male professionals), or a bit of both. Indeed, social relations are so complex that nearly everyone is privileged in some ways and disadvantaged in others. This does not mean, however, that everyone is equally advantaged and disadvantaged.

There are important connections between White privilege and inter-sectionality. White privilege refers to the collection of benefits that White people receive in societies where they top the racial hierarchy. As Peggy McIntosh exposed, this conveys an "invisible knapsack of privi-lege," including everything from Whiteness being equated with being "normal" to Whites having more representation in the media.[26] It encompasses daily supports while shopping, driving, and living with-out racial microaggressions. White privilege leads to White people being viewed as more honest and trustworthy than other groups, whether or not they have earned that trust. This form of privilege also means that White people can easily find products suitable for themselves—cosmetics, band-aids, and hosiery for their skin tones etc. While some of these priv-ileges might seem trivial, it is important to recognize that no form of privilege comes without its counterpart: oppression.

In a racist society, White skin allows for an array of unearned privi-leges unavailable to people of color. Accustomed to their social status and the benefits that accompany it, White people tend not to acknowl-edge their White privilege or, necessarily, to use it to confront myriad sources of minority oppression. It is invisible; hence, their value is assumed to be personal, not racial—legitimate, not unearned and grounded in White supremacy. Learning about the experiences of people of color, however, may prompt Whites to admit to the advan-tages they have in society. McIntosh's self-examination of her racial privilege as a White woman generated a list of fifty privileges that includes being regularly surrounded—in everyday life and in media representations—by people who look like you and having the ability to avoid those who do not.[27] These privileges also include not being inter-personally or institutionally discriminated against on the basis of race, never feeling afraid to defend oneself or speak out against injustice for fear of retaliation, and being viewed as normal and belonging, among others. The key point in McIntosh's list of privileges (not intended as exclusive) is that Americans of color do not typically enjoy or have access to them. In other words, they experience racial oppression—and White people benefit from this. And most insidiously, Whites do not notice or have awareness of their privilege, so the presence of inequality and their role or benefit from it becomes invisible.

By illuminating the many forms that White privilege takes, McIntosh urges readers to consider how our individual life experiences are connected to and situated within large-scale societal patterns and trends. Seeing and understanding White privilege is not about blaming White people for having unearned advantages. Rather, the point of reflecting on one's White privilege is to recognize that the social relations of race and the racial structure of society have created conditions in which one race has been advantaged over others. Further, McIntosh suggests that White people have a responsibility to be conscious of their privileges and to reject and diminish them as much as possible.

Social scientists and activists have expanded the conversation around privilege to include sex, gender, ability, culture, nationality, and class. This expanded understanding of privilege stems from the concept of intersectionality. When determining the level of privilege one has, sociologists today consider a number of social characteristics and classifications.

As society learns more about shared experiences across dimensions and layers, the compounded impact is astounding.[28] As a recent example, during the COVID19 pandemic, the economic impact of the pandemic was labelled by some as creating a "she-cession" due to the disproportionate impact on women, but more broadly, on an intersectional group of multiple identities. "We're seeing women and underrepresented groups—minorities, immigrants, youth, low-income, and lower-skilled individuals—disproportionately impacted."[29] This compounding effect is one of the reasons why understanding intersectionality is imperative to advancing equity and resiliency outcomes.[30]

We have emphasized that a major difference from traditional conceptual and theoretical insights about America's experiences with difference is that PVEST framing provides an inclusive life-course developmental perspective that incorporates intersubjective and intersectional perspectives.[31] Its framing encourages situating childhood and adolescence youth identity formation within everyday navigated situations through home, school, neighborhood, shopping malls, and online platforms. Risk and protective factors in the environment are not deterministic but are associated with accessible supports versus experienced challenges when stress occurs. The resulting psychological balance or imbalance is linked to the immediate reactive coping character. Thus, the experiences are conceptualized as an individual's vulnerability status, a status produced as one moves across contexts and deals with myriad encounters. Experiences require coping strategies specific to the particular developmental period (e.g., baby boys cry in response to frustration as stress, but adolescent boys may want to compete or fight).

An individual's vulnerability level is determined by experiences associated with cumulative social positionality and context-associated involvements. For many youths it involves the experience of interlocking systems of oppression and support (or lack of support). PVEST integrates the multiple identities of an individual with the psychological experience of identity and phenomenology-based interpretations or development-specific sense-making or unavoidable intersubjectivity. There is an embeddedness of the process for individuals and collectively for groups observed both across time and within ecological contexts, including physical contexts and social systems. PVEST brings key elements of intersectionality into developmental identity research by emphasizing youths' experience of multiple social positions and power structures, as sources of risk and support. Intersectionality is linked not only to those structures, but also to developmentally based sense-making.

PVEST: A Humanity Reframing of *Brown*

PVEST helps identify the ways in which *inhumanity* has been reinscribed. PVEST also provides scaffolding to construct shared *humanity*.

As previously discussed, portrayals of the adolescent period have consistently framed it stereotypically as "storm and stress."[32] Empirical research and cultural portrayals depict adolescent identity formation through chaotic, deficit-framed, and at-risk lenses, which are especially deterministic when speculating about marginalized groups of youth. Similar to the experiences of the early childhood period and particularly the so-called terrible twos, adolescence is highly stigmatized. Although much of adults' view of adolescent turmoil may be linked to the inability to acknowledge maturation-based physiological fluctuations precipitating not just significant physical growth but the prominence of sexuality-linked change, this is a time when cognition-supported opportunities for "seeing self and the world differently," and the socio-emotional consequences of this, as well, influence all youths' sense-making.[33] Perspectives that focus primarily on the risks and challenges faced by certain groups of youth narrowly conceptualize or ignore systems of oppression that trigger outcomes that society defines as maladaptive and antisocial.[34] The fact of resiliency and opportunities for ecological systems to provide support and afford opportunities for good outcomes are critical.[35]

PVEST is an identity-focused cultural ecological perspective that suggests significant and unavoidable plasticity.[36] *Recognizing the ability for change is a critical observation.* It is significant for the character of policies and practices intended to be supportive. It also aids in the identification of those having potential for increased vulnerability and negative outcomes. It recognizes intersubjective meaning-making and access to assets precipitating possibilities for resiliency and well-being in spite of static conditions.

PVEST combines an emphasis on individual perceptions with Bronfenbrenner's ecological systems theory. It links context and perception, giving fuller meaning to intersubjective processes and intersectionality.[37] As an example, Spencer and colleagues have challenged the widely disseminated explanation of the achievement gap as caused by minority students failing to adopt a Eurocentric value system.[38] They argue that this explanation fails to account for the way that high Afrocentricity can help students in forming high self-esteem and developing personal achievement goals.[39] This reveals a far more complex and significant process that includes own-group orientation and identification.

Too frequently, the human vulnerability variations and so-called gaps reflect the relationship between unacknowledged risks and frequently ignored privileges as protective factors. Supports matter given the obligation to confront the requirements of developmental tasks as well as to satisfy a hierarchy of needs.[40] There are few points across the life course other than adolescence (another is the first two years of life and, particularly, the neonatal period) when the invisible or unacknowledged character of vulnerability has more critical implications. Sources of assets and supports are multiple, such as responsive cultural practices including the arts, cultural socialization, and social movements that serve to benefit survival and in many cases provide thriving, resiliency, and protection. Many exemplars of good outcomes in the face of long-term oppression are well represented as authentic life outcomes for individuals and communities. Infrequently, however, do they make their way into programs of research and applications as factors promoting resiliency. For example, as suggested by Siddle-Walker's historical review, Black schooling provided core teaching and structural models for Black learning successes even when actively prohibited by Whites, evident during slavery and afterward.[41] According to Hope and Spencer, the civic engagement of communities also provided effective supports.[42] These insights are essential in the structuring of *Brown*'s implementation.

PVEST's theoretical perspective critically includes the chronosystem level of the ecology as well as the structured nature of dehumanizing systems for its palpable impact. Human development-linked intersubjectivity made the fact of their structured character and normative implementation of Black inhumanity practices another source of risk and stress experienced across developmental stages. The lack of efforts to acknowledge the history and to consider adequate supports for diminishing vulnerability and intergenerational trauma while increasing well-being through adaptive coping inputs is part of a pattern evident in the remedy implemented by *Brown* to address the complex manifestations, systems, and intersubjective meanings of inhumanity.

Tangibles requiring interrogation and considerations for authentic change are not enough. The intangibles are even more critical and remain unaddressed today. Individuals, families, and communities engage in reactive and stable identity strategies in myriad ways. The diverse strategies devised and utilized both individually and collectively (e.g., family-level and community-socialization-relevant coping devices) vary in efficacy. Many strategies have resulted in multiple instances of resiliency.[43] Not unexpectedly, evidence of high vulnerability persists four hundred years following the dehumanizing arrival of Blacks to North America. In addition—given significant levels of high risk and unaddressed challenges—coping responses include colorism traditions.[44] Graham's classic work investigates the impact of color and class within Black communities, demonstrating the impact and complexity of identity processes given context features even within race.[45]

Color and racial preferences and attitudes begin early and are noticeable features of children's palate of color categories as learned labels and associated connotative markers. For young children—as protected by cognitive ego-centered thinking—the evaluative associations for the colors black and white are not internalized but are "reported" as knowledge. They are not internalized but represent one's "store of knowledge" given social learning "opportunities." Because race awareness takes place in parallel with cognitive maturation, it is possible that children can share their strong learning of labels without an internalization of any associated affect.[46] Given the widely disseminated negative message about Black color and skin tone connotations versus positive associations of Whiteness, children report their knowledge of "social messages" regarding widely disseminated values, preferences, and attitudes about skin color and the colors black and white. However, cultural socialization provided for children by families and communities frequently prevent the internalization of preference and attitude labels.[47] Without the cultural socialization intervention and with the unavoidable fact of cognitive maturation and race awareness, children may be left to infer meanings about skin color and self-processes on their own. It is essential that we understand and utilize these interventions even while eliminating the need for them.

PVEST serves a critical interrogation needed for a rereading of *Brown*. As an inclusive conceptual device, it provides opportunity for a human development and context-sensitive explication of identity formation essential to *Brown*. More specifically, PVEST's phenomenological, ecological, and identity-focused framing provides a heuristic function in the interrogation of the remedy's efficacy for ending America's segregation problem given hundreds of years of Black dehumanization.

In the phenomenological tradition, utilizing phenomenology as a framing device is given a much wider range in our rereading. It addresses the meanings situations have in our experience; particularly notable is the significance of objects, events, tools, time, the self, and others providing sense-making as they are experienced in our "life-world." None of these human processes, which serve to protect and positively serve the self, were acknowledged in the implementation of *Brown*.

Phenomenology provides scaffolding. It remains foundational to the maturation, context, culture, and psychosocial life course-salient processes represented by PVEST.[48] The combined unavoidable meaning-making from intersubjective awareness expressly at adolescence and the intersectionality impact of protective factors, or their absence, make PVEST especially helpful for understanding adolescence and the life course for humans, but particularly those who are oppressed and dehumanized if one is concerned with supports having authentic impact. It is the unavoidable impact and awareness of intersubjective human processes and PVEST framing that make each helpful for appreciating why intersectionality is important.

Conclusion

The implications of intersectionality and identity processes observed from a phenomenological variant of ecological systems theory are clear. The ending of segregation provided by the *Brown* decision as implemented was never intended to provide freedom and equality for Black people. While in principle allowing little Black boys and girls to attend White, well-resourced schools with White girls and boys, hegemony was to be maintained within a particular and limited meaning of freedom. White freedom limits hierarchy placement to Whites. No matter the shared category demarcating status (i.e., race, gender, immigration status, body type, skin color, etc.), the demographics that have value are only those representing White bodies.[49]

As Jamelle Bouie notes:

If, as Stovall argues, "liberty and whiteness have been mutually reinforcing" throughout Western history and if "racial distinctions have played a key role in modern ideas of freedom," then the task of all those who seek a more inclusive and egalitarian freedom has been to challenge the hierarchies that have shaped and structured "freedom" as we understand it—along with the material realities that undergird and reinforce them.[50]

Experiences of intersectionality represent and impact all levels of the ecology navigated and experienced by all humans. Importantly, intersectionality exposes the points of overlap, which contribute to heightened experiences of oppression or privilege otherwise generally left invisible. PVEST makes it evident that intersectionality is exacerbated by context and is made worse by racial stigma.[51] The impact is evident across ecologies but remains functionally invisible. The implications for learning contexts are deeply unequal.

Our call for careful analysis and rereading of *Brown* suggests that all segregation-ending strategies may be lacking if intersubjectivity and intersectionality are ignored. Particularly salient for our rereading of *Brown*, then, is the need to consider the required critical character of risks, protective factors, supports, and challenges and the character of adaptive coping strategies leading to underperformance or resiliency.

The developmental core, the necessity of confronting, destroying, and dismantling the comprehensive scope of inhumanity, including the systems it has spawned and structured, is required by *Brown*'s central holding. We have deeply explored the developmental consequences of the failure to implement *Brown*'s mandate and the scope of what is required. PVEST provides the essential framework to implement that mandate. In part III we turn to implementation of Radical *Brown*. Chapter 9 provides policy analysis and argues for a robust set of factors for the interrogation needed for effective policies. Chapter 10 provides examples of effective programming options. The exemplars use the components of the innovative human development supports needed for authentic change. Both policy and specific exemplar programs incorporating humanity-acknowledging conceptualization and implementation strategies matter.

PART III

Implementing Radical *Brown*

CHAPTER 9

Policy

RADICAL *BROWN* is a guiding framework that drives a vision of equality requiring comprehensive implementation. Creativity is key. Essential to change is remaining focused on the goal of equal humanity, being responsive and agile in order to move forward, and holding steadfast against inevitable pushback. PVEST provides a framework for the complexity of the task.

The process of change requires long-term commitment and a recognition that radical change evolves. It involves a process of unfreezing, reconceptualization, and structural change to implement a new vision.[1] It begins with political and cultural commitment; that is what Radical *Brown* is about—the envisioning of the radical embrace of shared humanity.

Most importantly, policy frameworks must be devised to achieve the critical *intangible* goal of *Brown*, the goal of fostering every child's common humanity. This must include the differential tasks of dealing with issues of subordination as well as issues of privilege, to support equal worthiness in place of racial hierarchy and inequities. A policy of full national implementation ensures the principle not of mean-spirited, limited equality within a localized narrow definition, but of universal robust equality. At the same time, the scope of policy must include equal *tangible* factors in support of each child's humanity.

The core goal is humanity: accepting, recognizing, and valuing the humanity of all. It requires looking back to recognize the systemic and cultural depth of our task, how facially racially discriminatory policies as well as facially neutral policies with clear racially disproportionate effects sustained inequality. Looking back also ensures that we are clear about what must be accounted for by repair or reparations. Just as importantly, we must look forward. The core goal of humanity translates timeless principles ("We the People") into our current context. The key words of the Declaration of Independence, the Constitution, and the *Brown* decision—equality, freedom, liberty—must have present meaning in order to be meaning*ful*. Radical *Brown* articulates both the essential backward-looking context and the critical forward-looking vision of the meaning of equality, freedom, and liberty. The key is common humanity, a humanity not limited by the vision of the founders, but instead the humanity of the Reconstruction Amendments, Radical Reconstruction, and *Brown*. The focus is on Black Americans because it is their humanity that is the polestar. White racial identity, for too long fused with White supremacy, must be reconfigured to an egalitarian foundation.

We also argue that the core principle of Radical *Brown* necessarily extends beyond educational equality. Education intersects with a comprehensive environment of interlocking systems and culture that affect children. The racial justice framework of Radical *Brown* must be linked to other racial justice needs. *Brown* established a mandate that was not limited to schools; it was the basis for the dismemberment of Jim Crow, which remains incomplete. Radical *Brown* stands for multisystemic equality for all. Children may have unique claims for equal developmental support, but both children and adults should benefit from the full implementation of Radical *Brown*: to recognize and support the equal value and humanity of all persons.

We begin by suggesting framing principles for implementation. We then discuss educational policy, subdivided into intangible and tangible factors. In the final section we look to the intersecting systems that affect children's lives that are essential to achieve their equal humanity.

Framing Policy: Principles

The goal of Radical *Brown* is full personhood and citizenship. As Malcom X explained, "We have to keep in mind at all times that we are not fighting for integration, nor are we fighting for separation. We are fighting for recognition as free humans in this society.[2] Essential to Radical *Brown* is the recognition of the developmental, humanity-focused meaning of *Brown*, coupled with our legal analysis of *Brown*'s incorporation of that humanity focus by its embrace of the meaning of equality as comprehensive and "perfect."

Several perspectives must be incorporated in framing policy. One essential framing component is a robust notion of *equality*. "Equality" as currently interpreted constitutionally typically means "sameness." Sameness is often limited to the idea that each person gets the same benefits, or the same amounts of inputs. But sameness from the perspective of Radical *Brown* is the sameness of shared, "same" humanity, achieving inclusion by the *same* capability to exercise full humanity and citizenship. For children, equality means the support to develop to their *same* maximum developmental capacity. Sameness means same opportunities, outcomes, and equities. "Born equal, equally supported developmentally, children would arrive at the threshold of adulthood as equal social citizens."[3] It is critical to emphasize that sameness is in relation to *humanity*, not in relation to Whiteness. To say that equality means children of color have the same support, tangible and intangible, as White children makes Whiteness the standard of what is valued and thus worthy of support. It continues to racialize, create hierarchy, and sustain inequality amidst purported equality. Keeping identity in mind to achieve equality does not mean adopting, intentionally or unintentionally, Whiteness as the definition of full humanity. Humanity stands as its own definition. Sameness is the recognition and support of equal shared humanity. Sameness is the recognition that human processes are the same although the ecologies where intersubjectively is expressed may vary.

A second essential component is *equity*. Equity means fairness, accepting children where they stand—now and in the future—and ensuring the means for each child to develop to their maximum developmental capacity. As things currently stand, with gaping inequalities between children and their contexts, equity requires attending to each child's *needs* in order to achieve their full developmental capacity. If a child arrives at kindergarten not school-ready, that means providing all necessary resources to build their skills while creating the support systems to prevent the repetition of failed or missing early childhood policy. If a child is identified as having disabilities, it means providing the support to maximize their developmental capacity with the accommodations and additional supports to fully achieve. Equity must trigger the inquiry not only of "what happened to you" but also "what structures or policies failed you and caused or exacerbated the harm of what happened to you." Equity is a focus on needs. Equity must not be used to hide or excuse structural inequalities, but to respond to, expose, and dismantle them and refine our approach to maximize each child's developmental capacity.

A third critical component is *dignity*. Dignity has been defined by one scholar in three ways: as an inherent human characteristic, as a way of describing how one should be treated by others, and as affirmative state obligation to support each person through the provision of socioeconomic rights. All three meanings are essential to humanity, encapsulated in the concept of "worthiness."[4] Dignity requires the valuing of identities and cultures. It involves not merely respect or toleration, but empowerment. It means not only the recognition of Blackness as valued humanity, but also the rejection of Whiteness as the standard of value. It requires the reconfiguration of White identity away from supremacy and privilege toward shared humanity. For every person, it involves the freedom to explore and expand racial identity in individual ways while remaining dedicated to shared humanity.

A final component in the framing of policy incorporates *children's rights*. Children's rights, and specifically their equality rights, are distinctive because of their dependency on adults for their development. Their rights are inherently needs-based, and unique, because of their dependency. They are vulnerable throughout their development, vulnerability that changes over time but remains present until adulthood. Children have a distinctive relationship to society that justifies society's unique responsibility for them: children are our future, and as social citizens they are essential to our democracy. As Barbara Woodhouse has argued, each generation has a responsibility to the next to provide holistic support.[5]

This vision of universalism and shared humanity is dependent on close attention to the identities that define hierarchies among children. Priscilla Ocen reminds us that "presumptions of childhood" apply differentially by race, treating children of color as neither children nor as adults, to their disadvantage.[6] Khiara Bridges exposes how concepts like "privacy" as practiced are not inclusive of the marginalized, such as poor women and families.[7] This calls on us to infuse equality, equity, and dignity as well as children's rights with what Robin Lenhardt calls "race-attentive" inquiry to ensure that law and policy do not subordinate families along racial lines.[8] We must also use care so that children's rights are not "domesticated" to a universal standard that, like "color-blindness," hides a dominant norm and continues to reinforce hierarchies among children.

One last essential concept is *time*: a clear understanding of what came before and its persistence today, and how that operates developmentally as well as how it must be defeated and destroyed structurally. The key to this factor are the deep historical interconnected systems of racial hierarchy and inhumanity that persist and remain today; this infuses the cultural layers, and connects systems, structures, and policies at all developmental levels. This notion of time is captured by the concept of the *chronosystem* that we have referenced. The chronosystem impacts the life course and intergenerational replication inequalities. A chronosystem grounding helps identify harm and the scope of remedy and affirmative vision.

With these framing principles in mind, we move to suggest intangible and tangible components to Radical *Brown* policy implementation in public education.

Implementing Radical Brown in Public Education K–12
Intangibles
It is the intangible factors that lie at the heart of Radical *Brown*: equality requires recognition and support for the equal humanity and

developmental equality of every child. As the Court said in *Brown*, "We come then to the question presented: does the segregation of children in public schools solely on the basis of race, even though the physical facilities and other "tangible" factors may be equal, deprive the children of the minority group of equal educational opportunities? We believe that it does."[9]

A comprehensive approach to the intangible factors essential to the developmental equality of each child means engaging with developmental science to ensure the support for maximum developmental capacity. How do we teach and support humanity for each child's recognition of their identity and value, and their treatment of all other children as having equal humanity? Radical *Brown* would require continuous questioning and attentiveness to whether each child's humanity is supported. This requires multiple engagements across education in every intangible aspect.

Multicultural education in its most critical, radical, comprehensive form might be an example of a possible starting point. This would include curriculum, pedagogy, teacher training, and recruitment of multiracial faculty. As part of teacher training and student education, the insights of explicit and implicit bias are essential to engage in fostering equity rather than ignoring bias, as well as using anti-stereotyping interventions to undermine and eliminate hierarchies. The integral components of ethnic studies, Afrocentric curriculum, and antiracist education would be parts of a multicultural education lens. The goal would be to change K–12 education from a reinforcement of racial hierarchy, White supremacy, and the devaluing of students of color to an equality system. Rather than an "add-on" to existing educational content and methods, or a minimal part of teacher training and recruitment, this would require wholesale reorientation of all aspects of education in order to effect change in school culture. The content and the methods must be critically reexamined and reoriented to serve all students, not just a privileged subset of students.

As Sonia Nieto has noted, "At its core, multicultural education is a direct challenge to public education's Eurocentric focus and curriculum, as well as to the starkly uneven outcomes of education that have been particularly onerous for children whose race, ethnicity, native language, and social class differ from the majority group."[10] Nieto articulates five critical aspects of radical, reconceptualized multicultural education: (1) including power issues in regard to institutional policies and practices, (2) questioning *what* is taught with a multiracial curricular goal, (3) focusing on *how* the curriculum is taught, or critical pedagogy, (4) providing essential care to students, grounded in their lived realities, and (5) supporting the happiness and well-being of students, with a focus on their identities, perspectives, and experiences, and engaging them as active participants in their education.[11]

Education is not neutral, in content or in teaching. Paolo Freire argues that education can teach to reinforce hierarchy and conformity, or it can teach to encourage critical thinking and freedom.[12] Freire's model of education is intersubjective, with teachers and students mutually teaching and learning through their interaction. The goal is "humanization as a permanent process."[13]

Multicultural education requires the careful examination of content so as not to privilege only a single culture as a source of content or values and to ensure inclusion of all students by attentiveness to pedagogical methods. It must engage with the circumstances, ecologies, and identities of all children in the room. The multicultural perspective, in its strongest, most critical, most comprehensive form supports the common and equal humanity of every child by respecting the multiracial, multiethnic, multicultural contributions of all students. This is not a colorblind or neutral view of education, but instead a recognition of the necessity of a thoroughgoing reorientation of content to support every child's identity and development. It also challenges White identity's incorporation and sustenance of White supremacy.

Nieto defines multiculturalism as including "education for social justice."[14] Education for social justice exemplifies the affirmative, proactive education of every child in the meaning of equality, equity, and dignity; in the history and manifestations of racism; and in the methods and importance of valuing every peer in all their critical identities. Geneva Gay aptly calls this "curriculum desegregation and equity pedagogy."[15] Critical questions include, "Whose knowledge is it? Who selected it? Why is it organized and taught in this way? To this particular group?"[16] The content of curriculum is not neutral, nor should it purport to be so. The claim of neutrality too often hides the White gaze and White content. The result is the perpetuation of hierarchy, particularly exacerbated by the preponderance in K–12 education of White female teachers.

Radical multiculturalism is comprehensive, thorough, and ongoing, a transformative project rather than a diluted additive to White-centered education—critical and revolutionary by comparison to the policy and structure, the values and norms, of existing patterns of education.[17] Particularly important are issues of cultural identity and the organization of knowledge, emphasizing multiplicity and difference.[18]

Curriculum might also incorporate "racial literacy," a concept advocated by Katheryn Russell-Brown.[19] Russell-Brown suggests this as one way to reshape understanding and undermine mythology, by offering a preliminary index of "seminal laws, cases, incidents, and people [that] highlights the broad, deep, and historical ways that race works."[20] This example of substantive curricular change could be multiplied by many others.

As essential as curriculum is pedagogy. Identifying, reviving, and valuing African American pedagogy would provide an incredible resource.[21] Chike Akua identifies thirteen Afrocentric educational (ACE) standards. Three in particular illustrate parallel principles to critical multiculturalism: the incorporation of an African value system, promoting cooperation and collectivism; a social justice orientation; and an appreciation of multiple cultures.[22] We might also draw inspiration for critical pedagogy from bell hooks's call of "teaching to transgress,"[23] a model of empowering students while engaging teachers in growth.[24] Teaching requires self-critique, self-knowledge, and engagement with (all) students.

The engagement of teachers with all students must be complemented by attention to peer interactions. All the human interactions in the room must be grounded in freedom and equality. Michelle Fine, Lois Weis, and Linda Powell describe the creation of "desegregated spaces," defined in their work as equal spaces that work equally well for all kids.[25] They link this concept to Gordon Allport's contact theory concept of "equal status contact," generating less prejudice and bias as the result of intergroup contact under conditions of equality.[26] Optimal conditions according to Allport include four features: equal status of groups, common goals, intergroup cooperation, and the support of authorities, law, and custom.[27]

The factors in Allport's model are compatible with Radical *Brown*, going far beyond the "mere bodies" or numbers approach to "integration." It is a theory that imagines the value of multiracial students in a multiracial, multicultural curriculum as generating knowledge, understanding, and learning that promote equal valuing and social equality. Pettigrew and Tropp claim that multiracial youth relationships require "a sense of community; a commitment to creative analysis of difference, power, and privilege; and an enduring investment in democratic practice with youth."[28] They link what happens in school with what might happen for students as adults. This is a vision of an entirely different school culture consistent with Radical *Brown*.

The transformation of school culture, peer relationships, and teacher–student relationships might shift schools from what Elise Boddie calls "racial territoriality" to the humanization of school space.[29] "Racial territoriality occurs when the state excludes people of color from—or marginalizes them within—racialized white spaces that have a racially exclusive history, practice, and/or reputation."[30] The Whiteness of a space, with the intention or effect of exclusion and/or subordination, is based on "demographic data, patterns of current racial separateness and prior segregation, and reputational evidence regarding how both public and private actors have treated people of color in the space."[31] The opposite, Boddie suggests, is "spatial belonging."[32] Boddie elaborates on her vision by defining equality as "ordinariness": "the state of being treated as a full, complex person and a rightful recipient of human concern."[33] This standard of ordinariness connects to the comprehensive, pervasive nature of segregation and ongoing racism, "the quiet trauma that comes from being the persistent object of societal fear and resentment."[34] Ordinariness does not mean identity erasure or neutrality; rather, it is the embrace of the positivity of cultural and social differences in an everyday interaction of respect and value.[35]

There are difficulties and challenges in achieving inclusive school culture, learning, and curriculum. In our current climate a sustained assault on curriculum, particularly that surrounding racial history and identities, has coalesced around an attack on critical race theory. This attack not only misrepresents critical race theory, but also constitutes a thinly veiled attempt to erase the history and context that is foundational to Radical *Brown* and would be hostile to the creation of an inclusive, comprehensively equal school culture.

Tangibles

Adequate and equal funding of public education is one of the tangibles that has failed to be accomplished under *Brown* as implemented. Radical *Brown*, however, would include both tangible and intangible factors centered around the core proposition of equal support of the humanity and developmental support of every child to their maximum capacity. Equal, equitable funding to support every child's developmental equality is foundational, although not sufficient by itself.

Funding disparities are unconscionable and unacceptable under a Radical *Brown* framework. Inequities exist between states, within states, and within school districts. Funding inequities affect school facilities, equipment, books, technology, literally every aspect of the school budget. The experience level and competency of teachers is also disproportionately skewed against the kids with the greatest needs and away from poor kids and kids of color. Another tangible effect of funding inequality is the scope of the curriculum, literally what classes are offered.

Funding disparities are linked to the physical demarcation of school districts, with ongoing patterns of racially configured school attendance lines in urban and suburban school districts.[36] In some areas, the phenomenon of "secession" districts, literally districts created by leaving a multiracial school district, create predominantly White schools.[37] Patterns of disparate funding are defined by race and class, creating a monopolization of resources and "social closure" that benefit middle- and upper-class White students while excluding students of color.[38]

The Education Law Center's National Report Card uses four "fairness measures" to define funding equity: funding level (combining local, state, and federal resources), funding distribution (paying attention to poverty concentration and the need for more funds to address poverty related needs), effort (state spending relative to state fiscal capacity), and coverage (proportion of school-aged children attending public school versus private schools).[39] There also are equity models outside of the United States, in the countries to which we most commonly compare ourselves. The Organization for Economic Co-operation and Development (OECD) has been particularly concerned with socioeconomic inequities that create opportunity disparities in the absence of structures that explicitly ensure the maximum development of every child.[40]

A second area that is often treated as a tangible factor is achievement levels. In our view, this is a deficit approach that has focused on what students, parents, and communities lack rather than structural or systemic impediments. The data on the achievement gap can be used, however, to expose an "opportunity gap,"[41] or "receivement gap." The gap would expose patterns of support (or the lack of it) from systems, structure, policies, culture, and resources that disparately impact kids of color.[42] Or this might be framed as an affirmative community-based definition of equity as proposed by one group of scholars, grounded in the notion of educational debt owed to address subordinating structures and multiple gaps in teacher quality, teacher training, curriculum, funding, digital resources, wealth and income, employment opportunity, affordable housing, health care, nutrition, quality childcare, and integration.[43]

High performing schools, it turns out, have high expectations and great teachers and strong parental involvement. Majority minority schools succeed within this framework, although they are often treated as an exception.[44] Within those schools are likely additional keys to success.

Sean Reardon advocates the benefit of integrated schools for closing the achievement gap, emphasizing the benefits of not only racial integration but also socioeconomic integration.[45] Others as well have used the low socioeconomic status/poverty frame as an alternative to racial policies.[46] Tomiko Brown-Nagan argues for a "holistic" approach to educating children of poverty, including a trauma-informed approach to thinking about school culture and student support. Brown-Nagan's inclusion of culture as part of the equation of achievement is notable. She also looks at the intersection of housing and education.[47] This is a more comprehensive model with the goal of quality education, not achievement per se, focused on the structural problems that undermine education and that require solutions that reach beyond school walls.

The tangibles are important and significant. But just as a "mere bodies" approach misunderstands the scope of Radical *Brown*, so does equality solely focused on the tangible factors. Tangible factors provide support for equal humanity, but tangibles alone are not enough; they are merely one step.

A New Deal for Children: Interlocking Systemic Change

Radical *Brown* fully implemented, including both intangible and tangible components, would not be sufficient if it were only limited to schools. Fulfillment of every aspect of systemic educational equity would not be sufficient to achieve equality. It is clear beyond doubt that children's development, the maximization of their capacity, cannot be accomplished by schools alone. Pedro Noguera, at the sixtieth anniversary of *Brown*, argued that the core unresolved problem is the education of poor children of color in cities.[48] Educational inequity, then, is part of a host of inequities, although perhaps more morally reprehensible because, as currently structured, it often makes inequities worse instead of better.[49] Richard Rothstein, among many other scholars, emphasizes that economic and social conditions for the poorest children must change, as must the practice of concentrating the poorest kids in certain schools.[50]

What this points to as part of Radical *Brown* is the need for a comprehensive New Deal for Children. Equal education cannot flourish amidst other interlocking systems of inequality. The realization of Radical *Brown* in the public education system requires the systemic reform of all systems that touch on children's development as well as their interaction in the ecology of childhood. This includes the creation of systems of developmental support to ensure developmental equality, and the elimination of overarching, inter- and intra-systemic issues that transcend and infect specific systems: poverty and racism. As these system needs are essential to achieving children's equality, they are essential to Radical *Brown*.[51] They are linked, as *Brown* is, to dismantling not only segregation in public education, but all aspects of segregation's comprehensive, systemic, legal, and social manifestations.

Dowd coined the term "New Deal for Children" to describe the scope of system reform as well as system creation necessary to achieve children's equality.[52] Her New Deal for Children consciously draws on the New Deal of the 1930s as an example of comprehensive policy-making (as well as other comprehensive programs, such as the GI Bill and the Great Society Programs). At the same time, the New Deal for Children aims to improve on those previous historical examples, as they incorporated racial hierarchy into purportedly universal public policy.

The New Deal for Children assumes state responsibility for the developmental support of all children, therefore a "responsive state." State responsibility would include dismantling policies and structures that hinder children's development. It would focus on identities that mark existing children's hierarchies and would require paying attention to race and gender as well as other categories to monitor, correct, and dismantle structures and policies that create developmental challenges. Just as importantly, it would require affirmative support to foster children's development to their maximum capacity, building human capital and changing the macrosystem concerning the value and equality of all children. This would be grounded in concepts of children's rights as affirmative rights based on their dependency, vulnerability, and needs, and their preparation for equal social citizenship.

This comprehensive approach would require not only significant reform of existing systems critical to children that intersect with education (such as housing, income supports, health, and juvenile justice), but also system creation (such as early childhood and family supports). It requires addressing overarching problems that have multisystemic effects (poverty and racism). The vision of the New Deal is to ensure interconnection with the whole, rather than isolation of systems, and dedication to developmental equality for all children.

Within this comprehensive model, it is critical to sustain the focus on racial equality.[53] There are assuredly other patterns in the hierarchies among children that require our attention. But we should resist moving away from race. Racial inequalities among children should remain front and center, not be lost in a "universal" model. We should insist that *all* children be supported to develop to their maximum capacity, but we must be unflinching in our scrutiny of how race compromises and challenges the opportunities of children of color.

Can the intrusive state become a responsive state? Can the state be affirmative, respectful, and supportive? The notion of the responsive state is one supportive of all people, oriented to their needs, creating opportunities, and dedicated to equality, equity, and dignity. Nothing in the nature of the state prohibits this.

We have ample models of such a state. For example, in the Scandinavian countries and, more generally, in the countries of the European Union, the role of the state is understood as supporting the people as an expression of collective responsibility. By no means perfect, these models nevertheless provide examples of a responsive state. Their policies include income supports, housing, and health care in an equity framework. Education encompasses the support of all children with high-quality early childhood education through tuition-free post-secondary education.

Our recent policies in response to the COVID19 pandemic arguably are an American example of responsive state policy. Economic policies lifted more children out of poverty than at any other point in recent history. Yet the reversal of many COVID19 policies once the pandemic was declared over illustrates the limitations of situationally limited policy. Moreover, it cannot be ignored that we are in a particularly fraught moment concerning the role of the state. Many powerful forces call not for a responsive state but for an authoritarian state that dictates social, educational, and health policies in hierarchical, subordinating terms.

As Radical *Brown* makes clear, *Brown*'s mandate is to implement at all costs comprehensive humanity. Radical *Brown* is the promise of every child's humanity in a comprehensive system of equality for the benefit of all.

CHAPTER 10

Successful Programming Approaches

OUR RADICAL REREADING OF *BROWN* emphasizes the dilemma and impact of *not recognizing the humanity of Black and Brown humans* on all levels of American life. The existence of dehumanization as a normative context-linked process both affects and is inferred from everyday cultural traditions and policies, with voluminous and long-term consequences. It is essential in framing policy, or in the design of specific ground-up programs—such as the exemplars described in this chapter—to be mindful at all levels of design and implementation of the essence of humanity. This must infuse research undergirding social, health, and economic policies that affect the quality and efficacy of intended designated supports. Just as importantly, the essence of humanity must be the polestar for individual actions essential to the change envisioned by Radical *Brown*.

Individual Action: Engaging Humanity, Confronting "Missed Opportunities"

Myriad representations of unacknowledged fBIP demonstrate that there is no doubt that accumulated generations of inhumanity have embedded inequality structurally and systemically. And yet the significance of the nation's uncontested mores, the interpersonal relationships they solidify, the structured inequalities they codify, and the identities they impact can make "structural bias" an "innocent framing." The "innocence appearance" of the term and its dissonance utilization in fact ignore the problem of countless *tangible and intangible, visible and invisible forms of violence.* Structural bias embodies continually perpetrated cultural practices (e.g., intergenerationally practiced physical, interpersonal, and racial trauma), systematically and structurally imposed without core reflections about its contributions to a dehumanization process.[1] We do not deny structural bias; rather, we insist that individual beliefs, actions, and interactions are critical to understand where we are and also to acknowledge the role of *each of us* in order to move forward. This is our opportunity: the opportunity for individual, daily action that does not require policy or programs. At the same time, within policy and programs, individual meaning-making and identities are the key to collective equality and equity.

The importance of the individual perspective is best demonstrated by intergenerational socialization and its impact. Considered across four hundred years or twenty generations, for a hegemony-embracing White family—representing a "family line" of particular beliefs, attitudes, and assumptions about racial differences—think of the "conversation opportunities" about shared humanity. If we assume two family meals a week, approximately a hundred meals annually, consider those conversations over four hundred years. Annually, a family line will have experienced forty thousand "meal-time missed conversations" about shared humanity. This hypothesized number of estimated "missed socialization opportunities" for a family line of White families over generations informs practiced intangibles. The missed meal-time conversations acknowledge failure as opportunities to impact systemic Brown and Black dehumanizing language, assumptions, everyday practices, and organized traditions. It suggests the deep cultural practices and roots of White "harm invisibility." From a socio-emotional perspective, we hazard that this historic shortcoming contributes to hegemonic values and beliefs as well as character virtue. The lack of "socialization practice" facilitates conditions of dehumanization and experiences of trauma for those viewed as "other" and at the same time weakens positive reactive coping opportunities in responding to cultural differences. The situation is due to the many intangibles impacted by missed socialization opportunities to embrace shared humanity. Lost as well is the appreciation of a status of shared human vulnerability and shared expectations for the successful completion of developmental tasks expected of all citizens across the life course. Without a perspective of shared humanity and vulnerability, a failure to obtain success feeds into subsequent assumptions of intersectional perspectives about assumed inferiority.

Absent from everyday consciousness and achieved over four hundred years has been nothing less than highly effective *social amnesia*. We suggest, vis-à-vis collective memory, acts of knowledge suppression that matter.[2] Recent pushback against credentialing an African American history and culture AP course created by the College Board exemplifies social amnesia as well as knowledge resistance. AP course options have been offered long term for European history, United States history, and AP language and culture courses for Chinese, German, French, and Italian language and culture. Resistance to offering African American history contributes to social amnesia since it serves to diminish the knowledge pool critical for collective memory. Resisting the crediting of such courses suggests—vis-à-vis knowledge suppression—an ongoing organized struggle to demean, discredit, and ignore the history of the dehumanization of people of color. Such shortcomings maintain the tradition of physical and interpersonal racial trauma and the long-term impact on the human development of individuals of color.[3]

"We the People" has neither included people of color nor stood for practiced traditions of equality, inclusion, diversity, and adequate conditions and supports serving the needs of equity. Equity and equitable supports are those assistive to individuals' actual situations (i.e., events representing the phenomenology of individuals themselves rather than the preferences and perspectives of those having power to design and implement "intended" supportive change). It is for this reason that our rereading and interrogation of *Brown* has been framed from a particular identity focus and culturally sensitive theoretical stance. PVEST acknowledges the critical task of conceding individuals' meanings made from endogenously experienced authentic situations as opposed to assumptions inferred from exogenous sources (i.e., assumptions and

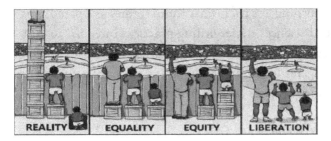

Figure 10.1 Illustrating equality vs. equity. *Source*: Shrehan Lynch, Sue Sutherland, and Jennifer Walton-Fisette, "The A–Z of Social Justice Physical Education: Part 1," *Journal of Physical Education, Recreation and Dance* 91, no. 4 (May 3, 2020): 8–13.

judgements made by those having power but lacking insights into culturally evolved traditions and shared identities). When the experience of liberty does not occur for particular populations, then, equity suggests the need for supports that fit the authentic need with the goal of a shared experience of liberation (see figure 10.1).[4]

Core Consideration Essential to Programs of Change

The intergenerational consistency of biases remains associated with a particular mindset that has prevented the realization of *Brown*. Moving beyond individual action to suggest the shape of ground-up collective actions for change, two successful exemplar programs are described that have been effective in withstanding the problem of dehumanization as a core challenge to Black children's thriving. Before describing the underlying assumptions and the specific practices of these programs, we emphasize two essential considerations.[5]

First, we caution that the use of science to construct programs requires great care. A perspective often used to exemplify the efficacy of science is its claim of objectivity; that is, the undergirding viewpoint is that the scientific implementation and analysis process is value neutral. Our perspective emphasizes the role of *character virtue* in the structuring of and implementation of accrued knowledge. Second, we draw attention to *group memory*. The respective contributions of each of these principles to the continuation of Black dehumanization traditions require nothing less than what Kuhn frames as a paradigmatic shift in the social sciences undergirding practices intended to sustain shared human development.[6] Functioning as impediments, the possibilities for well-being, resiliency, and thriving and demonstrations of developmental specific successes are undermined.[7]

Character Virtue

The foundational role of science in the maintenance of problematic social mores is highly salient in that it may misdirect and frame issues inappropriately. When it comes to deeply held cultural practices around "race difference beliefs" and "dehumanizing traditions" functioning as intangibles, strongly held traditions persist. Thus, seventy years after *Brown* and generations after Blacks' arrival in North America, the residual of such beliefs as repertoires of practice remains.[8] The content of interventions, programming, and learning traditions is impacted by the science from which it is produced and its leadership.

Character virtue is important and universal. Highly salient to character virtue development is education, as well as associated social policies, responsive socialization efforts (or their absence), interpersonal relations and interactive practices, linked academic curricula, and the scaffolding supports. In sum, education and social practices function as tools of control.

The scaffolding principles of character virtue represent a subset of social and emotional learning (SEL). The subset of SEL promotes specific traits, including honesty, compassion, self-discipline, and perseverance. Character virtue principles are represented in particular ways within the social and developmental science traditions. Desirable traits are often investigated and applied to research subjects. Judged evaluatively, the traits function as the focus of scholarly agendas and programs of research; they train practitioners who often deliver interventions determined by social science decision-makers. As topics—given their "treatment" and "representation" of various groups (e.g., as questions posed, variables selected, data analyses and their interpretation)—efforts contribute to literatures in the training of professionals and interpretation of interpersonal relationships among individuals and behaviors produced by them. This research provides national direction as policy, practice, and evaluation. In sum, knowledge production—represented particularly by social science leadership and attendant character virtue—matters profoundly. It serves as a cog in the wheel of influence, including what and who gets funded and by how much. Scholarly contributions—as a knowledge base—have implications for perspectives collectively shared as well as interpretations made of individuals' socio-emotional functioning.[9]

Our interrogation of and references to character virtue research references both the "producers of scholarship" and those who are represented as "the subjects" of social science efforts. There is frequently a failure to apply SEL-precipitated traits to our own individual and collective science traditions. Influenced by an anthropological perspective and cultural sensitivities, their emphasis as an epistemic contribution frames "culture as practice." It provides conceptual framing as scaffolding, incentivizing options, and sources of persistent intergenerationally dehumanizing bias. These shortcomings may result in cultural practices that are not of benefit to those for whom they are intended.[10]

Twenty or more generations of Black-White relational traditions and social structurally relevant variations of human vulnerability have institutionalized positionality. From a PVEST perspective, life course experiences, intergenerationally contributed and consciously structured levels of human vulnerability associated with "difference," suggest an uneven or imbalanced quality of vulnerability status. Accordingly, *equality* must focus on, and be inclusive of, the incorporated principle of *equity*, as we have articulated in chapter 9, as an essential, reality-centered policy goal given the status of high vulnerability for some (i.e., Blacks) and structured low vulnerability for others (i.e., Whites). Vulnerability is an unavoidable human status, suggesting particular interpersonal traditions. But vulnerability is not the same for all; it is highly unequal along race lines. Stable repertoires of practice require specific framing, structuring, and undergirding assumptions if an intervention is to be effective in reducing high vulnerability. Failing to do so only reifies inequality. Suggested here is that the tradition of particular cultural practices may limit the expression of promoted traits signaling charac-ter virtue.[11]

Collective Memory

In addition to the research and implementation of character virtue research for programs and policies, the role of memory processes as well has implications for the quality of programming and interventions needed for achieving authentic change. Making use of Erll's differenti-ation between remembrance and knowledge, Vinitzky-Seroussi and Maraschin hazard that social amnesia can be associated with a trau-matic event (such as a pandemic). This perspective is important in that it addresses the importance of admitting the knowledge pole in eval-uating collective memory. The events of American Slavery, Reconstruc-tion, and the aftermath together represent a significant collective memory.[12]

As suggested, historical memory refers to ways in which groups, col-lectivities, and nations construct and identify with particular narratives about historical periods or events. Scholars assume that memory exists beyond the individual's autobiographical experience and is linked to social frameworks and relationships extending across generations. Hal-bwachs went so far as to suggest that a completely isolated individual could not establish any memory at all, as these are built up, developed, and sustained in interaction with others in one's social groups.[13]

Memories of such diverse topics as self, race, and nation can draw from the same sources and materials as historical narrative and can be subject to the same bias, interpretation, and presentation while com-peting with and contesting other narratives. Political and cultural mem-ory are based on the selection and exclusion of memories, ordered and mediated toward a particular end. As Kansteiner notes, collective mem-ory is "as much a result of conscious manipulation as unconscious absorption and it is always mediated."[14]

Psychologists and neuroscientists have criticized human memory for being unreliable and prone to distortion. In the process of remem-bering, rediscovering, and reconstructing memory, there emerges the problem of false memories. These false memories can range from benign and mundane activities to abuse and trauma. A key element of collective memory which distinguishes itself from individual memory is in its ability to preserve the memory of events that some would prefer to forget. The politics of memory has been characterized as rhetoric about the past mobilized for political purposes or employing remembrance for specific aims. It can function as a means of creating "tradition," as an instrument of politics or as a political tool for reshaping understanding of the present by omitting shameful events in the past or reshaping national pasts for current interests. Multiple generations can interpret the same political events differently as mediated by political ideology or partisanship. These contests can take the form of official events such as commemorations, monuments, and truth and reconciliation commissions. They can also exist as intergenerational oral storytelling. Verovšek cautions that the study of the politics of memory should be principally concerned not with correcting people's historical misconceptions but, rather, with identifying where they "come from, how they spread, whose interests they serve and how they are deployed."[15]

Given the multiple ways that memory can function to serve the ego in diminishing experienced stress, its role deserves more research. At both the individual and group levels, the role of social emotional learning and the linked traits of honesty, compassion, self-discipline, and perseverance given the everyday observation of "difference" make the character virtue more complex. Issues of intersectionality matter and may have important implications. The complicating factors of habit, memory, and the significance of intersectionality afford important perspectives for exploration and interrogation; intersectionality is especially relevant when analyzed from a theoretical framing that allows for the consideration of stress, adaptation, and identity processes. Most certainly, information distortion suggests a reactive coping strategy abetted by both individual and collective memory processes.

Brown provided a symbol, linking the Constitution and the rule of law to civil rights and racial equality. Balkin maintains that *Brown* remains important and that the argument is over not whether it was correct but, rather, its meanings and implications. Balkin's perspective somewhat ignores the agency in persistence, which may be abetted by memory processes. Also salient are the everyday human traditions referred to as cultural practices. Of course, never was there mention of Black children's resilience and their requirements for thriving. Given the complicating impacts of character virtue and memory, determining what makes effective programming and thriving is critical.[16]

Resiliency

One final critical caution for programs implementing Radical *Brown* is how we think about resiliency. In our rereading of *Brown*, we have referenced the various ways in which scholars define resilience. While some earlier work characterized resiliency in terms of a quality of hardiness or invulnerability, there remains an ongoing debate as to whether resiliency represents an act, a process, or a personal quality or ability. Resiliency has been described as the "capacity to bounce back," an ability to adapt to adversity or risk. It has been called "ordinary magic" that enables people to obtain normative developmental outcomes in spite of severe challenges. Others have described it as a process of responding to challenges in a way that provides the individual with additional coping skills or protective factors, suggesting the importance of growth and improvement in resilience. Masten represents it as the ordinary normative processes and resources between the individuals, their families, and their broader community.[17]

Werner and Smith observed how the process of resilience builds upon each stage of the life course, noting how protective it appears throughout early childhood and adolescence and, as well, how it can predict the quality of adaptation to stressors later in adulthood. They note differences across gender, with protective factors such as autonomy, scholastic competence, and self-efficacy better contributing to female adaptation in adulthood than for males. On the other hand, protective factors such as family and community had greater impact on male adaptation. Other scholars connect adversity to the positive benefits that can come after a negative experience. Thus, they distinguish between threats and challenges, with the former producing harm and the latter often leading to improvements. Under this model, resilience represents a return to the status quo following the particular experience, whereas thriving refers to the improved state that follows.[18]

Overall, these perspectives seem to indicate the importance of moving forward through time as a critical factor in conceptions of thriving. Much of the literature suggests that thriving is less a state of being or a trait but, rather, a process of change reflecting an active individual functioning across time and adapting to changing contexts. The difficulty here, though, is the difference between conceptualizing thriving as a process while measuring it at a moment in time.[19]

There has been too little focus on supports that are significant enough to offset the "organized cultural traditions" that have undermined youths' resilience and thriving. Certainly, there are various perspectives on resilience and scaffolding needs for thriving; however, too few have juxtaposed the situations of risk and challenges against those viewed as assets for determining the processes that lead to good outcomes. Efforts such as Head Start programming and other early childhood efforts have been highly responsive to the human development needs of young children and their parents. Universal supports for such programming have consistently struggled due to the apparent character virtue shortcomings of policy makers. When race and low socioeconomic disadvantages intersect, dehumanization viewpoints suggest a vehicle for ineffective policies and a lack of critical supports. These practices guarantee long-term inequalities; worse yet, untoward outcomes are then blamed on those for whom intended developmentally relevant supports are most needed.

Exemplar Programs: Developmental and Culturally Relevant Practices

Too frequently, thriving- and resilience-focused research efforts are not included in the same studies that focus on risks and challenges. Intended supportive programming that confronts highly significant sources of risk and challenge suggest shortcomings in regard to basic human development needs; that is, too frequently, untoward context-linked cultural practices are ignored. The two programs that follow represent strategies for addressing biases experienced at the multiple levels of youth's ecologies of development. Their untoward experiences contributed to by fBIP are often made worse by either stereotyping about their underperformance or by assumptions that they "do not fit in." Particularly for youth designated as having "special needs" and those experiencing high risk due to economic disadvantage, stereotyping and social and emotional inferred exclusion are particularly detrimental.

Across the life course, the adolescent years are commonly the most critiqued, and individuals are considered "immeasurably difficult." The next section provides two programming exemplars that consider adolescents' developmental as well as cultural experiences and practices in ecologies of learning and development. The contextual situations, functioning as positive coping practices, include particular cultural traditions; they are intended to provide sources of significant assistance during adolescence given youths' normal human development needs. Each program described was framed and implemented as scaffolded by PVEST. Each project addresses both the psychological health and achievement supporting human development needs of youth; the inherent processes were positively impacted by the protective factors and assets provided as programming.[20]

1. Start-on-Success Scholars Program

A novel collaboration was designed and organized to assist underperforming students identified as having learning problems. Students had been previously assigned an individualized education plan (IEP). Even with the assumed educational benefits provided by IEP programming, high school graduation outcomes remained problematic. The responsive programming effort was organized with the specific human development goal of meeting IEP-supplied youths' adolescent needs. The Start-on-Success Program (SOS) was a unique collaboration between a local, urban-situated, Ivy League university, the National Organization on Disability (NOD), and a local public school system. The multimember community partnership had a clear mandate, which was to improve the learning experience and graduation rate of IEP recipients, who were predominantly African American and under-performing ninth- to twelfth-grade high school students. Largely funded by the school system, it was a collaboration with students and parents implemented on the university's campus, providing physical space for classes, a "college identification," and youth employment options. The program demonstrated the challenge and necessity of accounting for culture at multiple levels, including race, school, and work culture, for fully appreciating context character and its role in obtaining community buy-in, trust, and full participation. Assistance from teachers, job coaches, and work-site mentors provided a baseline condition of the program's implementation. Significant honesty and candor were required on the part of all collaborators and program implementers in regard to issues concerning race, class, culture, and context. The investigators knew that to address all issues effectively required a change in the context of learning and development for these high-vulnerability-status youths. In their prior educational contexts, untoward labels, including "not smart," were routinely used in youths' daily "learning environment" experience. Overcoming that particular stigmatizing contextual history was a major aspect of the "ecological change" required. It included everyone's candid involvement in the process of change as well as an engaged and authentic partnership with the community, its families, and the youthful participants.[21]

Another challenge was overcoming the notion that a "one size fits all" program would work, as well as confronting the quantity versus quality debate (i.e., the assumption that any support is "good enough[!]" and that all special needs were equivalent). The researchers' acknowledged reliance on the PVEST framework was represented in the program's design and intervention. Acknowledging and addressing developmental tasks, the program focused on academic programming as well as career counselling. Students were required to describe and build on their own identity (life events and lessons learned were explored with students). The workforce training challenge of the program included assisting with youths' internalization of new ways of thinking about effective responses to job situations. PVEST was used as an intervention to assist the adults in the workplace to identify, secure, and make use of new ways of thinking about and supporting young people. As a collaborative opportunity, it meant being very clear about expectations, roles, and responsibilities for all partners. Included in the implementation were required workshops and seminars for the adults as well as sustained and coordinated supervision of youths across the myriad program contexts. One of the major benefits of the model implemented was the added benefits given the alignments between the content of the program and its work responsibilities as parallel with the curriculum content.[22]

Students all had classifications of serious emotional disturbance (SED), learning disabled (LD), educable mentally retarded (EMR), and trainable mentally retarded (TMR). All of the work-based training occurred on the campus of the partnering university given its many job opportunities. Learning work transition skills in addition to academic content occurring in campus classrooms with inferred linked "college-associated identities" facilitated youths' acquisition of work-related skills, interpersonal competencies, academic content, self-efficacy, and the association with positive identifications. All aspects of the program mirrored and addressed the components of the identity-focused cultural ecological guiding framework, PVEST. For example, risks and supports as experienced and acknowledged by youth were invariably linked to context character. An example follows from an exit interview with two program participants, Katrina and Angel. They were asked why they desired program participation.[23]

> *Katrina:* They had a lot of choices and plus I didn't want . . . I mean, school is really not for me and I just thought the best thing to do was . . . dropping out and not going to school. Well this program, it did, it saved me. That's why I wanted to be in this program and I have a lot of opportunities. It's a lot of opportunities in here. It's a change, it's different, it's not the same as in school, you know. The change is good, that's what I like.
>
> *Angel* (male): Well it seem like the program had good things that I could use in the future like get training, training I can't get over there at Piney Ridge [high school, pseudonym] and I wanted to be with more professional people, you know people who are serious about their work and teach me a couple of things.

Interviewer: And what have you actually learned?

Angel (male): I learned a lot of things. Everything has improved. My mathematics has improved. My reading, because I was a little slow in reading also. I learned how to work with grown-ups and, you know, basically just work with more computers, because when I was over at Piney Ridge [pseudonym], we worked in computers but not like for money and things like that, not for business, just music.

The research questions were linked with the theory and resulted in qualitative findings that addressed each component of systems theory, including self-cognitions about risk and net level of support versus experienced stress. Linkages between net support versus stress and reactive coping were reported by program participants. Findings suggested the importance of making use of a theoretical framework that allows for greater understanding of how and why supports matter. Changes in the context have far-reaching implications for youths' resilience and thriving. The program also emphasized the importance of resources and the importance of "equity" as "equality." Youth without the stigmatizing label of IEP may need equity supports, but those with an additional source of risk (IEP label) require "equity"-level assistance that more closely matches their level of daily confronted risk.

In our interrogation of the implementation of *Brown*, the human development needs of Black and Brown children were never considered in this way. For twenty generations, there have been indelible experiences of structured inequality for some and unacknowledged privileges for others, including the periods of slavery, reconstruction, and Jim Crow. However, all individuals of color to this day continue to be burdened given the expectations to address life course developmental tasks but without needed supports representing equity.

2. Monetary Incentive Support Program

Parallel to the expectations and needs during adolescence noted for the IEP "card carrying students" described in the SOS program, the Monetary Incentive Support Program confronted a specific need.

Particularly salient during adolescence are expressed monetary "needs." Young people's too often and dramatically expressed monetary concerns are driven by wanting to be like others but lacking family resources (e.g., shoes, clothes, and other youthful accoutrements). These are "needs" taken for granted by privileged youngsters used to making requests of parents or having access to allowances. Using a novel strategy, this program directly addressed the economic needs of high performing but extremely low-resource students (i.e., students with a documented family status level-reflected family sustenance level within one standard deviation of the poverty line). The goal was to sustain youths' high performance. It provided yet another strategy for addressing the achievement gap by providing relevant supports for maintaining high performance and preventing dropping out of school for impoverished but high performing youths.[24]

PVEST was used as a framing device for the evaluation of a quantitative strategy designed for assessing monetary incentive impact programming to encourage and sustain academic achievement among a population of multiethnic students attending any one of dozens of schools in an urban environment. Although students were living in shared low-resource environments, student performance showed diversity. For students from ethnically diverse families functioning at or above the cutoff for poverty—which was individually assessed based upon family-level criteria, rather than school-level free lunch assumptions—programming assessed whether the receipt of a monthly monetary incentive was effective or meaningful for sustained achievement. Supported by National Institute of Mental Health (NIMH), the study explored whether a monthly monetary incentive delivered to economically high-risk high school students supports high academic achievement. Youth represented a large sample of economically high-vulnerability students, individuals showing high economic risk without adequate supports. Important to acknowledge is that the strategy was different for this multiethnic sample of youth. It assumed that given an objectively defined criterion, poverty, addressing it required a direct solution: reducing its impact by providing adolescents with resources or incentives designed to offset economic challenge.[25]

Importantly, the design and implementation of *Brown* was borne predominantly by Black students who were displaced to White schools, which only increased the situation of challenge and risk. However, the evaluation findings of the monetary-based incentive programming demonstrated why "equal resources" may not function similarly to equitable dispersion of resources. For some youths (i.e., African American males), the monetary incentives alone were not enough for offsetting the risks associated with poverty. Consistent with Jacqueline Irvine and other gender-focused and culture-sensitive researchers, untoward school-level characteristics are important and may potentially dampen the positive impact of supports, especially for African American males. At the same time, "model minority" positive stereotypes may heighten the incentivizing character of monetary incentives for Asian American impoverished high school students.[26]

The evaluation study of a randomized field trial involving high achieving, low-economic-resourced, ethnically diverse, and urban high school-attending adolescents yielded patterned findings. They suggest that equality of supports may not be experienced as equitable given individuals' simultaneous and phenomenological experiences of unique context character. Prior research had noted that monetary incentives, including welfare funding, can be effective in assisting youths' school completion. Youths receiving stipends demonstrated a greater likelihood of maintaining good grades after one year in comparison to those who received no monetary stipend. Consistent with a PVEST theoretical analysis, the findings suggest that youth inferred different meanings about receipt of the stipends and suggested various identity processes salient to the self (e.g., self-validation). Findings also suggested developmental differences in that ninth graders were more fragile than tenth graders; the latter pattern was assumed to be due to the younger students' need to adjust to a new school context given their recent arrival in high school and adjustment requirements in comparison to older students. As reported from telephone interviews with families and students, older students were more focused on postsecondary plans and, thus, found the receipt of a monetary stipend significantly more motivating and helpful given "next step" planning needs. An important and general finding was that students scoring high on a positive self-concept/identity scale were more likely to maintain good academic standing after one year. Consistent with PVEST, one might infer the stable protective role and coping device functioning provided by identity processes for maximum impact of stipend receipt.

While there were limitations to the study, an important finding was the efficacy of monetary stipends for encouraging the continuation of high performance for economically fragile adolescent students from ethnically diverse families. In particular, the evaluation included consideration of gender patterns and, as well, race/ethnicity (thus, intersectionality) suggesting individual-context perceptions and experiences. This variation of human experiences given demographics and context considerations was never inferred from the *Brown* decision. We hazard that humanity assumptions continue to be ignored into the twenty-first century.

Conclusions and Implications

Our interrogation and radical rereading of *Brown* make clear that humanity and human development assumptions matter and were absent vis-à-vis youth of color in the understanding and implementation of *Brown*. The complex ways in which individual characteristics, historical experiences within and across family lines, and human meaning-making impact individuals and groups all matter deeply. They show intersectionality across human characteristics and interact with context character given developmental tasks to be mastered and deeply engrained cultural traditions. Unavoidably, human meaning-making processes further complicate within- and between-group interactions, particularly when hegemonic beliefs formed and economic benefits go unaddressed. Distorted views about self and those defined as "others" function as uninterrogated identity. Theoretical responses abetted by social science shortcomings and their scaffolding of policy precipitate fears and further stereotyping, stigmatizing, and missed opportunities for authentic change. Precipitated are "invisible harms" and a failure to address intangibles for everyone. Consequent envisioned "supports" reflect dehumanizing beliefs about "difference." Significantly, such conceptual shortcomings fail to provide supports that function for all as sources of shared equity. Particular supports for Whites are required for offsetting 20 generations of "missed inclusive socialization opportunities" and an estimated 40,000 conversations that might have affirmed shared humanity. Equitable supports for people of color are required for offsetting generations of historical trauma as victims of dehumanizing, under-interrogated cultural repertoires of practice and undiagnosed social amnesia.

There are important implications for whether or not envisioned supports and socialization goals are realized as mechanisms supporting *everyone's humanity*. Using the two programs described above as exemplars of why they were more effective than the implementation of *Brown* thus far, both exemplar programs took into account that understanding the communities and repertoires of practice mattered (i.e., both communities *facilitating* shared humanity and those with traditions more *damaging* to shared humanity). Four hundred years of untoward cultural traditions as repertoires of practice represent and function as key requirements for designing and implementing programs intended and actually experienced as supportive. As authentic community partnerships, the exemplar programs recognized that "one size does not fit all." Thus, acknowledging malleability and providing context-linked incentives for and training of all parties is a key factor given differences in family lines of communication and character virtue values as potentially intrusive traditions. Particularly relevant to the SOS program, repertoires of practice required providing retraining opportunities given human vulnerability variations for youthful program recipients as well as the adult professionals intending to serve as sources of support.

For the SOS effort, PVEST was used to continually "tweak" program delivery for increasing the "match" between program character, youths' needs, and everyday practices (i.e., as experienced by youth when off and on campus). This ongoing process also dispelled the notion that supports viewed as "good enough" were, in fact, "good enough." The SOS effort also addressed the debate between "quality program delivery" versus an emphasis on "quantity of program" delivered. For guaranteeing customization opportunities, the collaborative SOS program opted for a "quality" approach, thus explaining the significant efficacy of outcomes; that is, it was possible to pay attention to the character of the context and needs for maximizing the best fit given the outcomes desired.

In the case of *Brown*, Black children's developmental needs and the representation of Whites, given their missed opportunities to understand shared humanity, meant that context character was ignored. Black children's humanity and basic required supports were overlooked. Unaddressed hegemony beliefs of Whites were ignored and functioned as sources of "invisible harm." In sum, our interrogation of *Brown* and critique of its lack of success seventy years post–launch date is specific. At the fundamental and foundational levels, not recognized—but experienced in myriad ways as fBIP—have have been twenty generations of social amnesia given the absence of accrued and acknowledged history. The tradition continues, and we speculate that for each family line, forty thousand missed opportunities and conversations have been obfuscated—with an ongoing tradition for its continuation—for maintaining a knowledge gap that supports the nation's social amnesia. The historical memory loss, then, compromises the authentic change needed for any inclusive "We the People" social fabric. Acknowledging that shortcoming, as a first step, would be one contribution to rectifying the nation's missed opportunities for a shared liberty status for all citizens—and particularly its youth.[27]

Brown mandated comprehensive equality to replace comprehensive inequality. It did so focused on the core, foundational principle of common humanity: embracing the radical understanding, then and still now, that every child, every person is valued, in every and all respects. That profound, essential, intangible principle is at the heart of comprehensive systems, structures, and culture. Radical *Brown* exposes the need to implement the principle of equal humanity. We demonstrate and translate what that means by exposing the life course developmental repercussions and cost of inhumanity within an intergenerational chronosystem of inequality as everyday American cultural traditions.

SUCCESSFUL PROGRAMMING APPROACHES

We have not escaped our past, because the flawed implementation of *Brown* in the past seventy years has ignored *Brown*'s true meaning.

Inequality and inhumanity harm us all but do so differently. That is also recognized in the social science underlying the core reasoning of the *Brown* decision. Black and Brown children and adults have suffered and continue to suffer disproportionately and comprehensively from the failure to implement *Brown*'s mandate of comprehensive equality. Whites have been affected differently, unfairly benefitting from skewed, privileging systems infused with beliefs in White supremacy and, at the same time, inflicting conditions of Black incapacity and inhumanity. Whites function on a construction of Whiteness that profoundly undermines their humanity, socio-emotional-associated character virtue, and potential for morality. Patterned Black–White differentials of experience and structured contextual variations mandate approaches informed by equity. We are not all situated the same; our way forward requires equity, necessitating solutions that recognize our differential positions in the inequality context in order to achieve real equality.

The way forward begins with unwavering dedication to *Brown*'s principle of shared humanity. It is the necessary polestar to guide the intangible and tangible goals of comprehensive equality. Common humanity is essential to each of us; it demands each of us to act. Radical *Brown* outlines both what is required and how to move forward. *Brown* then will no longer be used as a false apology to render inequality invisible but instead serve as the talisman for radical comprehensive equality.

Notes

Introduction

1. Margaret Beale Spencer, "Phenomenology and Ecological Systems Theory: Development of Diverse Groups," in *Handbook of Child Psychology*, vol. 1, *Theoretical Models of Human Development*, ed. R. M. Lerner and W. Damon, 6th ed. (New York: Wiley, 2006), 829–93; Margaret Beale Spencer, "Phenomenology and Ecological Systems Theory: Development of Diverse Groups," in *Child and Adolescent Development: An Advanced Course*, ed. W. Damon and R. M. Lerner (New York: Wiley, 2008), 696–735.

2. Walter Recharde Allen, Margaret Beale Spencer, and Geraldine K. Brookins, "Synthesis: Black Children Keep on Growing," in *Beginnings: The Social and Affective Development of Black Children*, ed. Margaret Beale Spencer, Geraldine K. Brookins, and Walter R. Allen (Hillsdale, NJ: Erlbaum, 1985), 301–14; Edgar G. Epps, "Forward," in *Beginnings*, xiii–xiv; Chester M. Pierce, "Afterword," in *Beginnings*, 315–316.

3. V. P. Franklin, "From Integration to Black Self-Determination: Changing Social Science Perspectives on Afro-American Life and Culture," in *Beginnings*, 19–28.

4. Margaret Beale Spencer et al., "Innovating Resilience Promotion: Integrating Cultural Practices, Social Ecologies and Development-Sensitive Conceptual Strategies for Advancing Child Well-Being," *Advances in Child Development and Behavior* 57 (2019): 101–48; Bronwyn Nichols Lodato, Jennifer Hall, and Margaret Beale Spencer, "Vulnerability and Resiliency Implications of Human Capital and Linked Inequality Presence Denial Perspectives: Acknowledging Zigler's Contributions to Child Well-Being," *Development and Psychopathology* 33, no. 2 (2021): 1–16.

5. Brown v. Board of Education, 347 U.S. 483, 496 (1954).

6. *Brown*, 347 U.S. at 492.

7. *Brown*, 347 U.S. at 494.

8. *Brown*, 347 U.S. at 493.

9. Bolling v. Sharpe, 347 U.S. 497 (1954).

10. *Bolling*, 347 U.S. at 499–500.

11. Brown v. Board of Education, 349 U.S. 294 (1955) (Brown II).

12. Nancy E. Dowd, *Reimagining Equality: A New Deal for Children of Color* (New York: NYU Press 2018), 11–18.

13. Sean F. Reardon and Ximena A. Portilla, "Recent Trends in Income, Racial, and Ethnic School Readiness Gaps at Kindergarten Entry," *American Educational Research Association Open* 2, no. 3 (2016): 1–18; Nancy E. Dowd and Teresa Drake, *Introduction: Early Childhood Symposium—Early Childhood Matters*, 71 Florida Law Review Forum 1 (2019).

14. Annie E. Casey Foundation, *Race for Results*, 2017 Policy Report, Kids Count, 34 (October 24, 2017), available at aecf.org.

15. Jaleesa Bustamante, "K-12 School Enrollment & Student Population Statistics," educationdata.org, June 9, 2019, https://educationdata.org/k12 -enrollment-statistics/.

16. Erica Frankenberg, "Assessing the Status of School Desegregation Sixty Years After Brown," *Michigan State Law Review* 2014, no. 3 (2014): 677, 688–89.

17. "K-12 Disparity Facts and Statistics," United Negro College Fund, https:// uncf.org/pages/k-12-disparity-facts-and-stats.

18. Jim Hilbert, "Restoring the Promise of Brown: Using State Constitutional Law to Challenge School Segregation" SSRN, August 31, 2016, http://dx.doi .org/10.2139/ssrn.2832964," 21.

19. Thandeka K. Chapman, "Is Integration a Dream Deferred? Students of Color in Majority White Suburban Schools," *Journal of Negro Education* 83, no. 3 (2014): 322.

20. Linda Darling-Hammond, "Inequality in Teaching and Schooling: How Opportunity Is Rationed to Students of Color in America 2001," in *The Right Thing to Do, The Smart Thing to Do: Enhancing Diversity in the Health Professions— Summary of the Symposium on Diversity in Health Professions in Honor of Herbert W. Nickens*, ed. Brian D. Smedley et al. (Washington, DC: National Academy Press, 2001), 208–233.

21. Darling-Hammond, "Inequality," 218.

22. "K-12 Disparity," United Negro College Fund, statistic #9.

23. Bustamante, "K-12 School Enrollment."

24. "K-12 Disparity," statistic #6.

25. U.S. Department of Education, "2013–2014 Civil Rights Data Collection: A First Look," revised October 28, 2016, https://www2.ed.gov/about/offices/list /ocr/docs/2013-14-first-look.pdf.

26. U.S. Department of Education, "2013–2014," 4.

27. Hilbert, "Restoring the Promise," 23.

28. Hilbert, 26.

29. Chapman, "Dream Deferred?" 311–326.

30. Chapman, 314.

31. Rita Kohli, Marcos Pizarro, and Arturo Nevárez, "The 'New Racism' of K-12 Schools: Centering Critical Research on Racism," *Review of Research in Education* 41, no. 1 (2017): 182–202.

Chapter 1

1. R. J. Havighurst, *Human Development and Education* (Oxford: Longmans, Green, 1953).
2. For phenomenological variant of ecological systems theory (PVEST), see Margaret Beale Spencer, "Phenomenology and Ecological Systems Theory: Development of Diverse Groups," in *Handbook of Child Psychology*, vol. 1, *Theoretical Models of Human Development*, 6th ed., ed. R. M. Lerner and W. Damon (New York: Wiley, 2006), 1:829–893; Margaret Beale Spencer, "Phenomenology and Ecological Systems Theory: Development of Diverse Groups," in *Child and Adolescent Development: An Advanced Course*, ed. W. Damon and R. M. Lerner (New York: Wiley, 2008), 696–735.
3. See Margaret Beale Spencer et al., "Understanding Hypermasculinity in Context: A Theory-Driven Analysis of Urban Adolescent Males' Coping Responses," *Research in Human Development* 1 (2004): 229–57; Margaret Beale Spencer, Suzanne G. Fegley, and Vinay Harpalani, "A Theoretical and Empirical Examination of Identity as Coping: Linking Coping Resources to the Self Processes of African American Youth," *Applied Developmental Science* 7 (2003): 188; Margaret Beale Spencer, Blanch Dobbs, and Dena Phillips Swanson, "African American Adolescents: Adaptational Processes and Socioeconomic Diversity in Behavioural Outcomes," *Journal of Adolescence* 11 (1988): 117; Margaret Beale Spencer and Carol Marstrom-Adams, "Identity Processes Among Racial and Ethnic Minority Children in America," *Child Development* 61 (1990): 290.
4. Spencer's model relies on but differs from that offered by Bronfenbrenner. Spencer, "Understanding Hypermasculinity," 231.
5. Spencer, 230 (emphasis added).
6. Spencer, 230; see also Margaret Beale Spencer, "Old Issues and New Theorizing about African-American Youth: A Phenomenological Variant of Ecological Systems Theory," in *African American Youth: Their Social and Economic Status in the United States*, ed. Ronald L. Taylor (Westport, CT: Praeger, 1995), 37.
7. Spencer, "Understanding Hypermasculinity," 233.
8. Spencer, 233.
9. Spencer, 233.
10. Margaret Beale Spencer, "Revisiting the 1990 Special Issue on Minority Children: An Editorial Perspective 15 Years Later," *Child Development* 77 (2006): 1149–54.
11. Spencer, "Revisiting the 1990 Special Issue."
12. Spencer, "Revisiting the 1990 Special Issue," 1151. See also Suniya S. Luthar and Bronwyn E. Becker, "Privileged but Pressured? A Study of Affluent Youth," *Child Development* 73 (2002): 1593; Suniya S. Luthar and Shawn J. Latendresse, "Adolescent Risk: The Costs of Affluence," *New Directions Youth Development* 95 (2002): 101; Claude M. Steele, Steven J.

Spencer, and Joshua Aronson, "Contending with Group Image: The Psychology of Stereotype and Social Identity Threat," *Advances in Experimental Social Psychology* 34 (2002): 379; Claude M. Steele, "The Psychology of Self-Affirmation: Sustaining the Integrity of the Self," *Advances in Experimental Social Psychology* 21 (1988): 261.

13. Margaret Beale Spencer, "Understanding Hypermasculinity," 232–33.
14. Kendra Cherry, "How Does Implicit Bias Influence Behavior? Explanations and Impacts of Unconscious Bias," Verywell Mind, September 18, 2020, https://www.verywellmind.com/ implicit-bias-overview-4178401.
15. Christiana Mair, Ana V. Diez Roux, and Jeffrey D. Morenoff, "Neighborhood Stressors and Social Support as Predictors of Depressive Symptoms in the Chicago Community Adult Health Study," *Health and Place* 16, no. 5 (September 2010): 811–19.
16. Dena Philips Swanson, Michael Cunningham, and Margaret Beale Spencer, "Black Males' Structural Conditions, Achievement Patterns, Normative Needs, and 'Opportunities,'" *Urban Education* 38, no. 5 (2016): 618.
17. Margaret Beale Spencer, "Resiliency and Fragility Factors Associated with the Contextual Experiences of Low Resource Urban African American Male Youth and Families," in *Does It Take A Village? Community Effects on Children, Adolescents, and Families,* ed. Alan Booth and Ann C. Crouter (Mahwah, NJ: Lawrence Erlbaum, 2001) 51, 53; Margaret Beale Spencer and Carol Marstrom-Adams, "Identity Processes Among Racial and Ethnic Minority Children in America," *Child Development* 61 (1990): 290; Margaret Beale Spencer, Blanch Dobbs, and Dena Phillips Swanson, "African American Adolescents: Adaptational Processes and Socioeconomic Diversity in Behavioural Outcomes," *Journal of Adolescence* 11 (1988): 117; Margaret Beale Spencer, Davido Dupree, and Dena Phillips Swanson, "Parental Monitoring and Adolescents' Sense of Responsibility for Their Own Learning: An Examination of Sex Differences," *Journal of Negro Educucation* 65 (1997): 30.
18. Erick H. Erikson, *Childhood in Society* (New York: Norton, 1950). Also, see Spencer, "Phenomenology and Ecological Systems," in *Handbook of Child Psychology*; Spencer, "Phenomenology and Ecological Systems," in *Child and Adolescent Development,* 696–735.
19. R. White, "Motivation Reconsidered: The Concept of Competence," *Psychological Review* 66 (1959): 297–333; R. White, "Competence and Psychosexual Development," in *Nebraska Symposium on Motivation,* ed. M. R. Jones (Lincoln: University of Nebraska Press, 1960); R. DeCharms, *Personal Causation: The Internal Affective Determinants of Behavior* (New York: Academy Press, 1968). Also, Havighurst, *Human Development and Education.*
20. R. DeCharms, *Personal Causation.*
21. Richard M. Lerner and Jacqueline V. Lerner, *Children in Their Contexts: A Goodness-of-Fit Model* (New York: Routledge, 1987).

22. Erikson, *Childhood in Society*; Spencer, "Revisiting the 1990 Special Issue," 1149; Spencer, "Phenomenology and Ecological Systems," in *Child and Adolescent Development*, 696–735.

23. Richard M. Lerner, "Developmental Contextualism and the Life-Span View of Person-Context Interaction," in *Interaction in Human Development*, ed. Marc H. Bornstein and Jerome S. Bruner (New York: Psychology Press, 1989), 217–39.

24. Roger G. Barker and Herbert F. Wright, "Psychological Ecology and the Problem of Psychosocial Development," *Child Development* 20, no. 3 (September 1949): 141–43; Herbert Wright, Roger G. Barker, and Paul V. Gump, *Big School, Small School: High School Size and Student Behavior* (Palo Alto, CA: Stanford University Press, 1964); Urie Bronfenbrenner, *The Ecology of Human Development* (Cambridge, MA: Harvard University Press, 1979).

25. Spencer, "Old Issues and New Theorizing," 37–69. Also see Spencer, "Revisiting the 1990 Special Issue," 1149; Spencer, "Phenomenology and Ecological Systems," in *Child and Adolescent Development*, 696–735.

26. Spencer, "Old Issues and New Theorizing," 37–69; Spencer, "Revisiting the 1990 Special Issue," 1149; Spencer, "Phenomenology and Ecological Systems," in *Child and Adolescent Development*, 696–735.

27. Gunnar Myrdal, *An American Dilemma: The Negro Problem and Modern Democracy* (New York: Harper and Bros, 1944).

28. Bronfenbrenner, *Human Development*.

29. Spencer, "Revisiting the 1990 Special Issue," 1149; Spencer, "Phenomenology and Ecological Systems," in *Child and Adolescent Development*, 696–735.

30. Havighurst, *Human Development and Education*; Spencer, "Revisiting the 1990 Special Issue," 1149; Spencer, "Phenomenology and Ecological Systems," in *Child and Adolescent Development*, 696–735.

31. See Margaret Beale Spencer et al., "Chapter Four. Innovating Resilience Promotion: Integrating Cultural Practices, Social Ecologies and Development-Sensitive Conceptual Strategies for Advancing Child Well-Being," in *Advances in Child Development and Behavior*, ed. Daphne A. Henry, Elizabeth Votruba-Drzal, Portia Miller (New York: Academic Press, 2019): 57:101–48.

32. Jean Piaget, *The Language and Thought of the Child* (New York: Harcourt, Brace, 1926); David Elkind, *The Hurried Child: Growing Up Too Fast Too Soon* (Reading, MA: Addison-Wesley, 1981); John H. Flavell, *The Development of Role-Taking and Communication Skills in Children* (New York: Wiley, 1968); Melvin Feffer, "Symptom Expression as a Form of Primitive Decentering," *Psychological Review* 74, no. 1 (1967): 16–28; Melvin H. Feffer, "The Cognitive Implications of Role Taking Behavior," *Journal of Personality* 27, no. 2 (1959): 152–68; Leonard S. Cottrell, "Interpersonal Interaction and the Development of the Self," in *Handbook of Socialization: Theory and Research*, ed. D. Goslin (Chicago: Rand McNally, 1969), 543–70.

33. Erikson, *Childhood in Society*.

34. Jean Piaget, "Piaget's Point of View," *International Journal of Psychology* 3, no. 4 (1968): 281–99; Elkind, *The Hurried Child*; see personification, Harry S. Sullivan, *The Interpersonal Theory of Psychiatry* (New York: Norton, 1953).

35. Barbara Woodward and Robert Costa, *Peril* (New York: Simon & Schuster, 2021).

36. Woodward and Costa, *Peril*.

37. See Peggy McIntosh, "White Privilege: Unpacking the Invisible Knapsack," *Peace and Freedom Magazine* 49, no. 4 (July/August 1989): 10–12; David R. Roediger, *The Wages of Whiteness: Race and the Making of the American Working Class* (New York: Verso, 1991).

38. See Spencer, "Resiliency and Fragility Factors," 51–77; Spencer, "Revisiting the 1990 Special Issue," 1149; Margaret Beale Spencer et al., "Understanding Vulnerability and Resilience from a Normative Developmental Perspective: Implications for Racially and Ethnically Diverse Youth," in *Developmental Psychopathology*, vol. 1, *Theory and Method*, 2nd ed., ed. Dante Cicchetti and Donald J. Cohen (Hoboken, NJ: Wiley, 2006), 627–672. Spencer, "Phenomenology and Ecological Systems Theory," in *Handbook of Child Psychology*.

39. Spencer, "Old Issues and New Theorizing," 37 (i.e., a "sense of self").

40. Keshia Lynette Harris, "'Somos Uma Salada de Fruta': Adolescent Achievement in Brazilian and Colombian Structures of Opportunity" (doctoral diss, University of Chicago, 2019).

Chapter 2

1. Edward E. Baptist, *The Half Has Never Been Told: Slavery and the Making of American Capitalism* (New York: Basic Books, 2014).

2. Dred Scott v. Sandford, 60 U.S. 393 (1856).

3. Orlando Patterson, *Slavery and Social Death, A Comparative Study* (Cambridge, MA: Harvard University Press, 2018), ix.

4. Patterson, *Slavery and Social Death*.

5. Patterson, chap. 12.

6. A. Leon Higginbotham Jr., "The Ten Precepts of American Slavery Jurisprudence: Chief Justice Roger Taney's Defense and Justice Thurgood Marshall's Condemnation of the Precept of Black Inferiority," *Cardozo Law Review* 17, no. 6 (1996): 1706.

7. William M. Wiecek, "The Origins of the Law of Slavery in British North America," *Cardozo Law Review* 17 (1996): 1711.

8. Wiecek, "Origins of the Law," 1791.

9. Thomas R. R. Cobb, *An Inquiry into the Law of Negro Slavery in the United States of America* (Athens: Georgia Press, 1999), first published in 1858 by W. Torne Williams (Savannah); Paul Finkelman, "Thomas R.R. Cobb and

the Law of Negro Slavery," *Roger Williams University Law Review* 5, no. 1 (Fall 1999): 75.

10. Finkelman, "Thomas R.R. Cobb," 97; Cobb, chap. 10.

11. Paul Finkelman, "The Crime of Color," *Tulane Law Review* 67, no. 6 (1993): 2065; see also Fran Lisa Buntman, "Race, Reputation, and the Supreme Court: Valuing Blackness and Whiteness," *University of Miami Law Review* 56, no. 1 (2001): 1–24.

12. Finkelman, "The Crime of Color," 2068.

13. Baptist, *The Half Has Never.*

14. Baptist, xxiii.

15. Baptist, xxi.

16. Baptist, xxiii, emphasis added.

17. Baptist, xxiii.

18. Baptist, xxv.

19. Wiecek, "Origins of the Law, 1777.

20. Daniel Farbman, "Resistance Lawyering," *California Law Review* 107, no. 6 (December 2019): 1877–954.

21. Patrick A. Dawson, "Slaves, the Law, and the Banality of Horror," *Journal of Southern Legal History* 23 (2015): 162.

22. Jenny Bourne Wahl, "Legal Constraints on Slave Masters: The Problem of Social Cost," *American Journal of Legal History* 41, no. 1 (1997): 1–24.

23. Adrienne D. Davis, "The Private Law of Race and Sex: An Antebellum Perspective," *Stanford Law Review* 51, no. 2 (January 1999): 221–88.

24. Farbman, "Resistance Lawyering."

25. A. Leon Higginbotham Jr. and Barbara K. Kopytoff, "Property First, Humanity Second: The Recognition of the Slave's Human Nature in Virginia Civil Law," *Ohio State Law Journal* 50, no. 3 (1989): 511–40; see also Lea Vandervelde, *Redemption Songs: Suing for Freedom Before Dred Scott* (New York: Oxford University Press, 2014); Alfred L. Brophy, "Book Review: Slaves as Plaintiffs," *Michigan Law Review* 115, no. 6 (2017): 895–914.

26. Vernon Valentine Palmer, "The Customs of Slavery: The War Without Arms," *American Journal of Legal History* 48, no. 2 (2006): 177.

27. Palmer, "Customs of Slavery," 177–218.

28. Peggy Cooper Davis, "Contested Images of Family Values: The Role of the State," *Harvard Law Review* 107, no. 6 (April 1994): 1363–64.

29. Davis, "Contested Images."

30. Davis, 1371–72.

31. Baptist, *The Half Has Never*, xxvii.

32. Baptist, 417.

33. Baptist, 419.

34. Ariela J. Gross, "Litigating Whiteness: Trials of Racial Determination in the Nineteenth-Century South," *Yale Law Journal* 108 (1998): 110–88.

35. Gross, "Litigating Whiteness," 156.

36. Nell Irvin Painter, "What Is Whiteness?," *New York Times*, June 21, 2015; see also Robert P. Baird, "The Invention of Whiteness: The Long History of a Dangerous Idea," *Guardian*, April 20, 2021.

37. 1 Stat. 103, chap. 3, Pub. L. 1–3 (1790).

38. Ian Haney Lopez, *White by Law: The Legal Construction of Race*, 10th anniversary ed. (New York: NYU Press, 2006), xxi–xxii.

39. Nell Irvin Painter, "White Identity in America Is Ideology, not Biology. The History of 'Whiteness' Proves It," NBC News, June 27, 2020, Opinion, https://www.nbcnews.com/think/ opinion/white-identity-america-ideology-not-biology-history-whiteness-proves-it-ncna1232200; Nell Irvin Painter, *The History of White People* (New York: W.W. Norton, 2010); Baird, "Invention of Whiteness."

40. Baird, "Invention of Whiteness."

41. Robin A. Lenhardt, "Understanding the Mark: Race, Stigma, and Equality in Context," *New York University Law Review* 79, no. 3 (2004): 803–931.

42. Lenhardt, "Understanding the Mark," 826.

43. Steven Hahn, *The Political Worlds of Slavery and Freedom* (Cambridge, MA: Harvard University Press, 2009), xvi.

44. Hahn, *Political Worlds*, chapter 2.

45. Sherri Burr, "The Free Blacks of Virginia: A Personal Narrative, A Legal Construct," *Journal of Gender, Race and Justice* 19 (Spring 2016): 4.

46. Burr, "Free Blacks of Virginia," 1–38.

47. Ira Berlin, "Introduction," in *Free Blacks in a Slave Society*, ed. Paul Finkelman (New York: Garland, 1989).

48. Berlin, "Introduction," 1.

49. David F. Forte, "Spiritual Equality, The Black Codes and the Americanization of the Freedmen," *Loyola Law Review* 43, no. 4 (1998): 569–612.

50. Ibram X. Kendi, *Stamped from the Beginning: The Definitive History of Racist Ideas in America* (New York: Bold Type Books, 2016), 1–14.

51. Ibram X. Kendi and Keisha Blain, *Four Hundred Souls: A Community History of African America, 1619–2019* (New York: One World, 2021).

52. Isabel Wilkerson, *Caste: The Origins of Our Discontents* (New York: Random House, 2020).

53. Wilkerson, *Caste*, 17.

54. Elise Boddie, "Adaptive Discrimination," *North Carolina Law Review* 94, no. 4 (2016): 1235–313.

55. Justin Collings, "The Supreme Court and the Memory of Evil," *Stanford Law Review* 71, no. 2 (2019): 265–339.

56. Eric Foner, *The Second Founding: How the Civil War and Reconstruction Remade the Constitution* (New York: W.W. Norton, 2019), xxix–xx.

57. Rhonda V. Magee Andrews, "The Third Reconstruction: An Alternative to Race Consciousness and Colorblindness in Post-Slavery America," *Alabama Law Review* 54, no. 2 (2003): 494.

58. Alexander Tsesis, "The Declaration of Independence and Constitutional Interpretation," *Southern California Law Review* 89, no. 3 (2016): 369-98.

59. W. E. B. Du Bois, *Black Reconstruction in America 1860–1880* (New York: Free Press, 1992), xix. First published 1935.

60. Eric Foner, *Reconstruction: America's Unfinished Revolution 1863–1877*, updated ed. (New York: Harper Perennial, 2014), 77-78.

61. Foner, *Reconstruction*, 110.

62. Foner, 78.

63. Foner, 96.

64. Foner, 119.

65. Foner, 278.

66. Foner, 288 (quoting from an Alabama convention in 1865).

67. Steven Hahn, *A Nation Under Our Feet: Black Political Struggles in the Rural South from Slavery to the Great Migration* (Cambridge, MA: Harvard University Press 2003); see also Hahn, *Political Worlds*.

68. Hahn, *Nation Under Our Feet*, 101.

69. Hahn, 115.

70. Hahn, 165.

71. Hahn, 165.

72. Hahn, 207.

73. Hahn, 266.

74. Hahn, 330–476.

75. Hahn, 476.

76. Katherine Franke, *Repair: Redeeming the Promise of Abolition* (Chicago: Haymarket, 2019), 110.

77. Franke, *Repair*, 3.

78. Franke, 8.

79. Franke, 9.

80. W. E. B. Du Bois, "Souls of White Folk," in *W.E.B. Du Bois: Writings* (New York: Library of America, 1987), 923-38, 937.

81. Du Bois, *Black Reconstruction*, 727.

Chapter 3

1. 163 U.S. 537 (1896).

2. C. Vann Woodward, *The Strange Career of Jim Crow*, 3rd rev. ed. (Oxford: Oxford University Press, 2002).

3. C. Vann Woodward, *The Strange Career of Jim Crow*, 2nd rev. ed. (Oxford: Oxford University Press, 1966), preface.

4. Gunnar Myrdal, *An American Dilemma: The Negro Problem and Modern Democracy* (New Brunswick, NJ: Harper and Row, 1962), lxxv-lxxvi.

5. Woodward, *Strange Career of Jim Crow*, 2002, 7.

6. Woodward, 2002, 7.

7. Woodward, 2002, 17.

8. Woodward, 2002, 18.

9. Woodward, 2002, 18–19 (quoting Leon F. Litwack, *North of Slavery: The Negro in the Free States, 1790–1860* [Chicago: University of Chicago Press, 1961]).

10. Richard Archer, *Jim Crow North: The Struggle for Equal Rights in Antebellum New England* (Oxford: Oxford University Press, 2017).

11. Brian Purnell and Jeanne Theoharis, with Komozi Woodard, eds., *The Strange Careers of the Jim Crow North: Segregation and Struggle Outside of the South* (New York: New York University Press, 2019).

12. Purnell, Theoharis, and Woodard, *Strange Careers*, 3–4.

13. Purnell, Theoharis, and Woodard, 13.

14. Purnell, Theoharis, and Woodard, 13; see also Douglas S. Massey and Nancy A. Denton, *American Apartheid: Segregation and the Making of the Underclass* (Cambridge, MA: Harvard University Press, 1993); Richard Rothstein, *The Color of Law: A Forgotten History of How Our Government Segregated America* (New York: Liveright, 2017).

15. Woodward, *Strange Career of Jim Crow*, 2002, 40.

16. Woodward, 2002, 69.

17. Woodward, 2002, 108.

18. Leon F. Litwack, "Jim Crow Blues," *OAH Magazine of History* 18, no. 2 (2004): 9.

19. Jerrold M. Packard, *American Nightmare: The History of Jim Crow* (New York: St. Martins Griffin, 2002), 173.

20. F. Michael Higginbotham, *Ghosts of Jim Crow: Ending Racism in Post-Racial America* (New York: New York University Press, 2013), 119 (quoting Eisenhower).

21. David Copp, "Corrective Justice as a Duty of the Political Community: David Lyons on the Moral Legacy of Slavery and Jim Crow, in rights, Equality and Justice: A Conference Inspired by the Moral and Legal Theory of David Lyons (prof of law at BU)," *Boston University Law Review* 90, no. 4 (August 2010): 1731–33.

22. Higginbotham, *Ghosts of Jim Crow*.

23. Jerrold M. Packard, *American Nightmare: The History of Jim Crow* (New York: St. Martins Griffin, 2002); Ana S. Q. Liberato, Dana Fennell, and William L. Jeffries IV, "I Still Remember America: Senior African Americans Talk About Segregation," *Journal of African American Studies* 12, no. 3 (2008): 229–42.

24. Packard, *American Nightmare*, 164–65.

25. Packard, 171.

26. Edward L. Ayers, *The Promise of the New South: Life After Reconstruction* (Oxford: Oxford University Press, 2007) (first published 1992).

27. Isabel Wilkerson, *The Warmth of Other Suns: The Epic Story of America's Great Migration* (New York: Vintage Books, 2011), 5.

28. Ayers, *Promise of the New South*, 145.

29. Khalil Girbran Muhammed, *The Condemnation of Blackness: Race, Crime and the Making of Modern Urban America* (Cambridge, MA: Harvard University Press, 2019), preface, xiii-xiv, 1.

30. Stephen A. Berrey, "Resistance Begins at Home: The Black Family and Lessons in Survival and Subversion in Jim Crow Mississippi," *Black Women, Gender + Families* 3, no. 1 (2009): 72.

31. Ana S. Q. Liberato, Dana Fennell, and William L. Jeffries IV. "I Still Remember America: Senior African Americans Talk About Segregation," *Journal of African American Studies* 12, no. 3 (August 2008): 229-42.

32. Anders Walker, *The Burning House: Jim Crow and the Making of Modern America* (New Haven, CT: Yale University Press, 2018).

33. Douglas A. Blackmon, *Slavery by Another Name: The Re-Enslavement of Black Americans from the Civil War to World War II* (New York: Anchor Books, 2008).

34. Blackmon, *Slavery by Another Name*, 5-6.

35. Blackmon, 402.

36. Purnell, Theoharis, and Woodard, *Strange Careers*, 4.

37. Woodward, *Strange Career of Jim Crow*, 2002, 192.

38. Purnell, Theoharis, and Woodard, *Strange Careers*, 4.

39. Purnell, Theoharis, and Woodard, 4.

40. Woodward, *Strange Career of Jim Crow*, 2002, 115.

41. Purnell, Theoharis, and Woodard, *Strange Careers*, 11.

42. Rothstein, *Color of Law*.

43. Jessica Trounstine, *Segregation by Design: Local Politics and Inequality in American Cities* (Cambridge, MA: Cambridge University Press, 2018).

44. Rothstein, *Color of Law*, vii.

45. Trounstine, *Segregation by Design*, 3.

46. Trounstine.

47. Trounstine, 13; Patrick Sharkey, *Stuck in Place: Urban Neighborhoods and the End of Progress Toward Racial Equality* (Chicago: University of Chicago Press, 2013).

48. Tom I. Romero II, "The 'Tri-Ethnic' Dilemma: Race, Equality, and the Fourteenth Amendment in The American West," *Temple Political and Civil Rights Law Review* 13, no. 2 (Spring 2004): 828.

49. Romero, "'Tri-Ethnic' Dilemma," 830.

50. Paul Ortiz, *An African American and Latinx History of the United States* (Boston: Beacon, 2018).

51. Ortiz, *African American and Latinx History*, 58-59.

52. Bruce A. Glasrud, "Jim Crow's Emergence in Texas," *American Studies* 15, no. 1 (1974): 47-48.

53. Julie M. Weise, "Mexican Nationalisms, Southern Racisms: Mexicans and Mexican Americans in the U.S. South, 1908-1939," *American Quarterly* 60, no. 3 (September 2008): 749-77.

54. Juan F. Perea, "Buscondo America: Why Integration and Equal Protection Fail to Protect Latinos," *Harvard Law Review* 117, no. 5 (2004): 1420-69.

55. Perea, "Buscondo America," 1429.
56. Monica Munoz Martinez, *The Injustice Never Leaves You: Anti-Mexican Violence in Texas* (Cambridge, MA: Harvard University Press, 2018), 6.
57. Martinez, *Injustice Never Leaves You*, 12.
58. Leslie Bow, "Racial Interstitiality and the Anxieties of the 'Partly Colored': Representations of Asians Under Jim Crow," *Journal of Asian American Studies* 10, no. 1 (February 2007): 1–30.
59. Davison M. Douglas, "The Limits of Law in Accomplishing Racial Change: School Segregation in the Pre-Brown North," *UCLA Law Review* 44, no. 3 (February 1997): 677–744.
60. Heather Andrea Williams, *Self-Taught: African American Education in Slavery and Freedom* (Chapel Hill: University of North Carolina Press, 2005).
61. Williams, *Self-Taught*, 13.
62. Williams, 16.
63. Williams, 24.
64. Williams, 39.
65. Williams, 69.
66. Williams, 75.
67. Williams, 95.
68. Williams, 125.
69. Williams, 139.
70. Williams, 174.
71. Williams, 195.
72. Williams, 197.
73. Williams, 197–98.
74. W. E. B. Du Bois, "The Economics of Negro Emancipation in the United States," *Sociological Review* 4, no. 4 (1911): 303–13.
75. James D. Anderson, *The Education of Blacks in the South, 1860–1935* (Chapel Hill: University of North Carolina Press, 1988).
76. William H. Watkins, *The White Architects of Black Education: Ideology and Power in America, 1865–1954* (New York: Teachers College Press, 2001).
77. Anderson, *Education of Blacks*, 182.
78. Davison M. Douglas, "The Limits of Law in Accomplishing Racial Change: School Segregation in the Pre-Brown North," *UCLA Law Review* 44, no. 3 (February 1997): 677–744.
79. Davison M. Douglas, *Jim Crow Moves North: The Battle over Northern School Segregation, 1865–1954* (New York: Cambridge University Press, 2005).
80. Roberts v. Boston, 59 Mass. (5 Cush.) 198 (1850).
81. Douglas, *Jim Crow Moves North*, 59; Plessy v. Ferguson, 163 U.S. 537, 544–45 (1896) (discussing *Roberts* in support of the principle of separate but equal as consistent with the meaning of equal protection in the Fourteenth Amendment).
82. Douglas, *Jim Crow Moves North*, 60.

83. Douglas, 123, 219.

84. Andrew R. Highsmith and Ansley T. Erickson. "Segregation as Splitting, Segregation as Joining: Schools, Housing, and the Many Modes of Jim Crow," *American Journal of Education* 121, no. 4 (August 2015): 563–95.

85. Katie R. Eyer, "The New Jim Crow Is the Old Jim Crow," *Yale Law Journal* 128, no. 4 (2019): 1032–33.

86. Eyer, "The New Jim Crow," 1049.

87. Eyer, 1074.

88. Adam Fairclough, *A Class of Their Own: Black Teachers in the Segregated South* (Cambridge, MA: Harvard University Press, 2007).

89. Vivian Gunn Morris and Curtis L. Morris, "Before Brown, After Brown: What Has Changed for African-American Children?," *University of Florida Journal of Law and Public Policy* 16, no. 2 (2005): 216.

90. Morris and Morris, "Before Brown, After Brown," 217.

91. Vanessa Siddle Walker, "Valued Segregated Schools for African American Children in the South, 1935–1969: A Review of Common Themes and Characteristics," *Review of Educational Research* 70, no. 3 (2000): 253–85.

92. Jean A. Patterson et al., "Remembering Teachers in a Segregated School: Narratives of Womanist Pedagogy," *Urban Education* 46, no. 3 (July 2010): 267–91.

93. Hilton Kelly, "What Jim Crow Teachers Could Do: Educational Capital and Teachers' Work in Under-Resourced Schools," *Urban Review: Issues and Ideas in Public Education* 42, no. 4 (2010): 329.

94. Morris and Morris, "Before Brown, After Brown," 228.

95. Morris and Morris, 221.

96. Morris and Morris, 221.

97. Michael Fultz, "The Displacement of Black Educators Post-Brown: An Overview and Analysis." *History of Education Quarterly* 44, no. 1 (Spring 2004): 11–45.

98. Mallory Lutz, "The Hidden Cost of Brown v. Board: African American Educators' Resistance to Desegregating Schools," *Online Journal of Rural Research and Policy* 12, no. 4 (2017), https://doi.org/10.4148/1936-0487.1085.

99. Maggie Blackhawk, "Federal Indian Law as Paradigm Within Public Law," *Harvard Law Review* 132, no. 7 (2019): 1787–877.

100. Ann Piccard, "Death by Boarding School: 'The Last Acceptable Racism' and the United States' Genocide of Native Americans," *Gonzaga Law Review* 49, no. 1 (2013/14): 154.

101. Nizhone Meza, "Indian Education: Maintaining Tribal Sovereignty Through Native American Culture and Language Preservation," *Brigham Young University Education and Law Journal* 2015, no. 1 (2015): 353–66.

102. Piccard, "Death by Boarding School," 151.

103. Piccard, 152–53.

104. Piccard, 137–86.

105. Piccard, 152.
106. Gabriel J. Chin and Daniel K. Tu, "Comprehensive Immigration Reform in the Jim Crow Era: Chinese Exclusion and the McCreary Act of 1893," *Asian American Law Journal* 23, no. 1 (2016): 39–68.
107. Chin and Tu, "Comprehensive Immigration Reform," 39–68.
108. Chin and Tu, 51–52.
109. Joyce Kuo, "Excluded, Segregated and Forgotten: A Historical View of the Discrimination of Chinese Americans in Public Schools," *Asian Law Journal* 5 (1998): 181–212.
110. Chin and Tu, "Comprehensive Immigration Reform," 39–68.
111. Perea, "Buscondo America," 1420–69.
112. Perea, 1425.
113. Perea, 1443–44.
114. Perea, 1439.
115. Daniel Aaron Rochmes, "Blinded by the White: Latino School Desegregation and the Insidious Allure of Whiteness," *Texas Hispanic Journal of Law and Policy* 13 (Spring 2007): 7–24.
116. José Roberto Juárez Jr. "Recovering Texas History: Tejanos, Jim Crow, Lynchings and the University of Texas School of Law," *South Texas Law Review* 52, no. 1 (Fall 2010): 85–100.
117. Rochmes, "Blinded by the White," 18.
118. Margaret E. Montoya, "A Brief History of Chicana/o School Segregation: One Rationale for Affirmative Action," *Berkeley La Raza Law Journal* 12, no. 2 (Fall 2001): 159–72.
119. Jeanne M. Powers, "On Separate Paths: The Mexican American and African American Legal Campaigns Against School Segregation," *American Journal of Education* 121 (November 2014): 29–55.

Chapter 4

1. Strauder v. West Virginia, 100 U.S. 303 (1880).
2. Brown v. Board of Education, 347 U.S. 483, 491 (1954) (emphasis added).
3. *Brown*, 347 U.S. at 483 n. 5 (quoting Strauder v. West Virginia, 307–308 [emphasis added]).
4. *Strauder*, 100 U.S. at 306.
5. Barbara J. Flagg, "Was Blind, But Now I See: White Race Consciousness and the Requirement of Discriminatory Intent," *Michigan Law Review* 91, no. 5 (1993): 957.
6. *Strauder*, 100 U.S. at 306 (emphasis added).
7. *Strauder*, 100 U.S. at 306.
8. *Strauder*, 100 U.S. at 306 (emphasis added).
9. *Strauder*, 100 U.S. at 307 (emphasis added) (citing Slaughterhouse Cases, 83 U.S. 36 [1873]).
10. *Strauder*, 100 U.S. at 307.

11. *Strauder*, 100 U.S. at 308.
12. *Strauder*, 100 U.S. at 308 (emphasis added).
13. Sanford V. Levinson, "Why *Strauder v. West Virginia* is the Most Important Single Source of Insight on the Tensions Contained within the Equal Protection Clause of the Fourteenth Amendment," *St. Louis University Law Journal* 90 (2018): 603; see also Eric Foner, *The Second Founding: How the Civil War and Reconstruction Remade the Constitution* (New York: W.W. Norton, 2019), 147; Michael J. Klarman, "The Plessy Era," *Supreme Court Review* 1998 (1998): 303–414.
14. Benno C. Schmidt, "Juries, Jurisdiction and Race Discrimination: The Lost History of *Strauder v. West Virginia*," *Texas Law Review* 61, no. 8 (1983): 1401-99.
15. Schmidt, "Juries, Jurisdiction and Race Discrimination," 1415.
16. Flowers v. Mississippi, 588 U.S.–, 139 S. Ct. 2228 (2019).
17. Slaughterhouse Cases, 83 U.S. 36 (1873).
18. Slaughterhouse Cases, 83 U.S. at 72.
19. Slaughterhouse Cases, 83 U.S. at 81.
20. The case involved two Black teenagers accused of killing a White man. A series of procedural devices were used to challenge the core injustice of the composition of the jury. The Court ultimately determined that the writ of *habeus* corpus used to challenge the jury composition was not proper, in essence that the wrong route was used to correct the constitutional violations.
21. 1866 Civil Rights Act, cited in Ex Parte Virginia, 100 U.S. 339 (1880), 317-18 (emphasis added).
22. Ex Parte Virginia at 318 (emphasis added).
23. The Court determined that not all violations of equal protection are subject to the removal statute: "The constitutional amendment is broader than the provisions of that section." Because of that, the defendants lose in this case—the removal statute authorizes removal only before trial. Constitutional violations during the trial are corrected by appeal to state courts and by the Supreme Court.
24. Ex Parte Virginia, 100 U.S. at 339.
25. Ex Parte Virginia, 100 U.S. at 344 (quoting 1875 statute, section 4, pt. 3).
26. Ex Parte Virginia, 100 U.S. at 344–345 (emphasis added).
27. Ex Parte Virginia, 100 U.S. at 346 (emphasis added).
28. Ex Parte Virginia, 100 U.S. at 349.
29. Plessy v. Ferguson, 163 U.S. 537 (1896).
30. *Plessy*, 163 U.S. at 542.
31. *Plessy*, 163 U.S. at 557 (Justice Harlan, dissenting).
32. *Plessy*, 163 U.S. at 559 (Justice Harlan, dissenting).
33. *Brown*, 347 U.S. at 494.
34. *Brown*, 347 U.S. at 483.

35. *Brown*, 347 U.S. at 497.

36. *Brown*, 347 U.S. at 493 (quoting Sweatt v. Painter, 339 U.S. 629, 634 [1950]).

37. U.S. Constitutional Amendment V.

38. Bolling v. Sharpe, 347 U.S. 497, 499 (1954).

39. *Bolling*, 347 U.S. at 497.

40. *Bolling*, 347 U.S. at 499.

41. *Bolling*, 347 U.S. at 500 (emphasis added).

42. Charles L. Black Jr., "The Lawfulness of the Segregation Decisions," *Yale Law Journal* 69, no. 3, (1960): 421–31.

43. Black, "Segregation Decisions," 423 (emphasis added).

44. Black, 422.

45. Black, 424.

46. Black, 424.

47. Black, 427.

48. Black, 428 (emphasis added).

49. Green v. County School Board of New Kent County, 391 U.S. 430 (1968), 436.

50. Richard Kluger, *Simple Justice: The History of Brown v. Board of Education and Black America's Struggle for Equality* (New York: Alfred A. Knopf, 1975), 749.

51. Paul Finkelman, "The Radicalism of Brown," *University of Pittsburgh Law Review* 66, no. 1 (2004): 56.

52. Finkelman, "Radicalism of Brown," 35–56.

53. David Southern, "Beyond Jim Crow Liberalism: Judge Waring's Fight Against Segregation in South Carolina, 1942–52," *Journal of Negro History* 66, no. 3 (1981): 209–27.

54. Peter H. Irons, *Jim Crow's Children: The Broken Promise of the Brown Decision* (New York: Penguin, 2002); Michael J. Klarman, *Brown v. Board of Education and the Civil Rights Movement*, abridged ed. of *From Jim Crow to Civil Rights: The Supreme Court and the Struggle for Racial Equality* (New York: Oxford University Press, 2007).

55. Cooper v. Aaron, 358 U.S. 1 (1958).

56. *Cooper*, 358 U.S. at 17.

57. *Cooper*, 358 U.S. at 19–20 (emphasis added).

58. Griffin v. County School Board of Prince Edward County, 377 U.S. 218 (1964), 223.

59. Bradley v. School Board of City of Richmond, 382 U.S. 103, 105 (1965).

60. Watson v. City of Memphis, 373 U.S. 526 (1963).

61. *Watson*, 373 U.S. at 533.

62. *Watson*, 373 U.S. at 535.

63. *Watson*, 373 U.S. at 530.

64. *Watson*, 373 U.S. at 530 n. 2.

65. *Watson*, 373 U.S. at 532 n. 4.

66. Jones v. Alfred H. Mayer Co., 392 U.S. 409 (1968) (property rights, restrictive covenants, links between slavery and present).

67. *Jones*, 392 U.S. at 440–43.

68. *Jones*, 392 U.S. at 445 (emphasis added).

69. *Jones*, 392 U.S. at 445–46.

70. Green v. County School Board of New Kent County, 436 (emphasis added).

71. Swann v. Charlotte-Mecklenburg Board of Education, 402 U.S. 1, 15 (1971).

72. *Swann*, 402 U.S. at 15–16.

73. *Swann*, 402 U.S. at 15–16.

74. Keyes v. School District No. 1, Denver, Colorado, 413 U.S. 189 (1973).

75. Milliken v. Bradley, 418 U.S. 717 (1974).

76. Board of Education of Oklahoma City Public Schools v. Dowell, 498 U.S. 237 (1991).

77. Missouri v. Jenkins, 515 U.S. 70 (1995).

78. *Keyes*, 413 U.S. at 218–19.

79. *Keyes*, 413 U.S. at 219.

80. Robert L. Hayman Jr. and Nancy Levit, "The Constitutional Ghetto," *Wisconsin Law Review* 1993, no. 3 (1993): 635.

81. *Jenkins*, 515 U.S. at 175 (Justice Ginsburg, dissenting).

82. San Antonio Independent School District v. Rodriguez, 411 U.S. 1 (1972).

83. Plyler v. Doe, 457 U.S. 202 (1982).

84. Civil Rights Act of 1964, title VI, section 601, 42 U.S.C. section 2000D et seq.

85. Public Law 89-10, Title 20-Education, chapter 70, "Strengthening and Improvement of Elementary and Secondary Schools."

86. Jim Hilbert, "School Desegregation 2.0: What is Needed to Finally Integrate America's Public Schools," *Northwestern Journal of Human Rights* 16, no. 1 (2018): 124.

87. Mildred J. Hudgon and Barbara Holmes, "Missing Teachers, Impaired Communities: The Unanticipated Consequences of Brown v. Board of Education on the African American Teaching Force at the Precollegiate Level," *Journal of Negro Education* 63, no. 3 (1994): 388–93.

88. Hilbert, "School Desegregation 2.0," 123. In 2017-2018, teachers of color accounted for 18% of the teaching workforce—7% Black, 9% Latinx, and 2% Asian.

89. Jeremy Anderson and Erica Frankenberg, "Voluntary Integration in Uncertain Times," *Phi Delta Kappan* 100, no. 5 (2019): 14–18.

90. Parents Involved in Community Schools v. Seattle School District No. 1, 551 U.S. 701 (2007), 746.

91. *Parents Involved in Community Schools*, 551 U.S. at 748.

92. *Parents Involved in Community Schools*, 551 U.S. at 864 (Justice Breyer, dissenting) (emphasis added).

93. *Parents Involved in Community Schools*, 551 U.S. at 867-68 (Justice Breyer, dissenting).

94. *Parents Involved in Community Schools*, 551 U.S. at 838–45 (Justice Breyer, dissenting).

95. Roper v. Simmons, 543 U.S. 551 (2005).

96. *Roper*, 543 U.S. at 570.

97. Graham v. Florida, 560 U.S. 48 (2010); Miller v. Alabama, 567 U.S. 460 (2012).

98. *Graham*, 560 U.S. at 68–69 (citing *Roper*, 543 U.S. at 570).

99. *Miller*, 567 U.S. at 471.

100. J.D.B. v. North Carolina, 564 U.S. 261 (2011).

101. *J.D.B.*, 564 U.S. at 10–11, slip opinion.

102. See, e.g., Carey v. Population Services International, 431 U.S. 678 (1977); Planned Parenthood of Central Missouri v. Danforth, 428 U.S. 52 (1976); Bellotti v. Baird, 443 U.S. 622 (1979)

103. Nancy E. Dowd, *Reimagining Equality: A New Deal for Children of Color* (New York: New York University Press, 2018), 53–96.

104. Dowd, *Reimagining Equality*, 53–96; Barbara Bennett Woodhouse, *The Ecology of Childhood: How Our Changing World Threatens Children's Rights* (New York: New York University Press, 2020).

105. Regents of University of California v. Bakke, 438 U.S. 265 (1978).

106. *Bakke*, 438 U.S. at 311–15 (diversity); *Bakke*, 438 U.S. at 315–320 (quotas).

107. Grutter v. Bollinger, 539 U.S. 306 (2003) (law school); Gratz v. Bollinger, 539 U.S. 244 (2003) (undergraduate).

108. *Grutter*, 539 U.S. at 328–33.

109. *Grutter*, 539 U.S. at 330.

110. *Grutter*, 539 U.S. at 332–33.

111. Fisher v. University of Texas at Austin, 579 U.S.365 (2016).

112. *Fisher*, 579 U.S. at 371–72.

113. *Fisher*, 579 U.S. at 388; see also discussion of diversity benefits at 579 U.S. 381–82.

114. Students for Fair Admissions, Inc. v President & Fellows of Harvard College, 600 U.S. 181 (2023).

115. *Students for Fair Admissions*, Opinion of the Court, (Chief Justice Roberts), 600 U.S.–(2023), slip opinion at Part III, and page 15, page 39. Justice Thomas's concurrence exhaustively argues for absolute colorblindness.

116. *Students for Fair Admissions*, 600 U.S.–(2023), Dissent of Justice Sotomayor, slip opinion at 1.

117. *Students for Fair Admissions*, 600 U.S.–(2023), Dissent of Justice Sotomayor, slip opinion at 2.

118. *Students for Fair Admissions*, 600 U.S.–(2023), Dissent of Justice Jackson, slip opinion at 1.

119. *Students for Fair Admissions*, 600 U.S.–(2023, Dissent of Justice Jackson slip opinion at 18.

120. Peggy McIntosh, "White Privilege: Unpacking the Invisible Knapsack," *Peace and Freedom Magazine* 49, no. 4 (July/August 1989): 10–12.

Chapter 5
1. Jamelle Bouie, "The Backlash Against C.R.T. Shows that Republicans are Losing Ground," *New York Times*, February 4, 2022.
2. Margaret Beale Spencer, "Phenomenology and Ecological Systems Theory: Development of Diverse Groups," in *Handbook of Child Psychology*, vol. 1, *Theoretical Models of Human Development*, 6th ed., ed. R. M. Lerner and W. Damon (New York: Wiley , 2006), 829–93; Margaret Beale Spencer, "Phenomenology and Ecological Systems Theory: Development of Diverse Groups," in *Child and Adolescent Development: An Advanced Course*, ed W. Damon and R. M. Lerner (New York: Wiley, 2008), 696–735.
3. Richard Lerner and Jacqueline Lerner, "Children in Their Contexts: A Goodness-of-Fit Model," in *Parenting Across the Life Span* (New York: Routledge, 2017), 377–404.
4. Lerner and Lerner, "Children in Their Contexts."
5. Adam I. P. Smith, "Why Is America Haunted by Its Past?," History Extra, June 15, 2020, https://www.historyextra.com/period/victorian/why-america-haunted-past-us-history-civil-war-misconceptions-revolution/.
6. Karl Marx, "The Eighteenth Brumaire of Louis Bonaparte," https://www.marxists.org/archive/marx/works/1852/18th-brumaire/ch01.htm.
7. Spencer, "Phenomenology and Ecological Systems," in *Handbook of Child Psychology*; Spencer, "Phenomenology and Ecological Systems," in *Child and Adolescent Development*.
8. Robert Havighurst, *Human Development and Education* (Oxford: Longmans, Green, 1953); Robert White, "Motivation Reconsidered: The Concept of Competence," *Psychological Review* 66: (1959), 297–333; R. White, "Competence and Psychosexual Development," in *Nebraska Symposium on Motivation*, ed. M. R. Jones, (Lincoln: University of Nebraska Press, 1960).
9. Spencer, "Phenomenology and Ecological Systems," in *Handbook of Child Psychology*; Spencer, "Phenomenology and Ecological Systems," in *Child and Adolescent Development*.
10. Spencer, "Phenomenology and Ecological Systems," in *Handbook of Child Psychology*; Spencer, "Phenomenology and Ecological Systems," in *Child and Adolescent Development*.
11. Walter R. Allen, Margaret Beale Spencer, and Geraldine K. Brookins, "Synthesis: Black Children Keep on Growing," in *Beginnings: The Social and Affective Development of Black Children*, ed. Margaret B. Spencer, Geraldine K. Brookins, and Walter R. Allen (Hillsdale, NJ: Erlbaum, 1985).
12. Smith, "Why Is American Haunted by Its Past?"
13. Margaret B. Spencer, Bronwyn Nichols Lodato, Charles Spencer et al., "Innovating Resilience Promotion: Integrating Cultural Practices, Social Ecologies and Development-Sensitive Conceptual Strategies for Advancing

Child Well-Being," *Advances in Child Development and Behavior* 57 (2019): 101–148. Bronwyn Nichols Lodato, Jennifer Hall, and Margaret Beale Spencer, "Culture, Diversity, Context and the Development of Coping: A Phenomenological Perspective," in *The Cambridge Handbook of the Development of Coping*, ed. E. Skinner and M. Zimmer-Gembeck (Cambridge: Cambridge University Press, 2023), 581–94.

14. Smith, "Why Is America Haunted by Its Past?"; Nichols Lodato, Hall, and Spencer, "Culture, Diversity, Context and the Development of Coping."

15. Smith, "Why Is America Haunted by Its Past?"

16. Molefi Kete Asante, *An Afrocentric Manifesto* (Oxford: Polity, 2007); K. Schwarz and A. Nicholson, "Collapsing the Boundaries Between De Jure and De Facto Slavery: The Foundations of Slavery Beyond the Transatlantic Frame," *Human Rights Review* 21 (2020): 391–414; also see Margaret Beale Spencer, Bronwyn Nichols Lodato, Charles Spencer et al., "Innovating Resilience Promotion: Integrating Cultural Practices, Social Ecologies and Development-Sensitive Conceptual Strategies for Advancing Child Well-Being," *Advances in Child Development and Behavior* 57 (2019): 101–48; Jennifer Hall, Bronwyn Nichols Lodato, and Margaret Beale Spencer, "Du Boisian Contributions to Phenomenological Variant of Ecological Systems Theory: Interrogating Thriving Efforts and Barbed-Wire Paths to Black Resiliency," in *The Oxford Handbook of W. E. B. Du Bois*, ed. Aldon Morris et al. (online edition, Oxford Academic, 2022), C33.P1–C33.S10.

17. Spencer, "Phenomenology and Ecological Systems," in *Handbook of Child Psychology*; Spencer, "Phenomenology and Ecological Systems," in *Child and Adolescent Development.*

18. Spencer et al., "Innovating Resilience Promotion."

19. Spencer et al., "Innovating Resilience Promotion"; Hall, Nichols Lodato, and Spencer, "Du Boisian Contributions."

20. William E. Cross, *Shades of Black: Diversity in African-American Identity* (Philadelphia: Temple University Press, 1991); Margaret B. Spencer, "Children's Cultural Values and Parental Child Rearing Strategies," *Developmental Review* 3 (1983): 351–70; Margaret B. Spencer, "Black Children's Race Awareness, Racial Attitudes, and Self-Concept: A Reinter-pretation," *Journal of Child Psychology and Psychiatry* 25 no. 3, (1984): 433–41; Margaret B. Spencer, "Risk and Resilience: How Black Children Cope with Stress," *Social Science* 71, no. 1 (1986): 22–26; Diane Hughes et al., "Parents' Ethnic-Racial Socialization Practices: A Review of Research and Directions for Future Study," *Developmental Psychology* 42, 5 (2006): 747–70.

21. Allen, Spencer, and Brookins, "Synthesis," 301–14; Fisher et al., "Research Ethics for Mental Health Science Involving Ethnic Minority Children and Youths," *American Psychologist* 57, no. 12: (2002): 1024–40; Fisher et al., "The National Conference on Graduate Education in the Applications of

Developmental Science Across the Life Span," *Journal of Applied Developmental Psychology* 14 (1993): 1–10.

22. Spencer et al., "Innovating Resilience Promotion," 2019.

23. S. Fajardo et al., "Positive Identity Development as an Immigration Integration Device: Reframing Alternative Conceptual Findings for Academically Resilient, Low Income Urban Youth," in *Re/Formation and Identity: The Intersectionality of Development, Culture, and Immigration*, ed. Debra J. Johnson, Susan S. Chuang, and Jenny Glozman (Cham, Switzerland, Springer Nature, 2021), 1–15; M. B. Spencer and B. Tinsley, "Identity as Coping: Youths' Diverse Strategies for Successful Adaptation," *Prevention Researcher* 15, no. 4 (2008), 17–21; M. B. Spencer, S. Fegley, and V. Harpalani, "A Theoretical and Empirical Examination of Identity as Coping: Linking Coping Resources to the Self-Processes of African American Youth," *Journal of Applied Developmental Science* 7, no. 3 (2003), 181–88; V. P. Franklin, "From Integration to Black Self-Determination: Changing Social Science Perspectives on Afro-American Life and Culture," *in Beginnings: The Social and Affective Development of Black Children*, ed. M. B. Spencer, G. K. Brookins, and W. R. Allen (Mahwah, NJ: Lawrence Earlbaum Associates, 1985), 19–28; Diana Slaughter and Gerald McWorter, "Social Origins and Early Features of Scientific Study of Black American Families and Children," in *Beginnings: The Social and Affective Development of Black Children*, ed. M. B. Spencer, G. K. Brookins, and W. R. Allen (Hillsdale, NJ: Erlbaum, 1985), 5–18.

24. Spencer, "Phenomenology and Ecological Systems," in *Child and Adolescent Development*.

25. Michelle Alexander, *The New Jim Crow: Mass Incarceration in the Age of Colorblindness*, (New York: New Press, 2010).

26. Smith, "Why Is America Haunted by Its Past?"; Bernestine Singley, *When Race Becomes Real: Writers Confront Their Personal Histories* (Carbondale, IL: Southern University Press, 2008).

27. Smith, "Why Is America Haunted by Its Past?"

28. Suniya Luthar, Samuel Barkin, and Elizabeth Crossman, "I Can, Therefore I Must": Fragility in the Upper-Middle Classes," *Development and Psychopathology* 25, no. 4, part 2 (2013): 1529–49.

29. Urie Bronfenbrenner, *The Ecology of Human Development: Experiments by Nature and Design* (Cambridge: Harvard University Press, 1979).

30. Robert Guthrie, *Even the Rat Was White: A Historical View of Psychology* (New York: Harper and Row, 1976).

31. Margaret Beale Spencer, "What You Ignore, Becomes Empowered: Social Science Traditions Weaponized to Resist Resiliency Research Opportunities," in *Race and Culturally Responsive Inquiry in Education*, ed. Stafford Hood et al. (Cambridge: Harvard Education Press, 2022), 63–80; Margaret Spencer, "Acknowledging Bias and Pursuing Protections to Support Anti-Racist Developmental Science: Critical Contributions of Phenomenological Variant

of Ecological Systems Theory," *Journal of Adolescent Research* 36, no. 6 (2021): 569–83.

32. Spencer, "Phenomenology and Ecological Systems," in *Handbook of Child Psychology*; Spencer, "Phenomenology and Ecological Systems," in *Child and Adolescent Development*.

33. Kimberlé Crenshaw, "Demarginalizing the Intersection of Race and Sex: A Black Feminist Critique of Antidiscrimination Doctrine, Feminist Theory and Antiracist Politics," *University of Chicago Legal Forum* 1989 (1989): 139–67.

34. Kimberlé Crenshaw, "Mapping the Margins: Intersectionality, Identity Politics, and Violence Against Women of Color," *Stanford Law Review* 43, no. 6 (July 1991), 1241–99; for public health, see Greta R. Bauer, "Incorporating Intersectionality Theory into Population Health Research Methodology: Challenges and the Potential to Advance Health Equity," *Social Science & Medicine* 110 (2014): 10–17; for the labor market, see Irene Browne and Joya Misra, "The Intersection of Gender and Race in the Labor Market," *Annual Review of Sociology* 29 (2003): 487–513, and Chenoa A. Flippen, "Intersectionality at Work Determinants of Labor Supply among Immigrant Latinas," *Gender & Society* 28, no. 3 (2013): 404–34; for self-perception, see Andrew Penner and Aliya Saperstein, "Engendering Racial Perceptions: An Intersectional Analysis of How Social Status Shapes Race," *Gender & Society* 27, no. 3 (2013): 319–44; for psychological health, see Dawn M. Szymanski and Destin N. Stewart, "Racism and Sexism as Correlates of African American Women's Psychological Distress," *Sex Roles: A Journal of Research* 63, no. 3–4 (2010): 226–38.

35. Hall, Nichols Lodato, and Spencer, "Du Boisian Contributions to Phenomenological Variant of Ecological Systems Theory."

36. Hall, Nichols Lodato, and Spencer.

37. W. E. B. Du Bois, *The Souls of Black Folk* (New York: Gramercy Books, 1994).

38. Jose Itzigsohn and Karida Brown, "Sociology and the Theory of Double Consciousness: W.E.B Du Bois's Phenomenology of Racialized Subjectivity," *Du Bois Review* 12, no. 2 (2015): 232.

39. Hall, Nichols Lodato, and Spencer, "Du Boisian Contributions to Phenomenological Variant of Ecological Systems Theory."

40. Margaret Beale Spencer et al., "Innovating Resilience Promotion."

41. Spencer, "Phenomenology and Ecological Systems," in *Handbook of Child Psychology*; Spencer, "Phenomenology and Ecological Systems," in *Child and Adolescent Development*.

42. Margaret Beale Spencer, "What You Ignore, Becomes Empowered"; Margaret Beale Spencer, "Character Virtue, Social Science, and 'Adept' Leadership: A Failure to Acknowledge Practice?," in *Critiquing Contemporary Approaches to Character Virtue Development*, ed. Richard Lerner and Michael Matthews (Routledge, in press).

Chapter 6

1. Brown v. Board of Education, 347 U.S. 494 (1954), quoting from the lower court opinion, Brown v. Board of Education 98 F. Supp. 797 (D. Kansas 1951).
2. *Brown*, 347 U.S. at 494, footnote 11.
3. Plessy v. Ferguson, 163 U.S. 537, 551 (1896).
4. Michael Heise, "Brown v. Board of Education, Footnote 11, and Multidisciplinarity," *Cornell Law Review* 90, no. 2 (2005): 279–320.
5. H. Hill and J. Greenberg, *Citizen's Guide to Desegregation: A Study of Social and Legal Change in American Life* (Boston: Beacon, 1955).
6. Edmond Cahn, *Jurisprudence, New York University Law Review* 30, no. 1 (1955): 150–70; Malik Edwards, "Footnote Eleven for the New Millennium: Ecological Perspective Arguments in Support of Compelling Interest," *Seattle University Law Review* 31, no. 4 (2008): 891.
7. L. T. Benjamin, E. M. Crouse Jr., and American Psychological Association, "The American Psychological Association's Response to Brown v. Board of Education: The Case of Kenneth B. Clark," *American Psychologist* 57, no. 1 (2002): 38–50.
8. Edwards, "Footnote Eleven," 891–910.
9. Dean Hashimoto, "Science as Mythology in Constitutional Law," *Oregon Law Review* 76 (1997): 111–53.
10. Kenneth B. Clark and Mamie K. Clark, "The Development of Consciousness of Self and the Emergence of Racial Identification in Negro Preschool Children," *Journal of Social Psychology* 10, no. 4 (1939): 591–99; Kenneth B. Clark and Mamie K. Clark, "Skin Color as a Factor in Racial Identification of Negro Preschool children," *Journal of Social Psychology* 11, no. 1 (1940): 159–69; Vinay Harpalani, Ahmad Qadafi, and Margaret Beale Spencer, "Doll Studies," in *Encyclopedia of Race and Racism*, 2nd ed., ed. Patrick L. Mason (Detroit: Cengage, 2013), 67–70; Diane Byrd et al., "A Modern Doll Study: Self Concept," *Race, Gender & Class* 24, no. 1–2 (2017): 186–202.
11. Margaret Beale Spencer, "Preschool Children's Social Cognition and Cultural Cognition: A Cognitive Developmental Interpretation of Race Dissonance Findings," *Journal of Psychology* 112 (1982): 275–96; Margaret Beale Spencer, "Black Children's Race Awareness, Racial Attitudes, and Self-concept: A Reinterpretation," *Journal of Child Psychology and Psychiatry* 25 (1984): 433–41; Harpalani, Qadafi, and Spencer, "Doll Studies"; William E. Cross, *Shades of Black: Diversity in African American Identity* (Philadelphia: Temple University Press, 1991); Margaret Beale Spencer and Carol Markstrom-Adams, "Identity Processes Among Racial and Ethnic Minority Children in America," *Child Development* 61 (1990): 290–96; Margaret Beale Spencer, "Black Children's Race Awareness, Racial Attitudes, and Self-Concept: A Reinterpretation," in *Annual Progress in Child Psychiatry and Child*

Development, ed. S. Chess and A. Thomas (1985), 616–30 (reprinted from Spencer, "Black Children's Race Awareness," 433–41).

12. Mary E. Goodman, *Race Awareness in Young Children* (Cambridge, MA: Addison-Wesley, 1964); Bentley Gibson, Erin Robbins, and Philippe Rochat, "White Bias in 3-7-Year-Old Children Across Cultures," *Journal of Cognition and Culture* 15, no. 3–4 (2015): 344–73; Byrd et al., "A Modern Doll Study"; Phillip Jordan and Maria Hernandez-Reif, "Reexamination of Young Children's Racial Attitudes and Skin Tone Preferences," *Journal of Black Psychology* 35, no. 3 (2009): 388–403.

13. Jordan and Hernandez-Reif, "Reexamination of Young Children's"; Erin A. Kaufman and Deborah L. Wiese, "Skin-Tone Preferences and Self-Representation in Hispanic Children," *Early Child Development and Care* 182, no. 2 (2012): 277–90; Katie Stokes-Guinan, "Age and Skin Tone as Predictors of Positive and Negative Racial Attitudes in Hispanic Children," *Hispanic Journal of Behavioral Sciences* 33, no. 1 (2011): 3–21.

14. Cara J. Averhart and Rebecca S. Bigler, "Shades of Meaning: Skin Tone, Racial Attitudes, and Constructive Memory in African American Children," *Journal of Experimental Child Psychology* 67, no. 3 (1997): 363–88; Suzanne G. Fegley et al., "Colorism Embodied: Skin Tone and Psychosocial Well-Being in Adolescence," in *Body in Mind, Mind in Body: Developmental Perspectives on Embodiment and Consciousness,* ed. Willis Overton, Ulrich Mueller, and Judith Newman (Mahwah, NJ: Lawrence Erlbaum, 2008), 281–311.

15. Kathy Russell, Midge Wilson, and Ronald Hall, *The Color Complex: The Politics of Skin Color Among African Americans* (New York: Anchor Books, 1992); Jane A. McDonald, "Potential Influence of Racism and Skin Tone on Early Personality Formation, *Psychoanalytic Review* 93, no. 1 (2006): 93–116; JeffriAnne Wilder and Colleen Cain, "Teaching and Learning Color Consciousness in Black Families: Exploring Family Processes and Women's Experiences with Colorism," *Journal of Family Issues* 32, no. 5 (2011): 577–604.

16. Verna M. Keith and Cedric Herring, "Skin Tone and Stratification in the Black Community," *American Journal of Sociology* 97, no. 3 (1991): 760–78. Michael Hughes and Bradley R. Hertel, "The Significance of Color Remains: A Study of Life Chances, Mate Selection, and Ethnic Consciousness Among Black Americans," *Social Forces* 68, no. 4 (1990): 1105–20; Howard Bodenhorn, "Colorism, Complexion Homogamy, and Household Wealth: Some Historical Evidence," *American Economic Review* 96, no. 2 (2006): 256–60; Howard Bodenhorn and Christopher Ruebeck, "Colourism and African-American Wealth: Evidence from the Nineteenth-Century South," *Journal of Population Economics* 20, no. 3 (2007): 599–620; Arthur Goldsmith, Darrick Hamilton, and William Darity Jr., "Shades of Discrimination: Skin Tone and Wages," *The American Economic Review* 96, no. 2 (2006): 242–45; Igor Ryabov, "Colorism and School-to-Work and School-to-College Transitions of African American Adolescents," *Race and Social Problems* 5, no. 1 (2013): 15–27.

17. Lance Hannon, Robert DeFina, and Sarah Bruch, "The Relationship Between Skin Tone and School Suspension for African Americans," *Race and Social Problems* 5, no. 4 (2013): 281–95; Jamilia Blake et al., "The Role of Colorism in Explaining African American Females' Suspension Risk," *School Psychology Quarterly* 32, no. 1 (2017): 118–30.

    Karletta White, "The Salience of Skin Tone: Effects on the Exercise of Police Enforcement Authority," *Ethnic and Racial Studies* 38, no. 6 (2015): 993–1010; Traci Burch, "Skin Color and the Criminal Justice System: Beyond Black-White Disparities in Sentencing," *Journal of Empirical Legal Studies* 12, no. 3 (2015): 395–420.

18. Meagan Jacobs et al., "Fifty Shades of African Lightness: A Bio-Psychosocial Review of the Global Phenomenon of Skin Lightening Practices," *Journal of Public Health in Africa* 7, no. 2 (2016): 552; Timothy Diette et al., "Skin Shade Stratification and the Psychological Cost of Unemployment: Is There a Gradient for Black Females?," *Review of Black Political Economy* 42, no. 1–2, (2015): 155–177; Dawne M. Mouzon, "Can Family Relationships Explain the Race Paradox in Mental Health," *Journal of Marriage and Family* 75, (2013): 470–85; Ellis P. Monk, "The Cost of Color: Skin Color, Discrimination, and Health Among African-Americans," *American Journal of Sociology* 121, no. 2 (2015): 396–444.

19. Maxine Thompson and Verna Keith, "The Blacker the Berry: Gender, Skin Tone, Self-Esteem, and Self-Efficacy," *Gender and Society* 15 (2001): 336–57; Mark E. Hill, "Skin Color and the Perception of Attractiveness Among African Americans: Does Gender Make a Difference?," *Social Psychology Quarterly* 65, no. 1 (2002): 77–91; T. Joel Wade and Sara Bielitz, "The Differential Effect of Skin Color on Attractiveness, Personality Evaluations, and Perceived Life Success of African Americans," *Journal of Black Psychology* 31, no. 3 (August 2005): 215–36; Tyhesha Goss Elmore, "Colorism in the Classroom: An Exploration of Adolescents' Skin Tone, Skin Tone Preferences, Perceptions of Skin Tone Stigma and Identity" (2009), https://repository .upenn.edu/dissertations/AAI3395695; Scyatta A. Wallace et al., "Gold Diggers, Video Vixens, and Jezebels: Stereotype Images and Substance Use Among Urban African American Girls," *Journal of Women's Health* 20, no. 9 (2011): 1315–24; Margaret L. Hunter, *Race, Gender, and the Politics of Skin Tone* (New York: Routledge, 2005).

20. Gail Ferguson and Phebe Cramer, "Self-Esteem Among Jamaican Children: Exploring the Impact of Skin Color and Rural/Urban Residence," *Journal of Applied Developmental Psychology* 28, no. 4 (2007): 345–59.

21. Hiroshi Wagatsuma, "The Social Perception of Skin Color in Japan," in *Color and Race*, ed. J. H. Franklin (Boston: Beacon Press, 1968), 129–65; Andre Beteille, "Race and Descent as Social Categories in India," in *Color and Race*, ed. J. H. Franklin (Boston: Beacon Press, 1968), 166–85; Ron E. Hall, *The Psychogenesis of Color Based Racism: Implications of Projection for*

Dark-Skinned Puertorriqueños (East Lansing: Julian Samora Research Institute, Michigan State University, 1987); Russell, Wilson, and Hall, *The Color Complex*; Evelyn Nakano Glenn, *Shades of Difference: Why Skin Color Matters* (Palo Alto, CA: Stanford University Press, 2009); Christopher Charles, "Skin Bleaching and the Prestige Complexion of Sexual Attraction," *Sexuality & Culture: An Interdisciplinary Quarterly* 15, no. 4 (2011): 375–90; Gerry Veenstra, "Mismatched Racial Identities, Colourism, and Health in Toronto and Vancouver," *Social Science & Medicine* 73, no. 8 (2011): 1152–62.

22. W. E. B. Du Bois, *The Souls of Black Folk* (New York: Gramercy Books, 1994).

23. Jennifer Hall, Bronwyn Nichols Lodato, and Margaret Beale Spencer, "Du Boisian Contributions to Phenomenological Variant of Ecological Systems Theory: Interrogating Thriving Efforts and Barbed-Wire Paths to Black Resiliency," in *The Oxford Handbook of W.E.B. Du Bois*, ed. Aldon Morris et al. (online edition, Oxford Academic, 2022), C33.P1–C33.S10; Karida Brown and Jose Itzigsohn, "Sociology and the Theory of Double Consciousness: WEB Du Bois's Phenomenology of Racialized Subjectivity," *Du Bois Review* 12, no. 2 (2015): 231–48.

24. Frantz Fanon, *Black Skin, White Masks* (New York: Grove, 1967); Du Bois, *Souls of Black Folk*.

25. Walter D. Mignolo, *The Darker Side of Western Modernity: Global Futures, Decolonial Options* (Durham, NC: Duke University Press, 2011); Nelson Maldonado-Torres, "Cesaire's Gift and the Decolonial Turn," *Radical Philosophy Review* 9, no. 2 (2006): 111–38.

26. Gurminder K. Bhambra, "Postcolonial and Decolonial Dialogues," *Postcolonial Studies* 17, no. 2 (2014): 115–21; Walter R. Allen, Margaret B. Spencer, and Geraldine K. Brookins, "Synthesis: Black Children Keep on Growing," in *Beginnings: The Social and Affective Development of Black Children*, ed. Margaret B. Spencer, Geraldine K. Brookins, and Walter R. Allen (Hillsdale, NJ: Erlbaum, 1985), 301–14; Margaret Beale Spencer and Tirzah Spencer, "Invited Commentary: Exploring the Promises, Intricacies, and Challenges to Positive Youth Development," *Journal of Youth & Adolescence* 43, no. 6 (2014): 1027–35; Gary Drevitch, "Psychology's WEIRD Problem," *Psychology Today*, April 15, 2020, https://www.psychologytoday.com/us/blog/non-weird -science/202004/psychologys-weird-problem; Glenn Adams et al., "Decolonizing Psychological Science: Introduction to the Special Thematic Section," *Journal of Social and Political Psychology* 3, no. 1 (2015): 213–38.

27. Mary Watkins, "Psychosocial Accompaniment," *Journal of Social and Political Psychology* 3 (2015): 324–41.

28. Kristie Dotson, "Tracking Epistemic Violence, Tracking Practices of Silencing," *Hypatia* 26, no. 2 (2011): 236–57.

29. Urie Bronfenbrenner, *The Ecology of Human Development* (Cambridge, MA: Harvard University Press, 1979).

30. Bronfenbrenner, *The Ecology of Human Development*.

31. Watkins, "Psychosocial Accompaniment."

32. Watkins, "Psychosocial Accompaniment"; Du Bois, *Souls of Black Folk*.

33. L. T. Benjamin, E. M. Crouse Jr., and American Psychological Association, "The American Psychological Association's Response to Brown v. Board of Education: The Case of Kenneth B. Clark," *American Psychologist* 57, no. 1 (2002): 38–50; D. M. Scott, *Contempt and Pity: Social Policy and the Image of the Damaged Black Psyche, 1880–1996* (Chapel Hill: University of North Carolina Press, 1997); S. Mody, "Brown Footnote Eleven in Historical Context: Social Science and the Supreme Court's Quest for Legitimacy," *Stanford Law Review* 54 (2002): 793–829.

34. David Brion Davis, *The Problem of Slavery in the Age of Emancipation* (New York: Knopf, 2014).

35. Davis, *The Problem of Slavery*.

36. V. P. Franklin, "From Integration to Black Self-Determination: Changing Social Science Perspectives on Afro-American Life and Culture," in *Beginnings: The Social and Affective Development of Black Children*, ed. M. B. Spencer, G. K. Brookins, and W. R. Allen (Mahwah, NJ: Erlbaum Associates, 1985), 19–28; Vanessa Siddle Walker, "Ninth Annual Brown Lecture in Education Research: Black Educators as Educational Advocates in the Decades Before Brown v. Board of Education," *Educational Researcher* 42, no. 4 (2013): 207–22; Cross, *Shades of Black*.

37. Wulf Kansteiner, "Finding Meaning in Memory: A Methodological Critique of Collective Memory Studies," *History and Theory* 41, no. 2 (2002): 179–97; Peter J. Verovšek, "Collective Memory, Politics, and the Influence of the Past: The Politics of Memory as a Research Paradigm," *Politics, Groups, and Identities* 4 (2016): 529–43.

38. Timothy M. Diette, Arthur H. Goldsmith, Darrick Hamilton et al., "Skin Shade Stratification and the Psychological Cost of Unemployment: Is There a Gradient for Black Females?" *Review of Black Political Economy* 42, nos. 1–2 (2015): 155–77.

39. Melvin Patrick Ely, *Israel on the Appomattox: A Southern Experiment in Black Freedom from the 1790s Through the Civil War* (New York: Random House LLC, 2010); Meghan Burke, "Colorism," in *International Encyclopedia of the Social Sciences*, vol. 2, ed. W. Darity Jr. (Detroit: Thomson Gale, 2008), 17–18; Margaret Hunter, "The Persistent Problem of Colorism: Skin Tone, Status, and Inequality," *Sociology Compass* 1, no. 1 (2007): 237–54.

Chapter 7

1. Urie Bronfenbrenner, *The Ecology of Human Development* (Cambridge, MA: Harvard University Press, 1979); W. E. B. Du Bois, *The Souls of Black Folk* (New York: Gramercy Books, 1994); Myrdal Gunnar, *An American Dilemma: The Negro Problem and Modern Democracy* (New York: Harper and Bros, 1944).

2. Peggy McIntosh, "White Privilege: Unpacking the Invisible Knapsack," *Peace and Freedom Magazine* 49, no. 4 (July/August 1989): 10–12; Richard Lerner, "Dialectics, Developmental Contextualism, and the Further Enhancement of Theory About Puberty and Psychosocial Development," *Journal of Early Adolescence* 12, no. 4 (1992): 366–88.

3. Margaret Beale Spencer, "Phenomenology and Ecological Systems Theory: Development of Diverse Groups," in *Handbook of Child Psychology*, vol. 1, *Theoretical Models of Human Development*, 6th ed., ed. R. M. Lerner and W. Damon (New York: Wiley, 2006), 829–93; Margaret Beale Spencer, "Phenomenology and Ecological Systems Theory: Development of Diverse Groups," in *Child and Adolescent Development: An Advanced Course*, ed. W. Damon and R. M. Lerner (New York: Wiley, 2008), 696–735.

4. Jamelle Bouie, "What Does 'White Freedom' Really Mean?," *New York Times*, December 17, 2021.

5. Bouie, "'White Freedom.'"

6. Bouie.

7. Bouie.

8. Bouie.

9. Suniya Luthar, Samuel Barkin, and Elizabeth Crossman, "'I Can, Therefore I Must': Fragility in the Upper-Middle Classes," *Development and Psychopathology* 25, no. 4 part 2 (2013): 1529–49.

10. Kenneth B. Clark and Mamie K. Clark, "The Development of Consciousness of Self and the Emergence of Racial Identification in Negro Preschool Children," *Journal of Social Psychology* 10, no. 4 (1939): 591–99; Kenneth B. Clark and Mamie K. Clark, "Skin Color as a Factor in Racial Identification of Negro Preschool Children," *Journal of Social Psychology* 11, no. 1 (1940): 159–69.

11. V. P. Franklin, "From Integration to Black Self-Determination," in *Beginnings: The Social and Affective Development of Black Children*, ed. Margaret Spencer, Geraldine Brookins, and Walter Allen (Hillsdale, NJ: Erlbaum, 1985), 19–28; Vanessa Siddle Walker, *Their Highest Potential: An African American School Community in the Segregated South* (Chapel Hill: University of North Carolina Press, 1996).

12. Spencer, "Phenomenology and Ecological Systems," in *Handbook of Child Psychology*; Spencer, "Phenomenology and Ecological Systems," in *Child and Adolescent Development*.

13. Brian Tinsley and Margaret Beale Spencer, "High Hope and Low Regard: The Resiliency of Adolescents' Educational Expectations While Developing in Challenging Political Contexts," *Research in Human Development* 7, no. 3 (2010): 183–201; Davido Dupree et al., "Identity, Identification, and Socialization: Preparation and Retention of African American Males in Institutions of Higher Education," in *Black American Males in Higher Education: Research, Programs, and Academe*, ed. H. T. Frierson, J. H. Wyche, and

W. Pearson (Bingley, West Yorkshire, England: Emerald Group, 2009), 1–20; Margaret Beale Spencer and Brian Tinsley, "Identity as Coping: Youths' Diverse Strategies For Successful Adaptation," *Prevention Researcher* 15, no. 4 (2008): 17–21; Margaret Beale Spencer, Michael Cunningham, and Dena P. Swanson, "Identity as Coping: Adolescent African-American Males' Adaptive Responses to High-Risk Environments," in *Racial and Ethnic Identity*, ed. Herbert W. Harris, Howard C. Blue, and Ezra E. H. Griffith (New York: Routledge, 1995), 31–52.

14. Spencer, "Phenomenology and Ecological Systems," in *Handbook of Child Psychology*; Spencer, "Phenomenology and Ecological Systems," in *Child and Adolescent Development*; Margaret Beale Spencer et al., "Understanding Vulnerability and Resilience from a Normative Developmental Perspective: Implications for Racially and Ethnically Diverse Youth," in *Developmental Psychopathology*, vol., *Theory and Method*, 2nd ed., ed. Dante Cicchetti and Donald J. Cohen (Hoboken, NJ: Wiley, 2006), 627–72.

15. Tasneem Mandviwala, Jennifer Hall, and Margaret Beale Spencer, "The Invisibility of Power: A Cultural Ecology of Development in the Contemporary U.S. Cross-Cultural Issues," *Annual Review of Clinical Psychology* 18 (2022): 179–99.

16. McIntosh, "White Privilege."

17. Jamelle Bouie, "'White Freedom.'"

18. Spencer, "Phenomenology and Ecological Systems," in *Handbook of Child Psychology*; Spencer, "Phenomenology and Ecological Systems," in *Child and Adolescent Development*.

19. Urie Bronfenbrenner, *Ecology of Human Development*.

20. Robert White, "Motivation Reconsidered: The Concept of Competence," *Psychological Review* 66 (1959): 297–333; Robert White, "Competence and Psychosexual Development," in *Nebraska Symposium on Motivation*, ed. M. R. Jones (Lincoln: University of Nebraska Press, 1960).

21. Margaret Beale Spencer, "Risk and Resilience: How Black Children Cope with Stress," *Social Science* 71, no. 1 (1986): 22–26; Nichols Lodato, Jennifer Hall, and Margaret Beale Spencer, "Vulnerability and Resiliency Implications of Human Capital and Linked Inequality Presence Denial Perspectives: Acknowledging Zigler's Contributions to Child Well-Being," *Development and Psychopathology* 33 (2021): 684–99; Jennifer Hall, Bronwyn Nichols Lodato, and Margaret Beale Spencer, "Du Boisian Contributions to Phenomenological Variant of Ecological Systems Theory: Interrogating Undermined Paths to Black Resiliency and Vulnerability," in *The Oxford Handbook of W.E.B. Du Bois*, ed., Aldon Morris et al. (Oxford: Oxford University Press, 2022).

22. Lerner, "Dialectics, Developmental Contextualism."

23. William E. Cross, *Shades of Black: Diversity in African American Identity* (Philadelphia: Temple University Press, 1991); William E. Cross, "Toward a

Psychology of Black Liberation: The Negro-to-Black Conversion Experience," *Black World* 20, no. 9 (1991): 13–27.

24. V. P. Franklin, *Black Self-Determination: A Cultural History of the Faith of the Fathers*, 2nd ed. (Brooklyn, NY: Lawrence Hill Books, 1985); V. P. Franklin, "From Integration to Black Self-Determination," in *Beginnings: The Social and Affective Development of Black Children*, ed. Margaret Spencer, Geraldine Brookins, and Walter Allen (Hillsdale, NJ: Erlbaum, 1985), 19–28; Vanessa Siddle Walker, "Ninth Annual Brown Lecture in Education Research Black Educators as Educational Advocates in the Decades Before Brown v. Board of Education," *Educational Researcher* 42, no. 4 (2013): 207–22; Vanessa Siddle Walker, "Valued Segregated Schools for African American Children in the South, 1935–1969: A Review of Common Themes and Characteristics," *Review of Educational Research* 70, no. 3 (Fall 2000): 253–85.

25. Erik H. Erikson, *Identity, Youth and Crisis* (New York: W. W. Norton, 1968); Spencer, "Phenomenology and Ecological Systems," in *Handbook of Child Psychology*; Spencer, "Phenomenology and Ecological Systems," in *Child and Adolescent Development*.

26. Margaret Beale Spencer, "Preschool Children's Social Cognition and Cultural Cognition: A Cognitive Developmental Interpretation of Race Dissonance Findings," *Journal of Psychology* 112 (1982): 275–96; Margaret Beale Spencer, "Children's Cultural Values and Parental Child Rearing Strategies," *Developmental Review* 3 (1983): 351–70.

27. Margaret Beale Spencer, "The Effects of Systematic Social (Puppet) and Token Reinforcement on the Modification of Racial and Color Concept Attitudes in Preschool Aged Children" (Master's thesis, University of Kansas, Lawrence, 1970); Margaret Beale Spencer and Frances Degen Horowitz, "Effects of Systematic Social and Token Reinforcement on the Modification of Racial and Color Concept Attitudes in Black and in White Pre-School Children," *Developmental Psychology* 9, no. 2 (1973): 246–54.

28. ABC News. *Black in White America*, 1989, https://www.youtube.com/watch?v =CSafZUWok98.

29. Spencer, "Social (Puppet) and Token Reinforcement"; Spencer and Horowitz, "Social and Token Reinforcement."

30. Spencer, "Social (Puppet) and Token Reinforcement"; Spencer and Horowitz, "Social and Token Reinforcement."

31. Anderson Cooper, *AC360 Degrees: Racial Biases in Children*, aired on CNN, May 14, 2010.

32. Spencer, "Social (Puppet) and Token Reinforcement"; Spencer and Horowitz, "Social and Token Reinforcement."

33. Spencer, "Preschool Children's Social Cognition"; Spencer, "Children's Cultural Values"; Margaret Beale Spencer, "Black Children's Race Awareness, Racial Attitudes, and Self-Concept: A Reinterpretation," *Journal of Child Psychology and Psychiatry* 25, no. 3 (1984): 433–41; Margaret Beale Spencer and

Carol Marstrom-Adams, "Identity Processes Among Racial and Ethnic Minority Children in America," *Child Development*. 61 (1990): 290–96.

34. Spencer, "Preschool Children's Social Cognition"; Spencer, "Children's Cultural Values"; Margaret B. Spencer, "Cultural Cognition and Social Cognition as Identity Factors in Black Children's Personal Social Growth," in *Beginnings: The Social and Affective Development of Black Children*, ed. Margaret Beale Spencer, Geraldine K. Brookins, and Walter R. Allen (Hillsdale, NJ: Lawrence Erlbaum, 1985), 215–30.

35. Cross, *Shades of Black*; Cross, "Toward a Psychology."

36. David Elkind, "Conceptual Orientation Shifts in Children and Adolescents," *Child Development* 37, no. 3 (1966): 493–98; David Elkind, "Egocentrism in Adolescence," *Child Development* 38, no. 4 (1967): 1025–34.

37. Spencer, "Preschool Children's Social Cognition"; Spencer, "Children's Cultural Values"; Spencer and Marstrom-Adams, "Identity Processes," 290.

38. Diane Hughes et al., "Parents' Ethnic-Racial Socialization Practices: A Review of Research and Directions for Future Study," *Developmental Psychology* 42, no. 5 (2006): 747–70.

39. Spencer, "Social (Puppet) and Token Reinforcement."

40. Elkind, "Conceptual Orientation Shifts,"; Elkind, "Egocentrism in Adolescence."

41. Lerner, "Dialectics, Developmental Contextualism."

42. Spencer, "Phenomenology and Ecological Systems," in *Handbook of Child Psychology*; Spencer, "Phenomenology and Ecological Systems," in *Child and Adolescent Development*; Erikson, *Identity, Youth and Crisis*.

43. Spencer, "Preschool Children's Social Cognition"; Spencer, "Children's Cultural Values."

44. Faustine Jones, *A Traditional Model of Educational Excellence: Dunbar High School of Little Rock, Arkansas* (Washington DC: Howard University Press, 1981); Walker, *Their Highest Potential*; Alison Stewart, *First Class: The Legacy of Dunbar, America's First Black Public High School* (Chicago: Lawrence Hill Books, 2013).

45. Walker, *Their Highest Potential*.

46. Adam Fairclough, *Teaching Equality: Black Schools in the Age of Jim Crow*, vol. 43 (Athens: University of Georgia Press, 2001); Sharon G. Pierson, *Laboratory of Learning: HBCU Laboratory Schools and Alabama State College Lab High in the Era of Jim Crow* (New York: Peter Lang, 2014); Vanessa Siddle Walker, *The Lost Education of Horace Tate: Uncovering the Hidden Heroes Who Fought for Justice in Schools* (New York: New Press, 2018).

47. Glenda Elizabeth Gilmore, *Gender and Jim Crow: Women and the Politics of White Supremacy in North Carolina, 1896–1920* (Chapel Hill: University of North Carolina Press, 1996).

48. Stephanie Rowley et al., "The Relationship Between Racial Identity and Self-Esteem in African American College and High School Students," *Journal*

of Personality and Social Psychology 74, no. 3 (1998): 715–24. Ken Resnicow et al., "Development of a Racial and Ethnic Identity Scale for African American Adolescents: The Survey of Black Life," *Journal of Black Psychology* 25, no. 2 (1999): 171–88; Russell B. Toomey and Adriana J. Umana-Taylor, "The Role of Ethnic Identity on Self-Esteem for Ethnic Minority Youth," *The Prevention Researcher* 19, no. 2 (2012): 8–12.

49. Rowley et al., "The Relationship Between Racial Identity and Self-Esteem in African American College and High School Students."

50. Roberta G. Simmons et al., "Self-Esteem and Achievement of Black and White Adolescents," *Social Problems* 26, no.1 (1978): 86–96.

51. Michael Hughes and David Demo, "Self-Perception of Black Americans: Self-Esteem and Personal Efficacy," *American Journal of Sociology* 95 (1989): 132–59; Judith Porter and Robert Washington, "Developments in Research on Black Identity and Self-Esteem: 1979-1988," *Revue Internationale de Psychologie Sociale* 2, no. 3 (1989): 339–53.

52. Toomey and Umana-Taylor, "Role of Ethnic Identity."

53. Michael Rutter, "Psychosocial Resilience and Protective Mechanisms," *American Journal of Orthopsychiatry* 57 (1987): 316–31.

54. Jean S. Phinney, Cindy L. Cantu, and Dawn A. Kurtz, "Ethnic and American Identity as Predictors of Self-Esteem Among African American, Latino, and White Adolescents," *Journal of Youth and Adolescence* 26, no. 2 (1997): 165 85.

55. Miwa Yasui, Carole LaRue Dorham, and Thomas J. Dishion, "Ethnic Identity and Psychological Adjustment: A Validity Analysis for European American and African Adolescents," *Journal of Adolescent Research* 19, no. 6 (2004): 807–25.

56. April Harris-Britt, Cecilia R. Valrie, Beth Kurtz-Costes et al., "Perceived Racial Discrimination and Self-Esteem in African American Youth: Racial Socialization as a Protective Factor," *Journal of Research on Adolescence* 17, no. 4 (2007): 669–82.

57. Jacquelynne S. Eccles, Carol A. Wong, and Stephen C. Peck, "Ethnicity as a Social Context for the Development of African-American Adolescents," *Journal of School Psychology* 44 (2006): 407–26.

58. Brendesha M. Tynes et al., "Online Racial Discrimination and the Protective Function of Ethnic Identity and Self-Esteem for African American Adolescents, *Developmental Psychology* 48, no. 2 (2012): 343–55.

59. Noni K. Gaylord-Harden et al., "Perceived Support and Internalizing Symptoms in African American Adolescents: Self-Esteem and Ethnic Identity as Mediators," *Journal of Youth and Adolescence* 36, no. 1 (2007): 77–88.

60. Christina Oney, Elizabeth Cole, and Robert Sellers, "Racial Identity and Gender as Moderators of the Relationship Between Body Image and Self-Esteem for African Americans," *Sex Roles* 65, no. 7–8 (2011): 619–31.

61. Bruce Compas, Pamela Orosan, and Kathryn Grant, "Adolescent Stress and Coping: Implications for Psychopathology During Adolescence," *Journal of*

Adolescence 16, (1993): 331–49; Amanda Guyer, Jennifer Silk, and Eric Nelson, "The Neurobiology of the Emotional Adolescent: From the Inside Out," *Neuroscience and Biobehavioral Reviews* 70 (2016): 74–85.

62. Granville Stanley Hall, *Adolescence: Its Psychology and Its Relation to Physiology, Anthropology, Sex, Crime, Religion, and Education*, vols. 1 and 2 (Englewood Cliffs, NJ: Prentice-Hall, 1904).

63. Albert Bandura, "The Stormy Decade: Fact or Fiction?," *Psychology in the School* 1 (1964): 224–31.

64. Thomas Armstrong, *The Power of the Adolescent Brain: Strategies for Teaching Middle and High School Students* (Alexandria, VA: ASCD, 2016).

65. B. J. Casey and Kristina Caudle, "The Teenage Brain: Self Control," *Current Directions in Psychological Science* 22, no. 2 (2013): 82–87.

66. B. J. Casey et al., "The Storm and Stress of Adolescence: Insights from Human Imaging and Mouse Genetics," *Developmental Psychobiology* 52, no. 3 (2010): 225–35.

67. Sarah-Jayne Blakemore, *Inventing Ourselves: The Secret Life of the Teenage Brain* (New York: Public Affairs Books, 2018).

68. B. J. Casey et al., "A Developmental Functional MRI Study of Prefrontal Activation During Performance of a Go-No-Go Task," *Journal of Cognitive Neuroscience* 9 (1997): 835–E47.

69. Farah Nayeri, "Remembering the Racist History of 'Human Zoos,'" *New York Times*, December 29, 2022.

70. Margaret Beale Spencer, Davido Dupree, and Tracey Hartmann, "A Phenomenological Variant of Ecological Systems Theory (PVEST): A Self-Organization Perspective in Context," *Development and Psychopathology* 9 (1997): 817–33.

71. Stephen M. Quintana, "Racial and Ethnic Identity: Developmental Perspectives and Research," *Journal of Counseling Psychology* 54, no. 3 (2007): 259–70; Margaret Beale Spencer, Dena Swanson, and Michael Cunningham, "Ethnicity, Ethnic Identity and Competence Formation: Adolescent Transition and Identity Transformation," *Journal of Negro Education* 60, no. 3 (1991): 366–87. James Youniss, Jeffrey McLellan, and Miranda Yates, "What We Know About Engendering Civic Identity," *American Behavioral Scientist* 40, no. 5 (1997); 620–31; Jeffrey Arnett, *Emerging Adulthood: The Winding Road from the Late Teens Through the Twenties* (Oxford University Press, 2004); Anthony D'Augelli and Charlotte Patterson, eds., *Lesbian, Gay, and Bisexual Identities and Youth: Psychological Perspectives* (New York: Oxford University Press, 2001); Margaret Rosario et al., "Sexual Identity Development Among Lesbian, Gay, and Bisexual Youths: Consistency and Change Over Time," *Journal of Sex Research* 43, no. 1 (2006): 46–58.

72. Gabriel M. Velez and Margaret Beale Spencer, "Phenomenology and Intersectionality: Using PVEST as a Frame for Adolescent Identity Formation Amid Intersecting Ecological Systems of Inequality," *New Directions for Child and*

Adolescent Development 4 (2018): 75–90; Baukje Prins, "Narrative Accounts of Origins: A Blind Spot in the Intersectional Approach?," *European Journal of Women's Studies* 13, no. 3 (2006): 277–90.

73. Seth Schwartz, "The Evolution of Eriksonian and Neo-Eriksonian Identity Theory and Research: A Review and Integration," *Identity: An International Journal of Theory and Research* 1, no. 1 (2001): 7–58; Dena Swanson, Margaret Beale Spencer, and Anne Petersen, "Identity Formation in Adolescence," in *The Adolescent Years: Social Influences and Educational Challenges*, ed. Kathryn Borman and Barbara Schneider (Chicago: University of Chicago Press, 1998), 18–41; Peggy McIntosh, "White Privilege: Unpacking the Invisible Knapsack," in *Understanding Prejudice and Discrimination*, ed. Scott Plous (Columbus, OH: McGraw-Hill, 2002), 191–96.

Chapter 8

1. Kimberle Crenshaw, "Mapping the Margins: Intersectionality, Identity Politics, and Violence Against Women of Color," *Stanford Law Review* 43, no. 6 (1991): 1241–99.
2. Crenshaw, "Mapping the Margins."
3. Margaret Beale Spencer, Davido Dupree, and Tracey Hartmann, "A Phenomenological Variant of Ecological Systems Theory (PVEST): A Self-Organization Perspective in Context," *Development and Psychopathology* 9 (1997): 817–33; Margaret Beale Spencer, "Phenomenology and Ecological Systems Theory: Development of Diverse Groups," in *Handbook of Child Psychology*, vol. 1, *Theoretical Models of Human Development*, 6th ed., ed. R. M. Lerner and W. Damon (New York: Wiley, 2006), 829–93; Margaret Beale Spencer, "Phenomenology and Ecological Systems Theory: Development of Diverse Groups," in *Child and Adolescent Development: An Advanced Course*, ed. Richard M. Lerner and William Damon, 6th ed. (New York: Wiley, 2008), 696–735.
4. Margaret Beale Spencer, "Preschool Children's Social Cognition and Cultural Cognition: A Cognitive Developmental Interpretation of Race Dissonance Findings," *Journal of Psychology* 112, no. 2 (1982): 275–86; Margaret Beale Spencer, "Personal and Group Identity of Black Children: An Alternative Synthesis," *Genetic Psychology Monographs* 106, no. 1 (1982): 59–84; Margaret Beale Spencer, "Children's Cultural Values and Parental Child Rearing Strategies," *Developmental Review* 3, no. 4 (1983): 351–70; Margaret Beale Spencer, "Black Children's Race Awareness, Racial Attitudes, and Self-Concept: A Reinterpretation," in *Annual Progress in Child Psychiatry and Child Development*, ed. Stella Chess and Alexander Thomas (New York: Bruner/Mazel, 1985), 616–30 (reprinted from *Journal of Child Psychology and Psychiatry* 25, no. 3 [1984]: 433–41).
5. Robert White, "Motivation Reconsidered: The Concept of Competence," *Psychological Review* 66, no. 5 (1959): 297–333; Robert White, "Competence

and Psychosexual Development," in *Nebraska Symposium on Motivation*, ed. M. R Jones (Lincoln: University of Nebraska Press, 1960), 3-32; Richard DeCharms, *Personal Causation: The Internal Affective Determinants of Behavior* (New York: Academy Press, 1968).

6. Robert J. Havighurst, *Human Development and Education* (Oxford, England: Longmans, Green and Company, 1953).

7. Urie Bronfenbrenner, *The Ecology of Human Development* (Cambridge, MA: Harvard University Press, 1979).

8. Ebony O. Mcgee and Margaret Beale Spencer, "The Development of Coping Skills for Science, Technology, Engineering, and Mathematics Students: Transitioning from Minority to Majority Environments," in *Urban Ills: Post Recession Complexities of Urban Living in the Twenty First Century*, ed. Carol Camp Yeakey, Vetta L.S. Thompson, and Anjanette Wells (Lanham, MD: Lexington Books, 2013), 351-78.

9. Association of American Medical Colleges, "Diversity in Medicine: Facts and Figures," 2019, https://www.aamc.org/data-reports/workforce /report/diversity-medicine-facts-and-figures-2019#:~:text=About%20 30%25%20to%2040%25%20of,and%2030.6%25% 20of%20White%20 physicians.

10. Tyler Stovall, *White Freedom: The Racial History of an Idea* (Princeton, NJ: Princeton University Press, 2021).

11. Roger G. Barker and Paul V. Gump, *Big School, Small School: High School Size and Student Behavior* (Palo Alto, CA: Stanford University, 1964); Herbert Fletcher Wright, *Recording and Analyzing Child Behavior with Ecological Data from an American Town* (New York: Harper and Row, 1967); Susan S. Stodolsky, "Ecological Psychology or What's Going on at Kansas," *American Journal of Education* 79, no. 4 (1971): 625-36; Jamelle Bouie, "Quantifying the Pain of Slavery," *New York Times*, January 30, 2022.

12. David Lat, "Criminal Injustice," *New York Times Book Review* (January 16, 2022): 1-1,16.

13. Margaret Beale Spencer, "Old Issues and New Theorizing About African American Youth: A Phenomenological Variant of Ecological Systems Theory," in *African-American Youth: Their Social and Economic Status in the United States*, ed. Ronald L. Taylor (Westport, CT: Praeger, 1995), 37-69; Spencer, "Phenomenology and Ecological Systems," in *Handbook of Child Psychology*; Spencer, "Phenomenology and Ecological Systems," in *Child and Adolescent Development*.

14. Spencer, "Phenomenology and Ecological Systems," in *Handbook of Child Psychology*; Spencer, "Phenomenology and Ecological Systems," in *Child and Adolescent Development*.

15. Jacqueline V. Lerner and Richard M. Lerner, "Explorations of the Goodness-of-Fit Model in Early Adolescence," in *Prevention and Early Intervention: Individual Differences as Risk Factors for the Mental Health of Children: A Festschrift*

for Stella Chess and Alexander Thomas, ed. William B. Carey and Sean C. McDevitt (1994), 161–69; Stovall, *White Freedom.*

16. Lat, "Criminal Injustice."

17. Suniya S. Luthar and Shawn J. Latendresse, "Adolescent Risk: The Costs of Affluence," *New Directions Youth Development* 95 (2002): 101–21; Peggy McIntosh, "White Privilege: Unpacking the Invisible Knapsack," *Peace and Freedom Magazine* 49, no. 4 (July/August 1989) : 10–12.

18. Lat, "Criminal Injustice"; Jamelle Bouie, "How the Domestic Slave Trade Worked," *The Reconstruction Era: Blog Exploring the World the Civil War Created,* January 30, 2022, https://thereconstructionera.com/jamelle-bouie-on-how -the-domestic-slave-trade-worked/.

19. Vanessa Siddle Walker, *The Lost Education of Horace Tate: Uncovering the Hidden Heroes Who Fought for Justice in Schools* (New York: New Press, 2018); Elan Hope and Margaret Beale Spencer, "Civic Engagement as an Adaptive Coping Response to Conditions of Inequality: An Application of Phenomenological Variant of Ecological Systems Theory (PVEST)," in *Handbook on Positive Development of Minority Children and Youth,* ed. Natasha J. Cabrera and Birgit Leyendecker (New York: Springer, 2017), 421–34.

20. Elisabeth Spelman, *Inessential Woman: Problems of Exclusion in Feminist Thought* (Boston, MA: Beacon, 1988).

21. Patricia Hill Collins, "It's All in the Family: Intersections of Gender, Race, and Nation," *Hypatia* 13, no. 3 (1998): 63.

22. Angela P. Harris, "Race and Essentialism in Feminist Legal Theory," *Stanford Law Review* 42, no. 3 (1990): 581–616.

23. Collins, "All in the Family."

24. Abby L. Ferber, *White Man Falling: Race, Gender and White Supremacy* (Lanham, MD: Rowman and Littlefield, 1998); Linda Burnham, "Introduction," in *Time to Rise: US Women of Color—Issues and Strategies. Report to the UN World Conference Against Racism, Racial Discrimination, Xenophobia and Related Intolerance, Durban South Africa Aug. 28–Sept. 7, 2001,* ed. Maylei Blackwell, Linda Burnham, and Jung Hee Choi (Berkeley, CA: Women of Color Resources Center, 2001).

25. Marilynn E. Brewer, "The Psychology of Prejudice: Ingroup Love and Outgroup Hate," *Journal of Social Issues* 55, no. 3 (1999): 429–44.

26. McIntosh, "White Privilege."

27. McIntosh.

28. Tania Amardeil, "Fostering Inclusion by Understanding and Embracing Intersectionality: TD's Inclusive Culture Enables Colleagues to Bring Their Whole Selves to Work—And It All Starts with an Understanding of Intersectionality," *Maclean's,* April 2021, S2, Gale in Context: Opposing Viewpoints.

29. Vivian Abdelmessih and Geoff Bertram, "Fostering Inclusion by Understanding and Embracing Intersectionality," Innovating Canada, 2020,

https://www.innovatingcanada.ca/diversity/fostering-inclusion-by-under
standing-and-embracing-intersectionality/.
30. Abdelmessih and Bertram, "Fostering Inclusion."
31. Spencer, "Phenomenology and Ecological Systems," in *Handbook of Child
Psychology*; Spencer, "Phenomenology and Ecological Systems," in *Child and
Adolescent Development.*
32. Granville Stanley Hall, *Adolescence: Its Psychology and Its Relation to Physiology,
Anthropology, Sex, Crime, Religion, and Education*, vols. 1 and 2 (Englewood
Cliffs, NJ: Prentice-Hall, 1904).
33. David Elkind, "Conceptual Orientation Shifts in Children and Adolescents,"
Child Development 37, no. 3 (1966): 493–98.
34. Lacey Hilliard et al., "Beyond the Deficit Model: Bullying and Trajectories of
Character Virtues in Adolescence," *Journal of Youth Adolescence* 43, no. 6 (2014):
991–1003.
35. Lerner and Lerner, "Goodness-of-Fit Model."
36. Spencer, "Phenomenology and Ecological Systems," in *Handbook of Child
Psychology*; Spencer, "Phenomenology and Ecological Systems," in *Child and
Adolescent Development.*
37. Crenshaw, "Mapping the Margins."
38. Margaret Beale Spencer and Vinay Harpalani, "What Does 'Acting White'
Actually Mean? Racial Identity, Adolescent Development, and Academic
Achievement Among African American Youth," in *Minority Status, Oppositional
Culture, and Schooling*, ed. John Ogbu (Mahwah, NJ: Lawrence Erlbaum, 2008),
223–39; Margaret Beale Spencer et al., "Identity and School Adjustment:
Revisiting the 'Acting White' Assumption," *Educational Psychologist* 36, no. 1
(2001): 21–30.
39. Spencer et al., "Identity and School Adjustment."
40. Havighurst, *Human Development and Education*; Abraham Maslow, "A Theory
of Human Motivation," *Psychological Review* 50, no. 4 (1943): 370–96.
41. Walker, *The Lost Education.*
42. Hope and Spencer, "Civic Engagement."
43. Walker, *The Lost Education*; Hope and Spencer, "Civic Engagement."
44. Keshia Harris, "'Somos Uma Salada De Fruta': Adolescent Achievement in
Utopian Brazilian and Colombian Structures of Opportunity" (PhD diss.,
University of Chicago, 2018), https://knowledge.uchicago.edu/record/1621
?ln=en.
45. Lawrence Otis Graham, *Our Kind of People: Inside America's Black Upper Class*
(New York: Harper Collins, 1999).
46. Spencer, "Personal and Group Identity"; Spencer, "Children's Cultural
Values"; Spencer, "Black Children's Race Awareness."
47. Spencer, "Personal and Group Identity"; Spencer, "Children's Cultural Values."
48. Margaret Beale Spencer, Davido Dupree, and Tracey Hartmann, "A Phenomenological Variant"; Spencer, "Phenomenology and Ecological Systems," in

Handbook of Child Psychology; Spencer, "Phenomenology and Ecological Systems," in *Child and Adolescent Development*; Margaret Beale Spencer and Vinay Harpalani, "Nature, Nurture, and the Question of 'How?': A Phenomenological Variant of Ecological Systems Theory," in *Nature and Nurture: The Complex Interplay of Genetic and Environmental Influences on Human Behavior and Development*, ed. Cynthia Garcia Coll, Elaine L. Bearer, and Richard M. Lerner (New York: Psychology Press, 2003), 53–77; Margaret Beale Spencer, Dena Phillips Swanson, and Vinay Harpalani, "Development of the Self," in *Handbook of Child Psychology and Developmental Science: Socioemotional Processes*, ed. Michael E. Lamb and Richard M. Lerner (New York: John Wiley and Sons, 2015).

49. Jamelle Bouie, "What Does 'White Freedom' Really Mean?," *New York Times*, December 17, 2021.

50. Bouie, "'White Freedom.'"

51. Spencer, "Phenomenology and Ecological Systems," in *Handbook of Child Psychology*; Spencer, "Phenomenology and Ecological Systems," in *Child and Adolescent Development*.

Chapter 9

1. Ursula Kilkelly and Pat Bergin, *Advancing Children's Rights in Detention: A Model for International Reform* (Bristol, England: Bristol University Press, 2022), ch. 11 and afterword (decade-long radical reform of Irish juvenile justice system); see also John D. Kotter, "The 8 Steps for Leading Change," https://www.kotterinc.com/8-steps-process-for-leading-change/ (business/organizational model for change).

2. Sonya Douglass Horsford, "School Integration in the New Jim Crow: Opportunity or Oxymoron," *Educational Policy* 33, no. 1 (December 13, 2019): 267 (citing NPR's *All Things Considered*, "Lost Malcolm X Speech Heard Again 50 Years Later." A podcast hosted by Guy Raz, February 4, 2012, https://www.npr.org/2012/02/04/146373796/lost-malcolm-x-speech-heard-again-50-years-later).

3. Nancy E. Dowd, "Children's Equality Rights: Every Child's Right to Develop to Their Full Capacity," *Cardozo Law Review* 41 (2020): 1395.

4. Dowd, "Children's Equality Rights," 1407–408.

5. Barbara Bennett Woodhouse, *The Ecology of Childhood: How Our Changing World Threatens Children's Rights* (New York: New York University Press, 2020).

6. Dowd, "Children's Equality Rights," 1413–14 (citing Priscilla A. Ocen, "(E)racing Childhood: Examining the Racialized Construction of Childhood and Innocence in the Treatment of Sexually Exploited Minors," *UCLA Law Review* 62 [2015]: 1586–641).

7. Khiara M. Bridges, "Privacy Rights and Public Families," *Harvard Journal of Law and Gender* 34, no. 1 (2011): 113–74.

8. Robin A. Lenhardt, "Understanding the Mark: Race, Stigma, and Equality in Context," *New York University Law Review* 79, no. 3 (June 2004): 803–931.

9. Brown v. Board of Education, 347 U.S. 483, 493 (1954).

10. Sonia Nieto, "Re-Imagining Multicultural Education: New Visions, New Possibilities," *Multicultural Education Review* 9, no. 1 (2017): 1–10.

11. Nieto, "Re-Imagining Multicultural Education," 5–7.

12. Paulo Freire, *Pedagogy of the Oppressed* (New York: Continuum, 1990).

13. Freire, *Pedagogy of the Oppressed*, 131.

14. Sonia Nieto, "Multicultural Education in the United States: Historical Realities, Ongoing Challenges, and Transformative Possibilities," in *Routledge International Companion to Multicultural Education*, ed. James A. Banks (New York: Routledge, 2009), 79–95.

15. Geneva Gay, "Beyond *Brown*: Promoting Equality Through Multicultural Education," *Journal of Curriculum and Supervision* 19, no. 3 (2004): 193–216.

16. Sonia Nieto et al., "Identity, Community, and Diversity: Retheorizing Multicultural Curriculum for the Postmodern Era," in *The Sage Handbook of Curriculum and Instruction*, ed. F. Michael Connelly, Ming Fang He, and JoAnn Phillion (Thousand Oaks, CA: Sage, 2008), 194 (citing Michael W. Apple, *Ideology and Curriculum*, 3rd ed. [New York: Routledge, 2004]).

17. Nieto et al., "Identity, Community, and Diversity," 178 (citing Christine E. Sleeter and Carl A. Grant, "An Analysis of Multicultural Research in the United States," *Harvard Educational Review* 57, no. 4 [1987]: 421–45); Christine Sleeter and Carl A. Grant, *Making Choices for Multicultural Education: Five Approaches to Race, Class, and Gender*, 4th ed. (Hoboken, NJ: John Wiley & Sons, 2003).

18. Nieto et al., "Identity, Community, and Diversity," 183.

19. Katheryn Russell-Brown, *The Color of Crime: Racial Hoaxes, White Crime, Media Messages, Police Violence, and Other Race-Based Harms*, 3rd ed. (New York: New York University Press 2021), 153–66, and see especially 157–60.

20. Russell-Brown, *The Color of Crime*, 156.

21. Melanie M. Acosta, Michele Foster, and Diedre F. Houchen, "'Why Seek the Living Among the Dead?' African American Pedagogical Excellence: Exemplar Practice for Teacher Education," *Journal of Teacher Education* 69, no. 3 (2018): 1–13.

22. Chike Akua, "Standards of Afrocentric Education for School Leaders and Teachers," *Journal of Black Studies* 51, no. 2 (2020): 114–21.

23. bell hooks, *Teaching to Transgress: Education as the Practice of Freedom* (New York: Routledge Taylor and Francis Group, 1994).

24. hooks, *Teaching to Transgress*, 21.

25. Michelle Fine, Lois Weis, and Linda C. Powell, "Communities of Difference: A Critical Look at Desegregated Spaces Created for and by Youth," in *Legacies of Brown: Multiracial Equity in American Education*, ed. Dorinda J. Carter,

Stella M. Flores, and Richard J. Reddick, HER Reprint Series (Cambridge, MA: Harvard Educational Review, 2004), 209–46.

26. Gordon W. Allport, *The Nature of Prejudice* (Reading, MA: Addison Wesley, 1954).

27. Allport, *The Nature of Prejudice.*

28. Thomas F. Pettigrew and Linda R. Tropp, "A Meta-Analytic Test of Intergroup Contact Theory," *Journal of Personality and Social Psychology* 90, no. 5 (2006): 752.

29. Elise C. Boddie, "Racial Territoriality," *UCLA Law Review* 58, no. 2 (2010): 406.

30. Boddie, "Racial Territoriality," 406.

31. Boddie, 406.

32. Boddie, 457–460.

33. Elise C. Boddie, "Ordinariness as Equality," *Indiana Law Journal* 93, no. 1 (2018): 57–71.

34. Boddie, "Ordinariness," 58.

35. Boddie, 63.

36. Erika K. Wilson, "Toward a Theory of Equitable Federated Regionalism in Public Education," *UCLA Law Review* 61, no. 5 (2014): 1416.

37. Erika K. Wilson, "The New School Segregation," *Cornell International Law Journal* 49, no. 3 (2016): 139.

38. Erika K. Wilson, "Monopolizing Whiteness," *Harvard Law Review* 134, no. 7 (2021): 2387.

39. Bruce Baker, Danielle Farrie, and David Sciarra, *Is School Funding Fair? A National Report Card,* 7th edition, Education Law Center (February 2018), page iii, available at edlawcenter.org.

40. Vibeke Opheim, *Equity in Education Thematic Review: Country Analytical Report: Norway* October 2004, https://www.oecd.org/education/innovation -education/38692818.pdf; Finnish Ministry of Education, *Equity in Education Thematic Review: Country Analytical Report, Finland,* March 2005, https://www .oecd.org/finland/38692775.pdf.

41. Hanover Research, *School Based Strategies for Narrowing the Achievement Gap* (Arlington, VA: Hanover Research, 2017).

42. Terah Venzant Chambers, "The 'Receivement Gap': School Tracking Policies and the Fallacy of the Achievement Gap," *Journal of Negro Education* 78, no. 4 (Fall 2009): 417, abstract; James Joseph Scheurich et al., "An Initial Exploration of a Community-Based Framework for Educational Equity with Explicated Exemplars," *Race Ethnicity and Education* 20, no. 4 (2017): 508–26.

43. Scheurich et al., "An Initial Exploration of a Community-Based Framework," 510–11.

44. David L. Kirp, *Improbable Scholars: The Rebirth of a Great American School System and a Strategy for America's Schools* (New York: Oxford University Press, 2013) (high achieving minority majority school in Union City, NJ).

45. Sean F. Reardon, "School Segregation and Racial Academic Achievement Gaps," *Russell Sage Foundation Journal of the Social Sciences* 2, no. 5 (August 2016): 34–57; Sean F. Reardon and Anne Owens, "60 Years After 'Brown': Trends and Consequences of School Segregation," *Annual Review of Sociology* 40, no. 1 (2014): 199–218; Sean F. Reardon and Lori Rhodes, "The Effects of Socioeconomic School Integration Policies on Racial School Desegregation," in *Integrating Schools in a Changing Society: New Policies and Legal Options for a Multiracial Generation*, ed. Erica Frankenberg and Elizabeth Debray (Chapel Hill: University of North Carolina Press, 2011), 187–207.

46. Tomiko Brown-Nagin, "Just Schools: A Holistic Approach to the Education of Impoverished Students," *University of Memphis Law Review* 49, no. 1 (2018): 185–204.

47. Brown-Nagin, "Just Schools," 195, no. 54.

48. Pedro A. Noguera, "Race, Education and the Pursuit of Equity in the Twenty-First Century," in *Race, Equity and Education: Sixty Years from Brown*, ed. Pedro Noguera, Jill Pierce, and Roey Ahram (New York: Springer International, 2016), 4.

49. Noguera, "Race, Education and the Pursuit," 11.

50. Richard Rothstein, "School Policy Is Housing Policy: Deconcentrating Disadvantage to Address the Achievement Gap," in *Race, Equity and Education: Sixty Years from Brown*, ed. Pedro Noguera, Jill Pierce, and Roey Ahram (New York: Springer International, 2016), 27–29.

51. Dowd, "Children's Equality Rights," 1370.

52. Nancy E. Dowd, "Children's Equality: The Centrality of Race, Gender and Class," *Fordham Urban Law Journal* 47, no. 2 (2020): 245–48; Nancy E. Dowd, *Reimagining Equality: A New Deal for Children of Color* (New York: New York University Press, 2018).

53. Robin A. Lenhardt, "The Color of Kinship," *Iowa Law Review* 102, no. 5 (2017): 2071–108; Robin A. Lenhardt, "Race Dignity and the Right to Marry," *Fordham Law Review* 84, no. 1 (2015): 53–68; Robin A. Lenhardt, "Race Audits," *Hastings Law Journal* 62, no. 6 (2011): 1527–78.

Chapter 10

1. Margaret Spencer and Tirzah Spencer, "Invited Commentary: Exploring the Promises, Intricacies, and Challenges to Positive Youth Development," *Journal of Youth and Adolescence* 43, no. 6 (2014): 1027–35; Margaret Beale Spencer, "Acknowledging Bias and Pursuing Protections to Support Anti-Racist Developmental Science: Critical Contributions of Phenomenological Variant of Ecological Systems Theory," *Journal of Adolescent Research* 36, no. 6 (2021): 569–83; Margaret Beale Spencer, "What You Ignore, Becomes Empowered: Social Science Traditions Weaponized to Resist Resiliency Research Opportunities," in *Race and Culturally Responsive Inquiry in*

Education, ed. Stafford Hood et al. (Cambridge, MA: Harvard Education Press, 2022), 63–80.

2. Spencer and Spencer, "Invited Commentary."

3. Margaret Beale Spencer, "Acknowledging Bias"; Spencer, "What You Ignore"; Spencer and Spencer, "Invited Commentary"; Vered Vinitzky-Seroussi and Mathias Jalfim Maraschin, "Between Remembrance and Knowledge: The Spanish Flu, COVID-19, and the Two Poles of Collective Memory," *Memory Studies* 14, no. 6 (2021): 1475–88.

4. Shrehan Lynch, Sue Sutherland, and Jennifer Walton-Fisette, "The A–Z of Social Justice Physical Education: Part 1," *Journal of Physical Education, Recreation and Dance* 91, no. 4 (2020): 8–13.

5. Kris D. Gutierrez and Barbara Rogoff, "Cultural Ways of Learning: Individual Traits or Repertoires of Practice," *Education Research* 32 (June 2003): 19–25.

6. Thomas S. Kuhn, *The Structure of Scientific Revolutions* (Chicago: University of Chicago Press, 1962).

7. Gutierrez and Rogoff, "Cultural Ways of Learning."

8. Kuhn, *Structure of Scientific Revolutions*; Gutierrez and Rogoff, "Cultural Ways of Learning."

9. Kuhn, *Structure of Scientific Revolutions*; Gutierrez and Rogoff, "Cultural Ways of Learning"; Spencer, "What You Ignore."

10. Barbara Rogoff, *Cultural Nature of Human Development* (Oxford: Oxford University Press, 2003); Barbara Rogoff et al., *Developing Destinies: A Mayan Midwife and Town* (Oxford: Oxford University Press, 2011); Gutierrez and Rogoff, "Cultural Ways of Learning."

11. Margaret Beale Spencer, "Old Issues and New Theorizing about African-American Youth: A Phenomenological Variant of Ecological Systems Theory," in *African American Youth: Their Social and Economic Status in the United States*, ed. Ronald L. Taylor (1995), 37–69; Margaret Beale Spencer, "Phenomenology and Ecological Systems Theory: Development of Diverse Groups," in *Handbook of Child Psychology*, vol. 1, *Theoretical Models of Human Development*, 6th ed., ed. R. M. Lerner and W. Damon (New York: Wiley, 2006), 829–93; Margaret Beale Spencer, "Phenomenology and Ecological Systems Theory: Development of Diverse Groups," in *Child and Adolescent Development: An Advanced Course*, ed. W. Damon and R. M. Lerner (New York: Wiley, 2008), 696–735; Margaret Beale Spencer, Davido Dupree, and Tracey Hartmann, "A Phenomenological Variant of Ecological Systems Theory (PVEST): A Self-Organization Perspective in Context," *Development and Psychopathology* 9 (1997): 817–33; Margaret Beale Spencer et al., "Understanding Vulnerability and Resilience from a Normative Developmental Perspective: Implications for Racially and Ethnically Diverse Youth," in *Developmental Psychopathology*, vol, 1, *Theory and Method*, 2nd ed., ed. Dante Cicchetti and Donald J. Cohen (Hoboken, NJ: Wiley, 2006), 627–72; Dorothy Prestwich, "Character Education in America's Schools," *School Community Journal* 14, no. 1 (2004): 139–50.

12. Astrid Erll, *Memory in Culture*, (London: Palgrave Macmillan, 2011); Astrid Erll, "Afterword: Memory Worlds in Times of Corona," *Memory Studies* 13, no. 5 (2020): 861–74; Vinitzky-Seroussi and Maraschin, "Between Remembrance and Knowledge."

13. Aleida Assmann, "Memory, Individual and Collective" in *The Oxford Handbook of Contextual Political Analysis*, ed. Robert E. Goodin and Charles Tilly (Oxford: Oxford University Press, 2006), 210–24; Peter J. Verovšek, "Collective Memory, Politics, and the Influence of the Past: The Politics of Memory as a Research Paradigm," *Politics, Groups, and Identities* 4, (2016): 529–43; Maurice Halbwachs, *On Collective Memory* (Chicago: University of Chicago Press, 1992); Noa Gedi and Yigal Elam, "Collective Memory: What Is It?," *History and Memory* 8, no. 1 (1996): 30–50; Tanja E. Bosch, "Memory Studies: A Brief Concept Paper," MeCoDEM, 2016, http://www.mecodem.eu/wp-content/uploads/2015/05/Bosch-2016_Memory-Studies.pdf.

14. Wulf Kansteiner, "Finding Meaning in Memory: A Methodological Critique of Collective Memory Studies," *History and Theory* 41, no. 2 (2002): 179–97, 180; Peter Verovšek, "Collective Memory, Politics, and the Influence of the Past: The Politics of Memory as a Research Paradigm," *Politics, Groups, and Identities* 4 (2016): 529–43; Anna Cento Bull and Hans Lauge Hansen, "On Agonistic Memory," *Memory Studies* 9, no. 4 (2016): 390–404.

15. Rauf Garagozov, "Painful Collective Memory: Measuring Collective Memory Affect in the Karabakh Conflict," *Peace and Conflict: Journal of Peace Psychology* 22, no. 1 (2016): 28–35; Henry Rousso, "The Vichy Syndrome: History and Memory in France Since 1944," trans. Arthur Goldhammer (Cambridge, MA: Harvard University Press, 1991); Jonathan Boyarin, "Space, Time and the Politics of Memory," in *Remapping Memory: The Politics of TimeSpace*, ed. Jonathan Boyarin (Minneapolis: University of Minnesota Press, 1994), 1–37; Steven Hoelscher and Derek Alderman, "Memory and Place: Geographies of a Critical Relationship," *Social and Cultural Geography* 5, no. 3 (2004): 347–55; Eric Hobsbawm and Terence Ranger, *The Invention of Tradition* (Cambridge: Cambridge University Press, 2000); Rousso, "The Vichy Syndrome"; David Lowenthal, *The Past Is a Foreign Country* (New York: Cambridge Univ. Press, 1985); Verovšek, "Collective Memory," 537; Lyn Spillman, *Nation and Commemoration: Creating National Identities in the United States and Australia* (New York: Cambridge University Press, 1997); Jeffrey K. Olick and Joyce Robbins, "Social Memory Studies: from Collective Memory to the Historical Sociology of Mnemonic Practices," *Annual Review of Sociology* 24 (1998): 105–40; Wiseman Chirwa, "Collective Memory and the Process of Reconciliation and Reconstruction," *Development in Practice* 7, no. 4 (1997): 479–82; Peeter Tulviste and James V. Wertsch, "Official and Unofficial Histories: The Case of Estonia," *Journal of Narrative and Life History* 4 (1994): 311–29; Qi Wang, "On the Cultural Constitution of Collective Memory," *Memory* 16, no. 3 (2008): 305–17.

16. Jack M. Balkin, *What Brown v. Board of Education Should Have Said: The Nation's Top Legal Experts Rewrite America's Landmark Civil Rights Decision* (New York: New York University Press, 2001); Barbara Rogoff, *Cultural Nature of Human Development* (Oxford: Oxford University Press, 2003); Rogoff et al., *Developing Destinies.*

17. Emily Werner and Ruth Smith, *Vulnerable but Not Invincible: A Longitudinal Study of Resilient Children and Youth* (New York: R. R. Donnelley and Sons, 1982); Adam Carle and Laurie Chassin, "Resilience in a Community Sample of Children of Alcoholics: Its Prevalence and Relation to Internalizing Symptomatology and Positive Affect," *Journal of Applied Developmental Psychology* 25, no. 5 (2004): 577–95; Ryan Santos, "Why Resilience? A Review of Literature of Resilience and Implications for Further Educational Research" (Claremont Graduate University and San Diego State University Qualifying Paper, 2012); Steven Wolin and Sybil Wolin, *The Resilient Self: How Survivors of Troubled Families Arise above Adversity* (New York: Villard, 1993); Ann Masten, Karin Best, and Norman Garmezy, "Resilience and Development: Contributions from the Study of Children Who Overcome Adversity," *Development and Psychopathology* 2 (1990): 424–44; Puja Iyer et al., "Investigating Asian American Adolescents' Resiliency Factors and Young Adult Mental Health Outcomes at 14-Year Follow-up: A Nationally Representative Prospective Cohort Study," *Journal of Immigrant and Minority Health* 25, no. 1 (2022): 75–85; Ann Masten, "Ordinary Magic: Resilience Processes in Development," *American Psychologist* 56 (2001): 227–38; Glenn E. Richardson et al., "The Resiliency Model," *Health Education* 21, no. 6 (1990): 33–39; Gina O. Higgins, *Resilient Adults: Overcoming a Cruel Past* (San Francisco: Jossey-Bass, 1994); Ann Masten J. et al., "The Structure and Coherence of Competence from Childhood through Adolescence," *Child Development* 66, no. 6 (1995): 1635–59.

18. Emmy Werner and Ruth Smith, *Overcoming the Odds: High Risk Children from Birth to Adulthood* (Ithaca, NY: Cornell University Press, 1992); Emmy Werner and Ruth Smith, *Journeys from Childhood to Midlife: Risk, Resilience, and Recovery* (Ithaca, NY: Cornell University Press, 2001); V. E. O'Leary and Jeanette Ickovics, "Resilience and Thriving in Response to Challenge: An Opportunity for a Paradigm Shift in Women's Health," *Women's Health* 1, no. 2 (1995): 121–42; Charles Carver, "Resilience and Thriving: Issues, Models, and Linkages," *Journal of Social Issues* 54, no. 2 (1998): 245–66.

19. Carver, "Resilience and Thriving"; Christina Theokas et al., "Conceptualizing and Modeling Individual and Ecological Asset Components of Thriving in Early Adolescence," *Journal of Early Adolescence* 25, no. 1 (2005): 113–43; Peter Benson and Peter Scales, "The Definition and Preliminary Measurement of Thriving in Adolescence," *Journal of Positive Psychology* 4, no. 1 (2009): 85–104.

20. Spencer, "Phenomenology and Ecological Systems," in *Handbook of Child Psychology*; Spencer, "Phenomenology and Ecological Systems," in *Child and Adolescent Development*; Spencer et al., "Understanding Vulnerability."

21. Joseph Youngblood and Margaret Beale Spencer, "Integrating Normative Identity Processes and Academic Support Requirements for Special Needs Adolescents: The Application of an Identity-Focused Cultural Ecological (ICE) Perspective," *Journal of Applied Developmental Science 6*, no. 2 (2002): 95–108; Margaret Beale Spencer and Joseph Youngblood, "Understanding Culture and Context: The Start On-Success Scholars Program (S-O-S) (Case Study 10)," in *Children's Mental Health Research: The Power of Partnerships*, ed. Kimberly Hoagwood et al. (New York: Oxford University Press, 2010), 118–21.

22. Youngblood and Spencer, "Integrating Normative Identity Processes"; Spencer and Youngblood, "Understanding Culture and Context," 120–21.

23. Youngblood and Spencer, "Integrating Normative Identity Processes," 102; Spencer and Youngblood, "Understanding Culture and Context," 118–21.

24. Robert J. Havighurst, *Human Development and Education* (Oxford: Longmans, Green, 1953).

25. Spencer, "Old Issues and New Theorizing"; Spencer, "Phenomenology and Ecological Systems," in *Handbook of Child Psychology*; Spencer, "Phenomenology and Ecological Systems"; Spencer et al., "Understanding Vulnerability"; Margaret Beale Spencer, Elizabeth Noll, and Elaine Cassidy, "Monetary Incentives in Support of Academic Achievement: Results of a Randomized Field Trial Involving High-Achieving, Low-Resource, Ethnically Diverse Urban Adolescents," *Evaluation Research+* 29, no. 3 (2005): 199–222.

26. Jacqueline Jordan Irvine, *Black Students and School Failure* (New York: Greenwood Press, 1990).

27. Vinitzky-Seroussi and Maraschin, "Between Remembrance and Knowledge."

Acknowledgments

We are grateful to Rich Milner, the series editor, and Jayne Fargnoli, our editor.

Each of us has drawn on the resources of our home institutions. The University of Florida College of Law provided generous research support. The support of Sherrice Smith and Victorica Redd has been invaluable, as well as that of Jerron Wheeler, Ebony Love, Courtney Bullock, Austin Vining, Adriane Carter, Levi Bradford, Marianna Hira, and Eric Petterson.

Research support from the University of Chicago, Social Sciences Division, has been ongoing, highly generous, and sincerely appreciated. Balancing research demands of the Urban Resiliency Initiative (URI) as well as editing and research support of this project have been consistently provided by Oliver Garland. His generous and untiring assistance has made this project possible.

We have intellectual debts to multiple colleagues. Nancy Dowd thanks Katheryn Russell Brown, Michelle Jacobs, Ken Nunn, Teresa Drake, Stephanie Bornstein, Stacey Steinberg, Jason Nance, Danaya Wright, Patricia Snyder, Maureen Conroy, Barbara Bennett Woodhouse, Angela Harris, R. A. Lenhardt, Angela Onwuachi-Willig, Jessica Dixon Weaver, Ursula Kilkelly, Frank Rudy Cooper, Clare Huntington, Naomi Cahn, Martha Fineman, Sacha Coupet, Ann McGinley, Catherine Smith, and Rachel Rebouche. Margaret Spencer credits long-term professional relationships that have contributed to her thinking over the years, including Drs. Walter Allen, Carol Camp Yeakey, Dena Swanson, Michael Cunningham, Howard Stevenson, and Cathy Cohen.

Our families influence us always. Nancy thanks her partner Paul W. Nichols, whose love, care, and support mean everything. Her children,

Zoe and Zack, inspire always. Margaret acknowledges fifty-six years of partnership, love, and support from Charles L. Spencer and the stimulation and inspiration from her loving children, Tirzah, Natasha (and Carrington Ward), and Charles A.—including the innovative STEM collaboration—and her grandchildren, Imani and Kofi, and her many friends and family members. Margaret particularly appreciates receipt of the Alphonse Fletcher, Sr., Fellowship (for scholarly and artistic works devoted to the legacy of 1954 *Brown v. Board of Education*).

This extraordinary collaboration, difficult to capture in words, hopefully speaks through this volume.

About the Authors

Margaret Beale Spencer is the Marshall Field IV Professor of Urban Education and Life Course Human Development in the Department of Comparative Human Development at the University of Chicago, emeritus. A prolific scholar, most recently she was awarded fellow status from the American Association for the Advancement of Science (2020) and was elected to the American Academy of Arts and Sciences (2019) and recognized with a Lifetime Achievement Award (2019) by the American Psychological Association. In addition, she was named recipient of the American Psychological Association Division 7 (Developmental Science) 2018 Urie Bronfenbrenner Award for Distinguished Contributions to Developmental Science and the Society for Research in Child Development (SRCD) Award for Distinguished Contributions to Cultural and Ecological Research. The author of a significant numbers of articles and chapters and three edited volumes, she also recently launched the Urban Resilience Initiative (URI) at the University of Chicago. As an innovative platform, URI supports and executes both basic collaborative developmental applied research initiatives and creative STEM-promoting private sector and university partnerships. URI is a national and community-emphasizing collaboration that synthesizes the "lessons learned" from several decades of theory-scaffolded basic research, theorizing efforts, and implementations of programming and evaluation efforts.

Nancy E. Dowd is a University of Florida Distinguished Professor and David Levin Chair in Family Law, University of Florida Levin College of Law, emeritus. She was the director of the Center on Children and Families from 2008 to 2015, fostering a broad range of work on juvenile law, nontraditional families, interventions into domestic violence, racial justice, gender and masculinities work, and children's rights. She held

263

the Distinguished Fulbright Chair at the Raoul Wallenberg Institute for Human Rights, at Lund University, Sweden, and served as the Distinguished Guest Professor at Aalborg University, Denmark, for two academic years. A prolific scholar, she is the author of eight books and numerous articles and the editor of the Families, Law, and Society series for New York University Press. Her interdisciplinary scholarship focuses on critical race, gender, feminist, and masculinities theory; children and children's rights; juvenile justice; fathers and fatherhood; and nontraditional families. Among her books are *The Man Question: Male Subordination and Privilege* (2010), *Redefining Fatherhood* (2000), and *In Defense of Single Parent Families* (1997). Her most recent book, *Reimagining Equality: A New Deal for Children of Color* (2018), is a critique of hierarchies among children that proposes a comprehensive structural strategy to achieve equality.

Index

educational diversity, Supreme
    Court on value of, 96–98
effort, outcomes and, 23–25
ego identifications, 22
Eisenhower, Dwight, 57, 63
Elementary and Secondary
    Education Act (ESEA), 93
Emancipation, 44, 48, 50, 51
Emancipation Proclamation, 45,
    135, 136
empathy
    sustained inhumanity and lack
        of, 109
    Whiteness and, 27–30
equality
    Brown and full, 1–2, 16, 73–74
    defined, 2, 46
    developmental Supreme Court
        cases and, 96
    disavowal of *Brown*'s radical,
        92–94
    Equal Protection Clause and,
        5–6
    equity and, 12, 199, 207
    equity *vs.,* 197
    lack of for freemen, 37
    linked by Supreme Court to
        liberty, 5–6
    meaning of in Fourteenth
        Amendment, 13
    need for affirmative state action
        to ensure, 75–76, 77–80
    policy to implement Radical
        Brown and, 181
    Reconstruction Amendments
        and, 45–46
    Reconstruction and meaning
        of, 50
    Slaughterhouse Cases and, 77–78,
        79

Strauder decision on meaning of,
    73, 74–76, 77–80
equal protection, *Bolling v. Sharpe*
    and, 86–87
Equal Protection Clause of
    Fourteenth Amendment
    meaning of equality in, 5–6
    race in college admissions and,
        97–98
    Strauder decision and, 74,
        75–76, 80
equal status contact, 186–187
equity
    equality and, 12, 199, 207
    equality *vs.,* 197
    need for supports that function
        as sources of, 211
    policy to implement Radical
        Brown and, 181–182
ethnic identity, self-esteem and,
    153
etiquette of Jim Crow, 57–58
Ex Parte Commonwealth of Virginia,
    82–83

facially neutral segregation, 53–53
facially racial segregation, 53, 54
false memories, 200–201
family
    resiliency and, 202
    slavery and disregard of, 41
Fanon, Frantz Omar, 129, 130–131,
    132
fBIP (functional Black Inhumanity
    Perspective), 125
    contrast between Black experi-
        ence and White's chrono-
        system support and,
        143–144
    group resistance to, 145